IN ITS OWN IMAGE

IN ITS OWN IMAGE

How Television
Has Transformed Sports

Benjamin G. Rader

THE FREE PRESS
A Division of Macmillan, Inc.
NEW YORK

Collier Macmillan Publishers
LONDON

The Free Press
A Division of Macmillan, Inc.
866 Third Avenue, New York, N.Y. 10022

Collier Macmillan Canada, Inc.

Printed in the United States of America

printing number

1 2 3 4 5 6 7 8 9 10

Library of Congress Cataloging in Publication Data

Rader, Benjamin G.
  In its own image.

  Bibliography: p.
  Includes index.
    1. Television broadcasting of sports—United States—
History.   2. Sports—United States—History.   I. Title.
GV742.3.R33   1984   070.4′49796′0973   84–47856
ISBN 0–02–925700–X

To Lydia Rader and Lowell Rader,
to whom I owe so much

Contents

Acknowledgments

The many persons who contributed directly to this book are too numerous to mention fairly. They include Richard Allen, William J. Baker, Joan M. Chandler, Esther Cope, Harry Coyle, Maxine Isenberg, Michael T. Isenberg, Frederick C. Luebke, Norma M. Luebke, Peter Maslowski, Thomas Merritt, Barbara S. Morris, John Olson, Joel Nydahl, Roberta Park, Val Pinchbeck, Jr., Stephen L. Rader, Jimmie L. Reeves, Joe Ricutti, Jay Rosenstein, Thomas L. Simons, Alex Sachare, and Douglas A. Skene. Personnel with the following organizations were of assistance: American Broadcasting Company, the Athletic Congress, Columbia Broadcasting Company, National Basketball Association, National Broadcasting Company, National Collegiate Athletic Association, National Football League, USA Network, and the United States Football League. Without the information provided by the authors (or the persons interviewed) cited in the text of this book and in the note on sources, this book could not have been written. And without a generous research fellowship granted by the University of Nebraska Research Council for 1983–84, the completion of this book would have been long delayed. None of these organizations or persons should be held accountable, however, for the contents of this book.

Two persons were indispensable to the book: Joyce Seltzer, my editor, who unrelentingly insisted upon greater clarity, and Barbara Koch Rader, my wife and best friend, who brought to the task keen insight, patience, and sustenance.

IN ITS OWN IMAGE

Prologue

At mid–twentieth century on a warm Saturday afternoon, you lounge on your cement patio, the latest suburban necessity. You read the newspaper and listen to your portable Philco radio. You hear your son's souped-up Studebaker roar out of the driveway; he is bound for the nearby drive-in movie to watch *The Jackie Robinson Story*, a film celebrating the acceptance of Negroes (not blacks, in the 1950s) into the National Game of baseball. Your Red-fearing neighbor is busy digging a bomb shelter in his backyard. The newspaper headlines are unpleasant, starkly declaring that China has fallen, that the Soviets have detonated an atomic bomb, and that there is treason in high places. Corruption reigns in Washington, on the nation's basketball courts, and even at the United States Military Academy at West Point.

Drowsiness descends like an evening fog. Across the street a kid in a Davy Crockett coonskin cap plays catch with his father. He hopes to join the Little League, a fast-growing movement spurred on by the enthusiastic endorsement of suburban parents. Next door, the Breen girl, pigtails streaming behind, dribbles her leather basketball down the driveway and places the ball gently against the backboard for an uncontested lay-up. "Don't worry," neighbors reassure her parents, "she'll grow out of it."

Like most Americans, you have never seen a live big-league baseball, football, or hockey game. Nearly all of the major league sport franchises are located in a tier of industrial cities in the

1

Northeast and upper Midwest. You own no television set, though several of your neighbors now have antennas sprouting from their roofs. Instead you listen to the games on your trusty Philco, where Stan Musial and Joe DiMaggio play baseball in the fertile recesses of your imagination.

Some thirty-five years later, you sit in your air-conditioned, glassed-in daylight basement, sipping a Budweiser Light with eyes riveted to your new twenty-four-inch color Sony. Enclosed, you do not hear your grandson roar off in his jeep, bound for a local punk rock concert. Your bomb shelter–building neighbor has become Rod the Roadrunner, the terror of the local jogging trails. The coonskin-capped kid has made it to the big leagues and is holding out for a salary of more than a million dollars a year. The Breen girl is now the coach of a college women's basketball team which features a man-sized budget and a man-sized recruiting program.

A kaleidoscope of full-color images dart across the screen, demanding your attention. Uneasily, you watch as—

- Having just won the U.S. Open, a golfer kisses a huge paycheck (made especially oversized for the television cameras).
- O.J. Simpson gracefully leaps through an airport for the Hertz Corporation.
- Magic Johnson, the ebullient guard of the Los Angeles Lakers, triggers the firing of coach Paul Westhead. Westhead's coaching system is "too dull," Johnson tells reporters.
- To inspire his team, Larry Canady, football coach at Eau Gaille High School in Florida, chomps off the heads of live frogs. "Our kids love it," Canady explains. "They say look how wild the coach is, let's get wild too. . . ."
- Digger Phelps, Notre Dame basketball coach, charges that the "going underground price" for top high school recruits is $10,000. Some fellow coaches angrily demand that Phelps name the wrongdoers; others smile and privately say that Digger placed the price too low.

Most Americans recognize, at least half-consciously, that the world of sports has experienced great changes in the last few decades. On one side of a mysterious boundary is the sports world—sometimes imaginary, sometimes real—of Judge Kenesaw Mountain Landis, Joe DiMaggio, Knute Rockne, Ebbets Field, and the Polo Grounds; of simple-minded athletes, benevolent owners, and play for its own sake. On the other side of the barrier is our own era, a time of division and strife; of player unions, strikes, and George Steinbrenner; of Pete Rozelle, Reggie Jackson, and Jackie Sherrill; of Texas Stadium and the Astrodome. Clearly on one side is radio, Red Barber, and boys playing baseball on empty lots or cow pastures; on the other lies television, Howard Cosell, and pre-adolescent boys playing on Pop Warner football teams, complete with plastic helmets, adult coaches, and briefly clad nine-year-old cheerleaders.

While these varied tendencies and discrete data defy simple explanation, one momentous fact stands at the center of the recent revolution in American sports. That fact is television. Television has had a large impact on the ethos of sports; on the motives and behavior of athletes, owners, and spectators; and on the organization and management of sports. In turn—and what is ultimately of more importance—the changes induced by television have altered the role that sports play in American life.

   Before the advent of television, Americans usually experienced sports as a unique form of human drama, a drama sharply different from other forms of entertainment. The drama contained a playful element akin to a kitten playing with a ball of yarn or a baby happily shaking a rattle. It also entailed genuine competition; there were winners and losers. But here, unlike in the marketplace, competition existed under ideal conditions. All players began with an equal chance to win, and explicit rules specified the competitive constraints. Furthermore, sports enlisted human skills and a concentration of purpose on behalf of a totally "useless" activity, one that made no direct contribution to material survival.

Yet the indirect contribution of such an experience to American society was a large one. For sports before television offered a wonderful release from everyday life; the experience transported players and fans alike into another realm of consciousness. Sports satisfied needs for fantasy and for the expression of childlike exuberance. The playing of the games enacted familiar ceremonies that reaffirmed society's core values. Being bracketed off from daily life, sports ideally exemplified how such opposing impulses as the individual versus the community, play versus work, and self-control versus indulgence could be contained or reconciled.

Players should strive to win, but not at all costs; winning should be subordinated to the rules of the game and the spirit of fair play. Sports should be serious, but not an activity that totally absorbed one's being. Players should play for the joy they found in the game, but simultaneously enlist their efforts on behalf of a larger cause: the game itself, the team, the community. Perhaps more than any other institution in American society, sports satisfied a hunger of the human spirit: They filled a need to witness the expression of beauty, excellence, and grace.

The history of televised sports can be divided into two principal eras. The first era extended from the 1940s into the mid-1960s; the second from the mid-1960s to the present. In the first era, television significantly affected such arena sports as wrestling, Roller Derby, and prizefighting, but quite differently than it would later alter the outdoor team sports of baseball and football. Since the drama of the arena sports could be easily translated to the small screen, they initially captured large television audiences. But each had to make important concessions to the cool medium: Wrestling became a completely theatrical exercise; Roller Derby featured stylized, fake violence; and boxing substituted slugfests for finesse.

Until the perfection of color television, slow motion, and replay shots in the 1960s, team sports could not be easily conveyed on the small screen. Nonetheless, the powers in charge of professional baseball and college football attributed their sports' sharp drop in attendance to the new medium. The colleges took collective action to reduce the number of telecasts, but professional baseball was unable to formulate a policy that would protect attendance. Professional football, on the other hand, not only devised a television policy that sheltered attendance but also used television to propel itself into a major form of entertainment.

The second era in televised sports began with a fundamental shift in television network policies. Until the 1960s, sports had constituted a small portion of network budgets and program time. Then ABC, a network which ranked a weak third in audience ratings, decided to make sports a centerpiece of its programming. Televised sports helped launch ABC's drive to the top of the ratings in the 1970s. In the mid-1970s, both NBC and CBS belatedly decided to follow the example of ABC. An all-out war between the networks for supremacy in sports television ensued. In the late 1970s and 1980s, new sports cable networks and superstations employing transmission satellites also joined in the fray.

These changes in network policy had profound consequences for sports. Within a decade, the hours of network television devoted to sports doubled. Rights payments for college and professional football, major league baseball, and the Olympic Games escalated to staggering heights. The moguls of sports quickly began to package their games so that they would be even more appealing to television. To obtain a larger share of the new largesse, athletes organized unions, held strikes, and sought assistance in the court system. The battle of the networks expedited the professionalization of the amateur sports of college basketball and football, of track and field, and of school sports. Even preadolescent youth sports began to ape the professional model.

The barrage of telecasts brought sports to millions of more people, and television's technological sophistication deepened and broadened the viewer's experience of sports. But the costs were large. By destroying the distance between the fan and the athlete, by displaying competing (i.e., non-sports) images of the athletes, and by encouraging the athletes to assume self-indulgent personas, television reduced the ability of sports to elevate athletes into heroes. By overwhelming the viewer with sensations extrinsic to the games, and by leading viewers to expect only the best, television sharply attenuated the traditional sporting experience. No longer did spectator sports enjoy the same capacity to release people from the ennui of daily life, to inculcate values, or to bind people together.

Television has essentially trivialized the experience of spectator sports. With its enormous power to magnify and distort images, to reach every hamlet in the nation with events from anywhere in the world, and to pour millions of additional dollars into sports, television—usually with the enthusiastic assistance of the sports moguls themselves—has sacrificed much of the unique drama of sports to the requirements of entertainment. To seize and hold the attention of viewers and thus maximize revenues, the authenticity of the sporting experience has been contaminated with a plethora of external intrusions. To capitalize upon the public's love of sports, television—again with the aid of sports promoters—has swamped viewers with too many seasons, too many games, too many teams, and too many big plays. Such a flood of sensations has diluted the poignancy and potency of the sporting experience. It has diminished the capacity of sports to furnish heroes, to bind communities, and to enact the rituals that contain, and exalt, society's traditional values.

1

Sports as They Once Were

Red Smith, a distinguished sportswriter, could not quite find the words to accurately evoke the drama of a classic sporting contest. His prose ricocheted between hyperbole and understatement. Describing the last half of the ninth inning of the final game of the New York Giants–Brooklyn Dodgers 1951 playoff for the National League championship, he wrote: "Now the story ends. And there is no way to tell it. The art of fiction is dead. Reality has strangled invention. Only the utterly impossible, the inexpressibly fantastic can ever be plausible again. Yet, the story remains to be told, the story of how the Giants won the 1951 pennant in the National League. Maybe this is the way to tell it: Bobby Thomson, a young Scot from Staten Island, delivered a timely hit in the ninth inning of an enjoyable game of baseball before 34,320 witnesses at the Polo Grounds."

But who could blame Red Smith? No mere words could describe the "miracle" at the Polo Grounds.

It all began in the midsummer of 1951. The Giants had been given up for dead; on August 11 they trailed the first-place Dodgers by thirteen and one-half games. Then Leo "The Lip" Durocher, former Dodger manager who was regarded by Brooklyn fans as a traitor, somehow led the Giants to victory streaks of sixteen and ten games. The Giants finished the season with a rush, winning their last four games, while the hapless Dodgers managed to win only three of their last seven games. The season ended in a dead heat, requiring a two-out-of-three game playoff for the National League pennant.

The Giants and the Dodgers divided the first two playoff games. In the decisive third game, when the Giants came to bat in the last half of the ninth inning, the Dodgers led, 4–1. This was the half-inning that caused Red Smith's prose to become unhinged. He was not alone. For at the conclusion of the inning, the Giants' radio broadcaster, Russ Hodges, insanely shouted, "The Giants win the pennant! The Giants win the pennant!" over and over again, and Dodger pitcher Ralph Branca slumped against the clubhouse wall and sobbed uncontrollably.

Alvin Dark led off the epic inning with a single; Don Mueller then slashed a single to right field, putting Giant runners on first and third. Monte Irvin popped up, but Whitey Lockman sliced a double to left field, scoring Dark. Charlie Dressen, the Dodger manager, waved in Ralph Branca from the bullpen to replace Don Newcombe, the struggling pitcher. Branca, another Dodger ace, threw a strike past Bobby Thomson. On the next pitch Thomson drove a fast ball into the lower left field seats of the Polo Grounds, bringing in three runs with a single swing of the bat. The pennant race was over. The Giants had won, 5–4.

The 1951 playoff game suggests how and why sports in the pre-television era had acquired such a powerful grip on the national psyche. Such intense feelings arose principally out of the *uniqueness* of the sports drama. For both the players and the fans, the 1951 playoff game was a live drama, a battle for victory, which could evoke feeling quite unlike anything found in day-to-day life or, for that matter, anything found on the stage or screen. Yet it was not the intrinsic drama of the game alone that seized the minds and emotions of the American people. The play of the game embodied art; it conveyed vividly and concretely one of the deepest yearnings of the species: to observe controlled physical performance at the highest levels of human potential. The world of sports, in which the 1951 playoff game was a quintessential event, embodied a set of values and aspirations that shaped the lives of millions of Americans. Indeed, the shared experience of sports helped to counter the centrifugal forces of race, religion, ethnicity, and class that always threatened to drive the nation asunder.

For the 34,320 fans present at the 1951 playoff game, those who watched the game on the first national television hookup for a baseball game, those who listened to the exciting radio description, and perhaps even those restricted to reading Red Smith's schizoid account, the game was high drama. And the drama of the sporting contest, unlike that in other forms of entertainment, is authentic. There are real winners and losers. In sports the performers—the athletes—actually feel pain and elation. The nine-year-old Little Leaguer may visibly tremble in anticipation of the next pitch. A baseball is hard, and the diminutive hitter knows that the big twelve-year-old on the mound may throw an errant pitch that could strike his body quite painfully. Basketballs jam fingers; spikes slice flesh; a hard tackle can cripple for life. Mistakes can induce genuine tears (witness Ralph Branca), and home runs can produce euphoria. The action on the field of play is closer to that of the battlefield than that on the stage.

Few forms of experience equal the intensity of sports. Like such classic forms of release as sex, drugs, or drink, a sporting event, such as the 1951 playoff game, transports fans and players alike into another realm of consciousness. Unlike alcohol or narcotics, however, the game achieves this state by intensifying and concentrating awareness. Unlike the drugs or alcohol "high," the sporting "high" can usually be achieved without the harmful side effects of hangovers, withdrawal pains, or perhaps permanent emotional upheaval. For the committed fan (derived, indeed, from the word "fanatic"), winning produces overwhelming exhilaration; defeat, deep depression. Yet never despair. For even in defeat there is always the next game, or the next season—the fresh chance to start over again.

Like religious mystics, athletes themselves, even when not performing before spectators, sometimes experience states of reverie seldom achieved in everyday life. When the teenager puts up one jump shot after another on the empty schoolyard basketball court, perhaps imagining himself to be a Larry Bird or a Magic Johnson, nothing of the outside world is likely to intrude upon his special pleasure. He temporarily forgets the fights with his sister, the quarrels with his mother, and the homework awaiting him on the kitchen table. Julius "The Doctor" Erving, National Basketball Association superstar, relates that when he was a boy, "If certain things troubled me or there was a conflict at home, I would take my ball, go out to the park and play by myself for a few hours. . . . It was utopia."

Playing can transform adult experience into childlike experience. In *Life on the Run*, Bill Bradley—Rhodes Scholar, star player for the New York Knicks, and now a United States Senator—stated it well: "In those moments on a basketball court I feel as a child and know as an adult. Experience rushes through my pores as if sucked up by a strong vacuum. I feel the power of imagination and the sense of mystery and wonder I accepted in childhood before my life hardened." In other terms, tennis star Billie Jean King described in her autobiography the near-transcendental feelings of the perfect shot: "My heart pounds, my eyes get damp, and my ears feel like they're wriggling, but it's also just totally peaceful. It's almost just like having an orgasm—it's exactly like that."

Coordinated team effort seems especially prone to produce moments of pure delight. Sometimes in professional basketball games, Bill Russell recalled in *Second Wind*, both teams achieved "magic spells." When three or four players suddenly "heated up," "the feeling would spread to the other guys, and we'd all levitate. Then the game would just take off and there'd be a natural ebb and flow that reminded you of how rhythmic and musical basketball is supposed to be." Both teams became totally engulfed in a "white heat of competition," so that Russell even found himself rooting for the other team to keep up the magic spell. Then suddenly the referee's whistle, an injury, or a bad play broke the reverie. Yet those rare moments, added Russell, "were sweet when they came, and the hope that one would come was one of my strongest motivations for walking out there."

In sports, fans ally themselves closely with the efforts of the athlete. "There was a magic going to a ball park," recalled Roger Kahn of the pre-television era of sport, "leaving the house, the trip to the field, being there." When cultural critic Michael Novak goes to a ball park, he reports feeling a sense of reverence identical to that of entering a great cathedral. Fans become so emotionally involved in the games that they cheer on their heroes and perhaps boo their opponents. When sports are played before audiences, the audience itself becomes a source of excitement. Then "we" the fans and "they" the players become inseparable actors in the same drama. For a few hours, fans and players may enjoy a community of shared experience—the experience not only of the game itself, but of the noise, the food, the brawls, and nature—the sun, the wind, the rain.

Sports help to satisfy the human need for artistic expression. "I feel that tennis is an art form," Billie Jean King explains, "that is capable of moving the players and the audience—at least a knowledgeable audience—in almost sensual ways. . . . When I'm performing at my absolute best, I think that some of the euphoria I feel must be transmitted to the audience." As with all the arts, innate skills must be combined with many hours of practice. Such common artistic standards as symmetry, grace, and beauty prevail in sports. Indeed, one of the most important virtues of sports, even in the age of television, has been the relative resistance of sports—as compared with the modern fine arts—to the collapse of standards. Excellence in sports, unlike as in many forms of art, is widely understood and appreciated. While only few receive the training essential to an appreciation of the beaux arts, countless Americans spend thousands of hours reading about, discussing, listening to, watching, and playing sports. They thereby gain the experience needed to appreciate the beauty of sports when they are performed at the highest levels of excellence.

Of course, this interpretation represents sports as ideally experienced. In fact, long before television a variety of motives drove athletes to play. Rather than simply the joy of the game itself, they might "play" for God, country, or money. When these motives became predominant, the athletes experienced the game as work rather than play. Playing the game became a means to achieve other ends. When the fans sensed that the athletes were at work rather than play, that the players had enlisted the games on behalf of projects other than the art form itself, the fans lost interest in the game. The joy of sports had been contaminated by ulterior motives.

In the pre-television era, however, the fans rarely concluded that the athletes were mere working men. Most fans recognized that a combination of motives drove athletes to play; they knew, for example, that big-league ball players received salaries and on occasion even "held out" in the spring for more money. But they believed that playing for money was incidental, that the compulsion to play on the part of professional and amateur athletes alike arose mostly from the joy found in the game itself. Fans were con-

fident that the athletes shared their pleasure in the sporting experience. And unless the cynical observer rejects the nearly universal
testimony of the athletes of the pre-television era, he must conclude that the belief of the fans rested on a firm foundation.

While the release furnished by sports from the rigors and monotony of daily life was certainly important, the significance of
sports as they existed before television extended far beyond this.
In the sports world, many Americans found a pillar of community
feeling and a unique kind of guidebook to daily living. But, unlike
those found in philosophical treatises, the values reflected in
sports required little or no interpretation; they seemed almost self-
evident. Though surrounded by the sea of artifice and greed found
in daily life, sports were often experienced as a celestial island of
the true and the good. On this island, rules prevailed over personal
whim, hard work over laziness, integrity over guile, self-control
over excess, and cooperation over individual aggrandizement.
Even in the twentieth century, when such values have come under
an unrelenting assault, sports continued to offer a stout refuge for
traditional values. In fact, for many Americans, sports conveyed a
more powerfully articulated and clearly perceived order of values
than could be found in religious doctrines, family maxims, or the
laws of the state.

In the sports world before television, Americans found a rich
history of fact and fancy, of legendary heroes, and of precise
benchmarks for measuring present performances. The history
taught in schoolbooks might seem to be a mishmash of vague,
confusing generalizations and discrete facts unconnected to any
larger meanings, but the history of sports revealed crystal-clear,
cyclical patterns. The fan always knew who won and who lost; the
reasons for success or failure could be easily identified. Statistics
permitted precise comparisons of performances, even between
athletes of the present and those of yesterday.

The sports drama encouraged various kinds of community.
All of those who observed the 1951 playoff game, whether fans of
the Giants or the Dodgers, radio listeners, casual television watchers, or readers about the game in the next morning's newspaper,
shared a common experience. To some fans, the game served as a
national symbol, similar to the flag, the National Anthem, or Un-
cle Sam. Baseball was the "National Game." Its common rules

and rich traditions gave the sport a changeless, universal quality that helped bind the entire nation together. "You pulled off the double play the same way for the Richmond County Juniors, the Auks or the White Sox," Tom Wicker has written about the baseball of the 1940s in *Esquire* (1975). "When I was in the press box in Lumberton or dying with shame when they stole second on me five times in Carthage, baseball was a common denominator; it had rules, symmetry, a beginning and an end, it challenged and rewarded, you could play or watch, it was the same one day as the next, in one town as another."

Competition, even when severely circumscribed by rules as in the case of sports, somehow stoked the fierce fires of tribalism. For deeply committed Giants and Dodgers fans, their professional baseball teams strengthened a sense of local community. The Dodgers were especially important to the residents of Brooklyn, for the team gave their borough a distinct identity, a powerful sense of being a separate community within greater New York City. Long before the 1951 playoff game between the Giants and the Dodgers, baseball games had become symbolic contests of great moment between cities. The last stanza of the classic poem "Casey at the Bat" expressed the emotional power of baseball for a town's residents:

> *Oh! somewhere in this favored land*
> *the sun is shining bright;*
> *The band is playing somewhere,*
> *and somewhere children's hearts are light.*
> *And somewhere men are laughing,*
> *and somewhere children shout;*
> *But there is no joy in Mudville—*
> *mighty Casey has Struck Out.*

After the mighty Casey struck out, Mudville, like Brooklyn in 1951, no longer had room for joy, laughter, shouting children, brass bands, or bright sunshine. A pall hung over the village. But there was always next season. Then Mudville and Brooklyn would again have the opportunity to experience the magic of sports.

Notre Dame football reveals an equally graphic example of the capacity of sports to engender allegiance and unity. By the 1920s, the small Catholic boys' school in South Bend, Indiana, had developed a frenzied level of support among Catholics everywhere, even among those who had never been near a college ("the subway alumni") and regardless of their ethnic origins. When Notre Dame met Army in their annual tilts in New York in the 1920s and 1930s, the passions of the city's large ethnic populations reached a fever pitch. "New York was never before, or since, so sweetly gay and electric as when Rock [Knute Rockne] brought his boys to town," Paul Gallico has written; "the city was wild with excitement." For a minority within a predominately Protestant nation, the Notre Dame football team became a great symbolic rallying point for the nation's Roman Catholic population.

Intercollegiate games frequently represented to fans symbolic battles for superiority between states or regions—sometimes between ethnic groups, religions, or ideologies. Citizens in states without a singular or conspicuously significant history, great civic monuments, or remarkable physical scenery might find in a winning state university football team a source of indisputable state pride. World War I supplied new built-in cheering sections for the two service academies. Those who had worn khakis in the war supported Army; bell-bottoms made one a Navy rooter.

Before mid-century, high school sports across the country helped give an identity and common purpose to many neighborhoods, towns, and cities. These geographical entities often lacked a rich history or collective goals. Varsity sports could coalesce the residents into a united front more effectively than anything else short of a natural disaster. Consequently, school boards typically paid coaches more than any other teacher and placed a higher priority on the construction of a gymnasium or a football field than they did on building a laboratory or a library. "You know that, if a principal is looking for a teacher, one of the first questions he asks frequently is: 'Can this man be of use in connection with athletics?'" reported Edwin H. Hall in *School Review* as early as 1905. In the 1920s in Indiana, a hotbed of high school basketball, the seating capacity of the school's gym sometimes exceeded the town's population.

In the pre-television era, heroes populated the world of sports. In 1951 the hero of Gotham was, of course, Bobby Thomson, who rather than striking out like the Mighty Casey of folklore, had struck the winning blow for his team. His home run, which had decided the entire baseball season, transcended the capabilities of ordinary men. He performed an extraordinary feat. At the most elemental level, the status accorded to Thomson by the residents of New York was in the same spirit as that bestowed upon the ancient Greek heroes for their superhuman strength, courage, and character. In turn, Thomson's act gave his admirers a sense of pride, inspiration, and self-worth. Perhaps men were, after all, akin to the gods.

In the sports world as it existed before television, the hero strengthened the will to act. How did the old man of the sea, a Hemingway protagonist, inspire himself to land the big fish? "I must have confidence and I must be worthy of the great DiMaggio who does all things perfectly even with the pain of the bone spur in his heel," said Santiago to himself. When Joe Louis knocked out Jim Braddock for the heavyweight championship on June 27, 1937, Malcolm X, "like every Negro boy old enough to walk wanted to be the next Brown Bomber." For novelist John Updike, as a boy in Pennsylvania, baseball slugger Ted Williams of the Boston Red Sox "radiated, from afar, the hard blue glow of high purpose." Athletic heroes have helped shape the resolve of countless others.

In the pre-television era, the heroes of sports assisted the public in coping with a rapidly changing society. The sports world made it possible for Americans to continue to believe in the traditional gospel of success: that hard work, frugality, and loyalty paid dividends; that the individual was potent and could play a large role in shaping his own destiny. As the society became more complicated and systematized, and as success had to be won increasingly in bureaucracies, the need for heroes who leaped to fame and fortune outside the system grew. By the 1920s, American heroes were no longer lone businessmen or statesmen, but more often the stars of movies, radio, and sports.

In sports, or so it seemed, one could still catapult to fame and fortune without the requirements of years of arduous training or acquiescence to the demanding requirements of bureaucracies. More than in most vocations, sheer natural ability coupled with a commitment to (in this case) sport for its own sake could propel the athlete to the top. Determining the level of success of a doctor, lawyer, or business manager might be difficult, but achievement in the world of sports was unambiguous: It could be precisely measured in home runs, knockouts, touchdowns scored, victories, and even salaries. Those standing on the assembly lines and those sitting at their desks in the bureaucracies increasingly found their greatest satisfaction in the athletic hero, who presented an image of all-conquering power. Thus they preferred the towering home runs of Babe Ruth to the "scientific" style of base hits, base stealing, sacrifices, and hit-and-run plays personified by Ty Cobb; they preferred the smashing knockout blows of Jack Dempsey to the "scientific" boxing skills displayed by Gene Tunney. Small wonder, perhaps, that boys now dreamed of becoming athletic heroes rather than captains of industry.

2

The Message and the Media

Televised sports in the United States got underway late in the afternoon of May 17, 1939, when someone threw a switch in the RCA Building in downtown New York City. The picture impulses picked up by the bulky Iconoscope television camera located at Columbia University's Baker Field traveled through a transmitter in a nearby truck and up an antenna fastened to the top of a flagpole, which then catapulted them through the sky to the eighty-fifth floor of the Empire State Building. From there the signal leaped to the RCA Building, and NBC's experimental station W2XBS was on the air. "Good afternoon, ladies and gentlemen!" came the nasal twang of Bill Stern, the famous radio broadcaster.

Several hundred people at the RCA pavilion watched the strange spectacle on a little silver screen. The baseball players, according to the *New York Times* report, looked "like white flies." "The ball was seldom seen except on bunts and other infield plays. . . ." The following Sunday, May 21, 1939, Orrin E. Dunlap, Jr., who covered the media for the *Times*, observed:

> The televiewer lacks freedom; seeing baseball on television is too confining, for the novelty would not hold up for more than an hour, if it were not for the commentator.
>
> To see the fresh green of the field as The Mighty Casey advances to the bat, and the dust fly as he defiantly digs in, is a thrill to the eye that cannot be electrified and flashed through space on a May day, no matter how clear the air.

What would Christy Mathewson, Smokey Joe Wood, Home Run Baker, Eddie Collins, Frank Chance, Tris Speaker, Ty Cobb, Rube Marquard and those old timers think of such a turn of affairs—baseball from a sofa!

The 1939 telecast touched off a long, ricocheting romance between the new medium and sports. Experimental station W2XBS continued to turn out sports firsts in 1939: The Eastern Grass Courts Tennis Championships, a baseball game between the Cincinnati Reds and the Brooklyn Dodgers, a college football game pitting Fordham University against Waynesburg College of Pennsylvania, a professional football game in which the Brooklyn Dodgers defeated the Philadelphia Eagles, 23 to 14. In 1940 the pioneering station carried the first televised hockey and basketball games and track meets. But few fans witnessed these early telecasts. "Television is trapped in a vicious circle," declared one engineer. "We can't sell sets because we haven't got enough good programs because there aren't advertisers to pay for them. And we can't find advertisers because we can't sell sets." During the war years, further experimentation with television ceased.

Long before the advent of television, various forms of the media had been intimately involved in the history of sports. Without media, the 1951 National League playoff game would have been lost in the byways of folk memories. As it was, the media firmly embedded the game in baseball history and gave it much more than local significance. Even in the nineteenth century, specialized sporting journals, mass-circulation newspapers, and sports fiction supplemented actual attendance as means by which Americans experienced the wonders of sports. Radio in the 1920s, and later television, in the 1940s, joined the print media in multiple marriages to sports.

Even early in the nineteenth century, print media—whether in the form of weeklies, newspapers, fiction, biography, or autobiography—enhanced public interest in sports. Before 1890 most of the sports news could be found in such weekly journals as the *Spirit of the Times*, the *New York Clipper*, the *National Police Gazette*, and the *Sporting News*. William T. Porter's *Spirit of the Times*, a weekly, began publication in 1831. By 1856 Porter claimed to have 40,000 subscribers scattered throughout the nation; the journal itself became a kind of national sporting center.

Sportsmen sent and received messages through the *Spirit*. An aspiring pedestrian (footracer) or prize fighter typically used the *Spirit* to issue public challenges. For example: "Billy Clarke of Birmingham [England] will fight any 104 lb. man in the United States give or take 2 lb., for $200 or $300 side [bets]. Money ready at William Clark's saloon, Laurens-street, near Bleecker street, New York." Unpaid, largely untutored authors from all over the nation sent in reports of sports, games, odd happenings, and curiosities. The weekly became a kind of central record-keeping agency for the sports of the nation. Porter himself served as the nation's principal arbiter of disputes; he strove to continue the best of the English sporting tradition in the United States.

At a remarkably early date, sporting journals recognized the importance of history to sports. William T. Porter had been acutely aware of the need to preserve the records of sporting events; in the 1860s, Henry Chadwick, the dean of baseball publicists, invented the box score and batting averages, marvelous quantitative devices that made it possible for fans to precisely compare present performances with those of the past. Regardless of the unpredictability and turmoil on the front page of the newspaper, fans, from the time of Chadwick on, expected to find on the sports page confirmation of orderliness and continuity.

To increase circulation, newspapers frequently became promoters of sports. As early as 1873, James Gordon Bennett, Jr., the eccentric owner of the New York *Herald*, began awarding cups and medals to intercollegiate track and field champions. He even sponsored Henry Stanley's exotic search for David Livingstone, who had been missing for several years in the African jungles. Stanley's eventual success in locating Livingstone became the stuff of a monumental legend.

Bennett's promotional ventures paled beside those of Richard Kyle Fox, the publisher and editor of the *National Police Gazette*. Printed on shockingly pink paper and distributed at discount rates to such all-male preserves as barbershops, livery stables, saloons, private men's clubs, and volunteer fire departments, the notorious weekly exploited to the fullest the nation's racial bigotry, secret sexual lusts, and thirst for the sensational. Repeated libel suits and efforts by the postal authorities to suppress the *Gazette* only served to increase its circulation. In the mid-1880s, *Gazette* subscriptions mounted to over 150,000, and each issue circulated through several hands. According to Fox, even Jesse James, the notorious train robber, regularly read the *Gazette*. To stimulate sales, Fox offered championship belts and prizes for, among other things, the world's championship of heavyweight boxing, teeth-lifting, hog butchering, "one-legged clog dancing," and female weightlifting.

In the 1920s, the large metropolitan daily newspapers also entered the arena of sports promotion. For example, the famous Golden Gloves boxing program got underway in the mid-1920s with the aid of Captain Joseph Medill Patterson, co-publisher of the Chicago *Tribune*. When Patterson became the publisher of the New York tabloid, the *Daily News*, in 1927, he introduced a similar boxing tournament open to all teenagers in New York City. In 1928, with the help of the sports staff of the *Tribune*, the Golden Gloves became a national tournament. By 1955, some 25,000 youngsters tried to fight their way through the regionals and become one of eight finalists. Arch Ward, longtime sports editor of the Chicago *Tribune*, was especially important as a promoter; he invented both the All-Star Baseball Game (1933) and the annual College All-Star Football Game (1934). On the local level, newspapers also frequently sponsored athletic teams and a wide variety of sporting events.

But sports stories were far more important than promotion by newspapers in enhancing the traditional sporting experience. Newspaper sportswriting in the pre-television era fell into three large, sometimes overlapping categories: the tall tale, verse, and the true story. The tall tale, the oldest form of sportswriting, sprang from oral accounts of the great feats of athletes, especially heroes along the roaring frontier of the American South and West. Often the bearer of tall tales depicted the hero as a comic figure; in these tales, the hero not only brought the forces of nature, man, and beast under his control through epic feats, but was often a clown and a braggart as well. On one occasion, Davy Crockett, perhaps the most popular hero of the tall tale, saved the world from disaster. During an especially frigid winter, the earth had frozen on its axis. Crockett squeezed some bear grease on the axis and over the face of the sun as he whistled, "Push along, keep movin'!" The earth grunted, groaned, and began to rotate once again. The tall tale has remained an integral part of sports folklore, but usually in the form of oral humor rather than written reports of sports events.

The early twentieth century witnessed the heyday of the age of poetry among sportswriters. Only poetry, they believed, could reduce the wonder of sports to human comprehensibility; but sometimes poetry furnished a vehicle for humor as well. Grantland Rice, the dean of the versifiers, took sports seriously. He had a gift for writing verse a cut above the popular commercial jingles of the day. Youngsters memorized his lines, coaches used them to inspire their teams, and moralists found in them reassurance of the ethical qualities of sports, as in his most famous line of verse: "When the one Great Scorer comes to write against your name he marks—not that you won or lost—but how you played the game." After Knute Rockne's 1924 Notre Dame team defeated powerful Army, Rice composed the best-known opening lines in sportswriting history: "Outlined against a blue-grey October sky, the Four Horsemen rode again. In dramatic lore they are known as Famine, Pestilence, Destruction, and Death. These are only aliases. Their real names are Stuhldreher, Miller, Crowley, and Layden." (Only a cynic would wonder, as Red Smith did, whether Rice was prostrate when he observed the Four Horsemen "outlined against a blue-grey October sky.") Sportswriters frequently dispensed on-the-spot immortality on athletes. Even the race horse Man O' War was immortal; he was the "horse of eternity."

Despite Rice's popularity, by the 1920s his form of sportswriting had begun to wane. A new group of sportswriters, led by (among others) Paul Gallico, Frank Graham, Damon Runyan, Ring Lardner, Westbrook Pegler, Heywood Broun, and Arch Ward, replaced the verse writers. These writers conceived of themselves as literary craftsmen rather than poets or investigative reporters. They saw their task to be the construction of an interesting story of what had happened or what was likely to happen—a conception of responsibility that led them to enhance rather than reduce the potency of the sports drama. After witnessing a contest, they looked for an "angle," or a theme to tie together the beginning, the middle, and the end. The best of them could weave a story as tersely and tightly as the strands in a steel cable. Apart from a coherent narrative, they employed powerful, often onomatopoetic, verbs, such as "smash" for "hit"; colorful figures of speech, such as "turf" for "field"; and outrageous nicknames. Alliterative nicknames came in a virtual flood: The Galloping Ghost (Red Grange), The Fordham Flash (Frankie Frisch), The

Sultan of Swat (Babe Ruth). They delighted in using all three names of people involved in sports—Grover Cleveland Alexander, Kenesaw Mountain Landis, or George Herman Ruth—thereby conferring upon them a kind of tongue-in-cheek dignity.

The literary school of sportswriting insulated the frailties of the athletes from their adoring admirers. "You know," a retired ball player once told Roger Kahn, "when I think of all the people I influenced, the fathers and sons who never met me, I get scared as hell. I was pretty much like any other guy. . . . It was only later looking back, that I thought, 'Son of a bitch, I was a hero.' That's what scares me. I got drunk, chased puss and down around home I had to carry out the garbage. I wasn't a very heroic guy." But the old-timer need not have worried, for the sportswriters felt obligated to protect the private lives of the athletes. Sometimes they apparently deluded themselves. Red Barber, a renowned baseball broadcaster who referred to every ball player as a gentleman, insisted that he never heard an obscenity spoken on a ball field.

Walter "Red" Smith, described by Ernest Hemingway as "the most influential single force in American sportswriting," bridged the generations of the storytellers and the modern sports essayists. Smith wrote with economy, candor, wit and keen intelligence. One could find references to the "yammer of radio announcers," the "conceit of managers," and a "bibulation of sportswriters" in his columns. As he grew older, Smith became more critical of the sports world. He crusaded against racism, against the reserve clause in player contracts, against owner arrogance, and against the influence of television on sports. His syndicated newspaper articles and essays in *Sports Illustrated* from the 1950s to the 1980s inspired many younger writers to embark upon their own crusades.

Although survivors of the literary tradition in sportswriting can be found on the sports pages of newspapers today, in the 1960s sportswriting began to take a new turn. Since presumably the fans could see for themselves (on television) the drama transpiring on the field of play, reporters tried to cover dimensions of the contest hidden from the cameras. Rather than trusting their own powers of observation and expression, and lacking faith in the power of the written word, reporters often turned to the opinions of others. Thus, in the age of television, the post-game interview of coaches and players became a kind of ritual. Stories might consist of little more than quotations of game participants strung together. A fan might look in vain for a coherent account of how and why the game turned out as it did. At best, such sportswriting contributed little or nothing to the drama of sports, or to the heroes who occupied the playing fields. "Reading sports pages and articles," Roger Kahn observed in a 1976 issue of *Esquire*, "one has little sense of strolling through a pantheon. Like the newly hirsute women of the girlie journals, athletes are becoming practically real."

Other modern sportswriters, influenced by the Vietnam War and the counterculture of the 1960s, attacked the sports world itself; they conceived their job to be the smashing of the false illusions that surrounded sports. They explored racism, sexism, drugs, religion, gambling, cheating, violence, and the business side of sports. A fan might find on the sports pages more about what happened in the courtroom, the boardroom, and the bedroom than what happened on the field of play. Making sociology or economics the central considerations in sports reporting also detracted from the games themselves and often offended sports fans. The sports page, fans believed, should be free of wars, politics, murder, and matters of salary, discrimination, and high finance. Indeed, the fan read the sports page to find relief from daily turmoil; the sports page should convey the mystery, wonder, continuity, and heroism of sports.

Radio, which began to have an impact on sports in the 1920s but did not reach its apogee until the 1940s and 1950s, brought a totally new experience of sports to the fan. Now the fan did not have to await his morning newspaper; he instantly shared the drama transpiring on the playing field. Rather than witnessing the event live or reading about it, the fan heard a mellow-voiced radio announcer describe the drama. While remaining loyal to the basic facts, the announcers could add drama by resorting to hyperbole or altering the rhythm and inflection of their deliveries. Radio inspired the imagination. Since listeners could not see what was happening, they were free to take liberties with the content of what they heard on the radio. Rather than visualizing that the shortstop had merely stopped a routine ground ball, the listener might imagine that it had been a hard smash; an ordinary fly ball might be transformed into a long drive; a mediocre pass from the quarterback might become a beautiful spiral; and a defensive left hook to the jaw might become a crushing left to the chin.

Initially, radio aired only the more spectacular sporting events rather than regularly scheduled contests. Since the first stations failed to realize the potential profitability of advertising, they sought only to create a demand for more radio sets. To sell more sets, they attempted to grab the attention of would-be listeners by broadcasting big prize fights, classic college football encounters (Army versus Notre Dame, for example), and the World Series.

A special 1921 broadcast of the Georges Carpentier–Jack Dempsey heavyweight championship of the world fight held in Jersey City, New Jersey, furnished an early indication of some of the potentialities of radio sports. While Tex Rickard, the leading sports impresario of the day, set out to convince the public that they were about to witness the "Battle of the Century"—the debonair war hero of France (Carpentier) versus the dark-visaged peasant (Dempsey)—David Sarnoff hired Major J. Andrew White, an experienced radio man, to solve the engineering problems that arose from broadcasting a bout held in an open air arena far away from existing radio transmitters. White borrowed a transmitter from the United States Navy and strung an aerial between two Lackawanna Railroad towers in Hoboken. He convinced the railroad to permit him to place his equipment in a nearby metal shack used by porters as quarters for dressing and sleeping; the vigorous protests of the porters went for naught. On the day of the fight, White, sitting alongside a nervous Sarnoff, spoke into a microphone connected to the shack in Hoboken. At the shack, a technician listened to the description furnished by White and wrote down the pertinent details for another technician, J. O. Smith, to read over the air.

The broadcast created something of a sensation. Fight fans from as far away as Florida reported hearing the broadcast. Shopkeepers in New York City rigged up phonograph horns to magnify the voice coming over their radio sets; listeners could then hear the fight either in the street or inside the stores. Perhaps as many as 200,000 persons simultaneously heard the classic sporting event.

Even after advertising became a major source of revenue for radio, prize fighting remained a staple of sports broadcasting. As early as 1923, an estimated two million fans listened to the broadcast of the Luis Firpo–Jess Willard heavyweight fight. Four years later, probably fifty million Americans heard Graham McNamee's excited account of the second Jack Dempsey–Gene Tunney fight. According to *Radio Digest*, 127 fight fans dropped dead during McNamee's tense description. In 1938, perhaps two-thirds of the American people heard Joe Louis knock out Max Schmeling, the darling of the Nazis, in the first round. And because radio had developed the know-how to tape events, those who missed it live were able to hear a replay of the knockout ad nauseam. Probably no other event in radio history, including Franklin D. Roosevelt's famous fireside chats, enjoyed such a large audience.

Until they were upstaged by television in the 1950s, the radio broadcasts of baseball's World Series became an annual rite. The *New York Times* deemed the broadcast of the 1926 Series to be such a pioneering venture that it carried the entire narrative in its sports section. By the mid-1930s, Judge Kenesaw Mountain Landis, the indomitable Commissioner of Baseball, was successfully insisting that advertisers pay dearly for association with the Series. The Ford Motor Company paid $100,000 for the privilege of sponsoring the 1934 Series on all three major networks of the day: NBC, CBS, and the Mutual Broadcasting Company. In 1939 the Gillette Safety Razor Company began its thirty-two year stint as the regular sponsor of the Series.

Landis oversaw the contents of the broadcasts with a firm hand. He required that the Series announcers omit the names of visiting Hollywood celebrities for fear that they might steal the limelight from the games. He also asked that the play-by-play men refrain from questioning the decisions of umpires or the wisdom of team managers. When Ted Husing, CBS's premier sportscaster, criticized some of the decisions of the umpires in the 1933 Series, Landis banned him from the World Series broadcast booth for life. Such ironclad control over announcers by the moguls of professional sports, or their representatives, continued in the age of televised sports. Members of the sports establishment never perceived broadcasters as journalists. The first obligation of play-by-play men, as they saw it, was to promote, not report, the sport.

Radio broadcasts of regular season big-league games caught on much more slowly than World Series broadcasts. Chicago was an exception; by the late 1920s it had become a hotbed of early baseball broadcasting. Unlike most baseball owners, William Wrigley, the chewing gum magnate and owner of the Chicago Cubs, welcomed radio coverage; he believed radio accounts stimulated interest in big-league baseball and increased attendance. Initially, Wrigley charged the stations nothing for the privilege of doing the broadcasts. Consequently, as many as seven Chicago radio stations sometimes carried Cubs games. Wrigley continued to hold a similar attitude when television intruded its way into major league baseball. In 1949, all three Chicago television stations carried Cubs games. Wrigley Field, the home of the Cubs, looked "like a forest of TV cameras," according to Harold Rosenthal of the *New York Times*.

In New York and most other big-league cities, baseball magnates feared the worst from radio. Owners worried lest radio play-by-play accounts encourage the fans to stay at home rather than make their way to the park. In 1932 the major leagues came close to banning regular season baseball broadcasts entirely. Two years later the Yankees, Giants, and Dodgers, all in New York City, agreed to a pact outlawing radio accounts of their games for five years. During the final year of the ban, Larry MacPhail, a baseball promoter who had introduced night baseball, cigarette girls in satin pants, and red player uniforms while serving as general manager of the Cincinnati Reds, became the new head man of the Dodgers. He secretly negotiated a deal with General Mills to sponsor all Dodger games in 1939 for $70,000. The contract compelled both the Giants and Yankees to capitulate; they began to permit broadcasts of road games while continuing to resist the airing of home games. By 1945, when World War II ended, all big-league teams sold the rights to their regular season broadcasts. Each year the sums received from advertisers mounted. In 1933 the teams averaged less than $1,000 each from broadcasts; in 1950 each franchise received an average in excess of $200,000 from radio.

Even in the age of televised sports, radio continued to be an important medium for the transmission of regular season baseball games. Between 1945 and 1950 the number of locally operated AM radio stations doubled; these stations often turned to baseball to fill program gaps. For instance, in the 1950s the Mutual Broadcasting Company sent its "Game of the Day" to nearly 500 stations scattered across the country. In parts of the Far West a listener could hear baseball broadcasts from 11:00 in the morning until 11:00 at night. In the late 1940s and early 1950s, the St. Louis Cardinals regional network, one of the largest, regularly included some 120 stations spread out over nine states. On weekends the arrival of busloads of Cardinal fans from cities located several hundred miles from St. Louis furnished visible testimony of the capacity of radio to create and enhance fan loyalty over a large regional area.

Until the mid-1950s, many baseball broadcasts consisted of "re-creations" rather than live play-by-play coverage. Since sending a crew to a far-off location (not to mention telephone charges) could be excessively expensive, stations would re-create sports events from Western Union reports. Miles from the site of the game, a Western Union operator would receive a Morse code report of the game and would transcribe the dots and dashes into a shorthand version of the contest. The announcer then described the game from the shorthand version as though he were actually witnessing the live event. As a backdrop, sound technicians furnished recordings of crowd noises. Sometimes loud cheering broke out on the recording at an entirely inappropriate time. The announcer would quickly invent a spectacular catch of a foul ball by a fan or perhaps a rhubarb between the umpire and a manager. Sometimes the Western Union ticker broke down; radio fans then might be treated to a batter hitting a dozen fouls in succession or a sudden, inexplicable rain shower.

Roger Angell recalled in 1982:

> I remember . . . me at ten or eleven, with my ear next to the illuminated, innerly-warmed gold celluloid dial of the chunky, polished-wood family radio, from which there emerges, after an anxious silence, the clickety, train-depot sounds of a telegraph instrument suddenly bursting with news. . . . "*Uh*-oh . . . Hafey really got a hold of that delivery from Fat Freddie. The ball is rolling all the way to the wall in left and here come two more Cardinal runs across the plate. . . ." The front door slams—my father home from work, with the New York *Sun* under his arm (and the early-inning zeros of the same Giants road game on the front page, with the little white boxes for the rest of the line score still blank), and I get up to meet him with the bad news.

The costs of re-creations were so low that many stations relied totally upon such broadcasts. Station WHO in Des Moines, Iowa, for example, used a popular local announcer, Ronald "Dutch" Reagan, to re-create all the games of the Chicago Cubs. But a court ruling in 1955 that stations and networks had to pay sports franchises for re-creations and the growing popularity of televised sports sharply reduced the number of re-created broadcasts.

For many decades, millions of Americans found in the radio coverage of baseball games both an escape from the humdrum of everyday life and a separate wonderland of the imagination. "Radio—mysterious, disembodied, vivid as a dream—screamed for fantasy response," wrote Bil Gilbert in the July 28, 1969 issue of *Sports Illustrated* of his experiences listening to the games of the Detroit Tigers while a youngster in the 1930s. Even when not listening to Tiger games, Gilbert imitated the Detroit broadcaster's voice as he described to himself the tossing of a ball on the roof of his home or throwing stones at a target. In his private world, where Gilbert always had his beloved Tigers crush rivals, he never suffered from the humiliation of defeat. On a remote farm in southern Missouri, Harry Caray's vivid descriptions of St. Louis Cardinals games led two young brothers to invent an entirely mythical league populated by ball players who performed only in accordance with the dreams and imaginations of their creators. For Gilbert, the Missouri youths, and millions like them, television intruded upon the imagination; it reduced the magic of baseball. "Thereafter baseball was never again serious," Gilbert has written. "The trouble is that it is very hard to have bigger-than-life imaginary playmates when smaller-than-life, but photographically accurate models of the real thing are living-room intimates."

Although radio often featured sporting events of national interest, it was most potent in strengthening the bonds between fans and their local teams. Besides both major league and minor league baseball games, local stations often carried local high school football and basketball games. They might also air the games of nearby colleges or the state university. Unlike the fan who sits down before his television set on a weekend afternoon to watch a professional baseball or football game of national importance but of little local significance, the fan listening to the games of the local team on radio invariably had an emotional stake in the contest.

Early radio men soon discovered that sports fans wanted announcers who were something more than disembodied voices objectively and dispassionately describing the action. The fans wanted announcers capable of becoming celebrities in their own right. Graham McNamee, a baritone singer of small repute in New York, became the first star of the new medium. In 1923, McNamee wandered into WEAF in New York City (which in 1926 became the flagship station of the newly organized NBC radio network) and immediately obtained a job as an announcer. McNamee enjoyed a remarkable capacity for using his voice to span the gamut of emotions—of, as a contemporary put it, "becoming audibly excited at crucial moments, using the popular idiom, putting the spirit of every punch, every pitch, every run into his voice, speeding up his voice with the tensions of the play, letting it subside with the aftermath of calm." Universally hailed as "The World's Most Popular Announcer," he received over 50,000 letters from infatuated fans in the wake of his descriptions of the 1925 World Series. For NBC, McNamee also covered prize fights; major college football games; important live news developments, such as the arrival of Charles A. Lindbergh in Paris in 1927; and national political conventions. Other sports announcers, such as Ted Husing and Bill Stern in the 1930s and 1940s, received national recognition, but none quite equaled the stature of McNamee until Dizzy Dean arrived on the national broadcasting scene in the 1950s.

But on the local scene, regular season baseball broadcasters became virtual institutions. To the fans, they were often inseparable from the team and its fate. The voice of the Boston Red Sox was Curt Gowdy, that of the Philadelphia Phillies, By Saam. The Pittsburgh Pirates' man was Bob Prince, the Cincinnati Reds' Waite Hoyt, the St. Louis Cardinals' Harry Caray. In New York, Russ Hodges represented the Giants, Mel Allen the Yankees, and Red Barber the Dodgers. Mel Allen and Harry Caray were masters of the "Gee Whiz" style of broadcasting, which sometimes elevated the ordinary play into the realm of the immortal. Red Barber, on the other hand, relied on precise description—along with the eloquence and Southern drawl he shared with Allen—to enchant Brooklyn fans. Barber began his career doing Cincinnati Reds games for a mere $25 a week in 1934; by 1954, when Barber joined the Yankees, his salary had risen to $50,000 annually. But annoyed by Barber's candor, the Yankee management fired him in 1967. Mel Allen had been replaced two years earlier, by ex-player Joe Garagiola. Other former players—George Kell, Ralph Kiner,

Richie Ashburn—were invading the radio-television booths of many big-league clubs.

The requirements of strict accuracy in reporting rarely inhibited the mellow-voiced radio announcers. Since their listeners were not present to see things for themselves, the announcers could take unbridled freedom with the truth. McNamee himself was notorious for the absence of precision in his broadcasts. If he asserted that the wrong back was toting the ball in a football game, he would try to correct himself by quickly declaring that the ball had been lateraled to the player who was actually carrying it. After sitting alongside McNamee during his broadcast of a World Series game, Ring Lardner observed that "the Washington Senators and the New York Giants must have played a double-header this afternoon—the game I saw and the game Graham McNamee announced."

Sports also sometimes furnished the raw material for radio melodrama masquerading as true stories. For nearly a decade bridging the 1930s and the 1940s, Bill Stern, a CBS announcer, hosted an immensely popular program, "Colgate Sports Newsreel," that deliberately falsified reports of athletes and sports events for dramatic effect. From his deathbed, Abraham Lincoln, according to Stern, summoned a nearby general. "Keep baseball going. The country needs it," said Lincoln. The general's name, Stern cried triumphantly, was Abner Doubleday. Stern told of a dejected Frankie Frisch, who was on the verge of quitting Fordham University and ending his life. A sympathetic priest saw Frisch and urged him to give his life "to the great game of baseball. And that priest's name," Stern exuberantly shouted, "was Eugenio Pacelli. Yes, the same Eugenio Pacelli who is famous the world over today as Pope Pius." Few doubted; millions listened in wonderment.

Stern admitted that "these . . . dramatized stories . . . were aimed solely at entertaining those who listened to my show. . . . Diversion was my stock in trade and I thrived, rightly or not, on the same fanciful principles used by other communications media which lift audiences out of a humdrum, monotonous existence of mundane fact and insipid incident." On "Newsreel," as radio critic John Crosby observed, Stern "created his own little world of sportsdom, where every man is a Frank Merriwell, every touchdown an epic feat of arms, and coincidence stretches like a rubber band to fit every conceivable situation.'' Athletes, since they were invariably cast in superheroic dimensions, were only too happy to appear on Stern's program. While a razor-thin line separated Stern's free-wheeling liberties with authenticity from the frankly dramatic radio series based on sports, such as ''Jack Armstrong— The All-American Boy,'' Stern probably did not reduce the public's love of sports. He may have added to it.

Radio has been—and even continues to be—a major medium for the transmission of the sporting experience to the American people. Radio encouraged interest in sports at all geographical levels: locally, regionally, and nationally. Perhaps more ominously, some sports announcers became celebrities in their own right, thereby potentially detracting from the fans' undiluted experience of sports. On a more mundane level, radio's experience with sports exercised a powerful influence upon early television coverage of sports. The early announcers brought with them the knowledge and habits they had gained from doing radio coverage. Likewise, club owners, league commissioners, and college authorities often approached the new medium of television based on the knowledge they had gained from dealing with radio broadcasts of sports.

Few dreamed that after World War II the new medium of television would exert a far more profound influence on the history of American sports than had magazines, newspapers, and radio. At mid-twentieth century, at the very moment that the power of sports appeared to be so ascendant in American life, sports and television began to consummate a series of marriages. Ultimately, the marriages radically transformed the ways in which Americans experienced sports.

3

Torrid but Short Romances

The inaugural issue of the new magazine *Sports Illustrated*, released in mid-August, 1954, proclaimed that "The Golden Age Is Now." "For world-wide interest, for widespread participation, for shattered records, for thrilling triumphs of the human spirit," declared *Sports Illustrated* feature writer Gerald Holland, "this is the greatest sports era in history." While Holland admitted that the 1950s had not yet produced a galaxy of superstars equal to that of the 1920s, he cited impressive evidence to support his claim that the nation had entered a "new golden age" of sports. Statistically, the number of bowling alleys, fishing and hunting licenses, golfers, and softball players had reached all-time highs. Swimming records seemed to be falling almost monthly; at the British Empire Games, Roger Bannister and John Landy had both just completed the mile run in under four minutes; and Florence Chadwick had recently shaved a full hour off of Gertrude Ederle's record for swimming the English Channel. Finally, according to Holland, the new medium of television was creating millions of new sports fans.

Yet beneath the surface of sports prosperity lurked omens of trouble. Something was awry in the national game of baseball. Angered by the independence displayed by A. B. "Happy" Chandler as Commissioner, the owners fired him in 1951; they hired an innocuous former sportswriter, Ford Frick, to replace Chandler. Major and minor league attendance fell for the second year in a row. A string of ugly stories about corruption in college sports leaped to the headlines of the nation's press. The United States Military Academy acknowledged that all but two members of its vaunted varsity football team had been dismissed for cheating on examinations. The public soon learned that college basketball was the victim of the biggest scandal in the history of American sports; in exchange for keeping the point spread of games within the range called for by certain gamblers, players had been paid cash by the gamblers. Perhaps a more significant harbinger of the future of sports occurred in St. Louis, where in a desperate effort to attract fans, Bill Veeck, the owner of the lowly Browns, hired a midget as a pinch hitter.

Unknown to the keenest observers of the early 1950s, the nation had entered a new age of sports. While additional millions began to watch sports on television, attendance at sporting events fell, and it would take nearly a decade before full recovery could be achieved. In Washington, D.C., men and women sitting at wooden desks with electric adding machines toted up the grim figures. Consumption expenditures on spectator sports, the Census Bureau reported, had averaged $282.2 million in constant dollars for the 1947–49 era. Then the descent began; for the decade of the 1950s the annual average was $252.4 million. Attendance at nearly all forms of public entertainment—major and minor league baseball; college football; even high school football games, boxing, and the movies—dropped precipitously.

The Great Sports Slump of the 1950s reflected a revolution in the ways that Americans had begun to spend their spare time. Television was only one of the ways, albeit perhaps the most important of all. In the post–World War II era, there was a shift from inner-city, public forms of recreation to private, home-centered forms of recreation. This increased privatization of leisure resulted in a decline in attendance at most sporting events and thus a curtailment of the direct involvement of fans in the drama of sports.

In the past, urban dwellers usually looked to the inner city for entertainment. There they might find concert halls, museums, shopping streets, theaters, vaudeville houses, ball parks, gymnasiums, restaurants, and later movie houses. Saloons were a favorite retreat for all-male groups; others without the wherewithal to patronize commercial entertainment might visit neighbors and friends on their front porches or their stoops.

Then after World War II, when millions of Americans moved to the suburbs, their spare-time activities moved with them. In suburbia residents might bowl more, play softball, attend church, go to the beach or a nearby lake, or hunt and fish, but they often left behind them public entertainment located in the inner city. Above all else, suburbanites spent more of their spare time at home. There, they made home repairs, tried to conquer the crabgrass frontier, explored sex as an at-home sport, raised children, listened to music on high-fidelity phonographs, and watched television.

Earlier movements of people to the exteriors of American cities paled beside the great waves of the post–World War II era. For nearly two decades, the Great Depression of the 1930s and the great war of the early 1940s had stunted family life and the building of adequate housing. Returning veterans married, set off a "baby boom," and bought houses in the suburbs. Subsidies by the Federal Housing Administration and the Veterans Administration, bold subdividers with a knack for building houses en masse, and soaring automobile sales soon transformed cornfields and cow pastures into acres and acres of suburbs. In the suburbs, one hoped to escape the crowding, crime, dirt, and racial tension of the city, to be closer to nature, to own a house, and to have one's own yard so that one's son could grow up with grass stains on the knees of his blue jeans. The home became a self-sufficient recreational center, or a "family playpen," to use anthropologist Margaret Mead's apt phrase. The enjoyment of children and "family togetherness," according to the popular media of the postwar era, became virtually a moral obligation.

Suburbia, in conjunction with television, fractured older all-male relationships. Beginning in adolescence, males in the past often established a close network of friendships based upon meetings at their workplaces, taverns, bowling alleys, or even street corners. In the 1920s, William Foote Whyte had brilliantly analyzed such a male, working-class, Italian-American group in Boston. But in the 1950s, in a neighborhood less than a mile from the one described by Whyte, Herbert Gans found that the male social system had broken down. Instead of joining their friends at the saloon or streetcorner, the Italian-American men were now inside their homes with their wives watching television. The traditional night or nights out with the boys had become an obsolete social practice. Men attended fewer sporting events, and when they did go to the fights or a baseball game, they took their wives or girl friends with them.

After having crept through enormous traffic jams to get in and out of the city by day, weary suburban husbands had little desire to return at night. In the late 1940s, and especially in the early 1950s, downtown public recreation fell into a deep slump. Inner-city restaurants closed, and movie attendance nosedived. In Newark, New Jersey, which was to become one of the more blighted American cities, only fourteen out of an original sixty-five movie theaters survived. In the past, because of the oppressive heat in the summer and the absence of warmth in the winter, the house or apartment had been a place to leave. But suburban houses, with their central heating and air conditioning, invited one to stay inside. Fewer Americans found any reason to "waste" time and money by going out to a restaurant, movie, concert, or baseball game when in the family living room they could watch "I Love Lucy" and the New York Yankees on television free.

The ubiquitous television set, often located on a swivel so that it could be watched from anywhere in the room, was at the center of the revolution in leisure. "And so the monumental change began in our lives and those of millions of other Americans," recalled one man about the effects of the purchase of the family's first television set in 1950. "More than a year passed before we again visited a movie theater. Money which previously would have been spent for books was saved for TV payments. Social evenings with friends became fewer and fewer still." By 1950, nearly four million Americans owned sets. According to a study published in the *American Psychologist*, each family had the set turned on for an average of five hours each day. By 1956, over 75 percent of all families owned a television set.

The shifting patterns of leisure embraced more than television and other forms of at-home entertainment; direct participation in a host of activities ranging from softball playing to fishing and hunting grew at unprecedented rates. Until the mid-1930s, softball had hardly existed as a sport, but play by defense workers in World War II, along with cheap lighting (which permitted play at night), resulted in some 20 million people playing the sport by

1955. In certain youth groups the car itself became a major source of recreation; youths customized their cars, used them for drag or stock car racing, and took them to suburban drive-in movies. The car and additional income permitted more Americans to tour, to hunt and fish, and to visit National Parks. By the mid-fifties, fifteen times more people visited National Parks than in the 1930s. The sale of hunting and fishing licenses doubled between 1947 and 1953. Interest in water sports flourished. On weekends, everyone, it seemed, rushed to nearby lakes, rivers, or ocean beaches. Instead of going to watch the local Knoxville Smokies play minor league baseball, according to J. Anthony Lukas in *Harper's* (1967), men now spent warm lazy evenings lolling by a beer cooler in the back of their boats on Norris Lake (part of the TVA chain), trolling for walleyes and bluegills. Little wonder that minor league and major league baseball attendance tumbled downward.

After World War II, television quickly began to make significant headway as a popular source of entertainment. By 1948, factories were turning out 140,000 new sets a month. Reception was still unpredictable. The Orthicon camera, affectionately called "Doctor Cyclops" by crewmen, often failed to convey a picture or beamed blinking images blurred with white smudges that viewers described as "snow." Delays could last up to an hour. Viewers expected to be treated to numerous "PLEASE STAND BY" signs, sometimes decorated with little symbols of crossed bats or a pair of boxing gloves. Patient viewers even sent the networks letters evaluating the artwork of their apologies.

In the late 1940s and early 1950s, sports constituted a major part of television programming, including even prime evening hours. In New York and other large cities one could see hours and hours of wrestling, Roller Derby, and boxing; baseball, basketball, and football received almost no prime time coverage. Sports seemed perfectly suited to the pioneering stage of the new medium's development. Compared with other forms of programming, the beaming of sports events was economical. Many sports moguls also thought television hyped the live gate; thus they were eager to have their sport shown on television. They often charged little or nothing for their television rights. The networks and early television stations put little money into the production of sporting events; often they used only a single camera and a small crew of less than half a dozen men. But, as more people purchased sets and advertising revenues mounted, the networks poured more money into programming. Then sports had to compete with the likes of "Gunsmoke," "Twenty-One," and "The Untouchables." After the mid-1950s, of all the sports shown earlier in the decade, only boxing remained a regular feature of prime time network television; in the 1960s it too would disappear from prime time.

In the 1950s, television technology placed severe constraints on sports telecasts. Satisfactory color television, for instance, did not develop until the 1960s. Without the use of multiple cameras, multiple lens, instant replays, and slow motion shots—all of which awaited the 1960s—the chaotic action of football could not be easily translated to the small screen. In the 1950s, with television limited to the use of only one or perhaps two cameras and a single lens, individual sports fared much better on the screen than team sports. In addition, early television favored those sports which graphically displayed individual acts of violence or faked violence. Thus in the late 1940s and the early 1950s, television gave over more hours to wrestling and boxing than to baseball, basketball, and football. When after mid-decade the networks began to produce more and more drama series devoted to brutality and violence, the ratings for wrestling and boxing fell.

Even in the 1950s the new medium already tended to alter the fundamental nature of the spectator's experience of sports. Wrestling and Roller Derby, two of early television's favorite "sports," featured fake, stylized forms of physical violence rather than genuine athletic competition; television encouraged the players to engage in even more extravagant showmanship. Television altered more radically the traditional mode of prize fighting. Sensing that most of the viewers—many of whom were persons who had never witnessed a live prize fight—wanted to see more brutal action, producers urged slugfests at the expense of boxing finesse.

Professional wrestling was a notorious example of the fusion of the real and the unreal in televised sports. Prior to the twentieth century, wrestling matches sometimes consisted of two sweating giants frozen for several hours in mutual hammerlocks. Facing possible extinction, pro wrestling—even before television—had gradually begun to transform itself into a giant morality play, one which increasingly bore little resemblance to a genuine sport.

Everywhere the routine was the same. One wrestler incarnated absolute good, the other absolute evil. Speaking gibberish and glowering wickedly, the villain repeatedly broke the rules and brought chaos to the ring. The evil wrestler stomped the hero with his feet, slammed his head against the ring posts, and pulled his hair. Yet in the end the hero, always relying only upon fair means, subdued the villain. Fans then had the satisfaction of seeing justice and order restored. Unlike day-to-day existence, where ambiguity if not injustice often reigned supreme, the world of wrestling was an intensely moral one. Good and evil stood in sharp contrast.

As a morality play, televised wrestling incorporated all of the techniques of theater. The wrestlers cooperated in a "combat ballet." They donned theatrical costumes and assumed theatrical names: The Swedish Angel, The Zebra Kid, Gorgeous George, Mr. America, Ricki Starr, and Antonino Rocca. Gorgeous George, the first television wrestling superstar, sported long, flowing curls. Television even brought to the viewers lady and midget wrestling. In due time the events became even splashier; contestants made grand entrances complete with entourages of fan bearers, slave girls, and sedan chair carriers.

Theatrical wrestling became the rage of early television. Spectators crowded into bars and in front of furniture store showroom windows to watch the televised matches. While the speed of team sports and the large number of participants might obscure the drama, in wrestling the action centered on only two athletes. No replay or slow motion shots were needed, for the wrestlers perfected the art of excessive gestures. Their histrionics projected in stark clarity the progress of the match. A wrestler thrown to the mat, for instance, dramatized the event by appearing to be totally powerless. To hype the gate, television encouraged the wrestlers to make outrageous remarks about each other, a promotional strategy later used effectively by Muhammad Ali in boxing. For television the wrestlers adopted a more gymnastic style, one that included aerial moves such as drop kicks, flying head scissors, and backward flips; these replaced the more tedious arm and head locks.

The crowds and the television announcers became part of the show. The viewers loved the antics of ringside fanatics; they took special delight in "Hatpin Mary," who, sitting at ringside, regularly stuck the villains with a deadly hatpin. The DuMont network's man at ringside, Dennis James, who was later to become a game show host, probably did even more to popularize wrestling on television. He came equipped with dog biscuits (which he threw out to the hungry "beasts" in the ring), walnut shells and pieces of wood (which he cracked in front of the microphone to simulate breaking bones), and balloons (which he rubbed together to give the impression of agonizing groans). When a grappler was thrown across the ring, James would quickly play a cadenza on his harmonica. James baited the "bad guys" and egged on the "good guys." *Newsweek* declared in 1948 that James had "become a minority celebrity" in his own right—an important harbinger of things to come in television sports. Ladies, according to *Newsweek*, were especially infatuated with the handsome announcer.

Eventually over 200 stations carried at least one wrestling match each week, but by the mid-1950s televised wrestling had faded from the network television scene. In the face of other kinds of programming and perhaps audience saturation, ratings fell. Nonetheless, wrestling remained strong on the fringes of the television industry. Promoters used late night and non–peak hour televised matches to tantalize viewers into attending local wrestling cards. As a gimmick to hype local matches, theatrical wrestling continues today to be a staple of local television stations.

Roller Derby may have represented an even more notorious instance of television's fusion of the genuine and the fake. In a desperate effort to attract fans to half-filled big city arenas in the 1930s, Leo A. Seltzer of Chicago, who was also responsible for the dancing marathon craze of the depression years, designed Roller Derby on a kitchen table cloth in 1935. But Roller Derby, which consisted of both male and female roller skaters dashing madly around a steeply banked arena, caught on only with the advent of television. Fans seemed to love the rough-and-tumble, partly faked violence. The violence included body checks, sometimes pulled hair, fist fights, and outrageous grandstanding. Male fans seemed especially enamored with the spectacle of female skaters belting one another. Midge "Toughie" Brasuhn, "the toughest tomato on skates," became a household name; she regularly whacked fellow female skaters with a deadly forearm or her fists.

During the performance, a circus-like barker urged the crowd to cheer their heroes or heroines and boo the unscrupulous deeds of the villains.

Tied directly to television, the success of the Derby roller-coasted between long valleys of depression and two short peaks of prosperity. Like local television wrestling producers, Seltzer used televised Roller Derby to increase gate attendance; he received little revenue directly from the medium. By 1950, the Derby shared the prime time television limelight with boxing, wrestling, and Milton Berle. In 1951, the Derby attracted 82,000 fans to five engagements at Madison Square Garden. Then the bubble of prosperity burst. By the fall of 1951 the Derby was off network television; endless hours of Derby telecasting had apparently jaded the public.

Yet, in due time, the "sport" rebounded. In 1972, Roller Derby, dubbed by one wag as the sport of the "human bumper cars," peaked again. It drew over five million often hysterical fans to arenas and eighteen million viewers for its weekly television slot. Then the Roller Derby industry suddenly splintered into warring factions, and by the mid-1970s, competing promoters had nearly hyped the "sport" to death for a second time.

No sport experienced the impact of the media more decisively in the late 1940s and the 1950s than prize fighting. Historically, the "manly art" had been a sport supported by an unusual alliance of "outsiders"—blacks, ethnics, and workingmen—on the one hand and a hedonistic fringe of well-to-do "insiders" on the other. Always in the background was the shady world of racketeers, hit men, scalpers, thugs, and bookies. Since the days of the peerless John L. Sullivan in the 1880s and 1890s, the sport, as the ultimate metaphor of masculine conflict, had enjoyed a large following; its mystique for men may have exceeded that of any other sport. In the 1920s, clandestine fights on barges, in the backrooms of saloons, and in isolated rural spots gave way to fights held in huge outdoor stadiums and glittering arenas. Tex Rickard, the Phineas T. Barnum of fight promoters, and radio gave prize fighting a new respectability among the middle class. Most states dropped their legal bans on fights. The Great Depression and World War II temporarily set back boxing, but in the immediate post-war years television lifted the sport into a new Golden Age.

Yet in time the new medium dealt it a blow from which it never fully recovered.

From their very first encounter, television and prize fighting were locked in a passionate embrace. Only a few days after the historic telecast of the Columbia University baseball game, specifically on June 1, 1939, experimental station W2XBS of New York telecast a fight between Max Baer and Lou Nova held in Yankee Stadium. While NBC's cumbersome Iconoscopic camera had been terribly awkward in trying to cover the baseball game, it could easily focus on the details of the boxing ring. Viewers usually saw a sharp, steady picture. Several stores displayed sets turned on to the fight. Perhaps 20,000 people (more than those at Yankee Stadium) saw the fight on television. A media reviewer for the *New York Times* was "amazed and bewildered by the magic of it all. To see a prize fight telecast is 10,000 times more interesting than listening sightless to a broadcast announcer." He predicted that "carnage" would someday be the "dream of television."

And indeed it was. In the late 1940s, the passionate affair between television and professional fighting turned into orgy. Viewers in the bars of major cities and on their home screens (if they could afford sets) watched one or more fights nearly every night of the week. They could even see the best fighters perform: Rocky Graziano, Tony Zale, Sugar Ray Robinson, Jersey Joe Walcott, and Ezzard Charles. (Only the heavyweight championship fights usually remained off the small screen.) In New York City, Madison Square Garden, the Eastern Parkway Arena, St. Nicholas Arena, and Sunnyside Gardens were for a time virtually television boxing studios. Television even transformed people merely associated with the sport into celebrities. Bill the Bartender (Bill Nimmo), who hawked Pabst Blue Ribbon beer between rounds on Wednesday nights, became a household name; Ruby Goldstein, a boxing referee, was booked on the "Ed Sullivan Show"; and Dr. Joyce Brothers, a psychologist who had become famous for her display of boxing knowledge on "The $64,000 Question," assisted Jack Drees in his coverage of the Wednesday night fights.

Until television sets became commonplace in the home, "fight nights" at bars often attracted full houses. Patrons sometimes had to wait outside before they could obtain a place inside to watch. According to a *New Yorker* magazine account of a fight night at the Knife and Fork Tavern on Bleecker Street and West

Broadway in New York, the fans claimed that they liked television boxing better than going to the arena itself. Barroom stools are "a hell of a lot better than a ringside seat" that might cost a "hundred bucks," agreed the boxing barflies. But sometimes the early viewers had little patience with the limitations of the medium. When long-range shots reduced the size of the ring to a tiny square of brightness "with a couple of germs swimming in it," customers shouted to the bartender: "Fix it, Lou. We can't see nothing" or "Put us back on ringside, Lou."

To sell their products, breweries, tobacco companies, and razor blade makers exploited the public's enthusiasm for televised boxing. In 1944 the Gillette Company signed a pact with Madison Square Garden to sponsor weekly fight telecasts. For many Americans, the Friday night Gillette fights became an institution. Decades later the Gillette Cavalcade of Sports jingle (which is used here by permission of The Gillette Company's Safety Razor Division) could still evoke a deep nostalgia among veteran fight watchers:

> *To LOOK sharp*
> *Every time you shave,*
> *To FEEL sharp*
> *And be on the ball,*
> *Just BE sharp—*
> *Use Gillette Blue Blades*
> *For the quickest, slickest shaves*
> *Of aw-ll.*

Playwright David Trainer recalled in *TV Book* that he would sometimes climb into his father's lap to watch the fights. His father would drink Labatt's India Pale Ale, "and the heady aroma that arose when he poured the brew from the bottle to his glass often made me sleepier than I had been upstairs in bed." In preparation for each bout, Trainer and his father would read newspaper articles and make their own predictions. They usually made up scorecards and awarded rounds to fighters as they saw fit; sometimes they even made small wagers on the bouts. When Emile Griffith killed Benny "Kid" Paret in a 1962 televised fight, Trainer and his father stopped watching boxing matches.

Even after the heady days of early television had stabilized, the NBC and CBS networks continued to beam weekly fight cards.

As late as 1955, the Pabst Blue Ribbon telecast on Wednesday night and the Gillette Cavalcade of Sports fight on Friday night were among the highest rated shows on network television. The paychecks for fighters soared; boxers on network television received up to $4,000 a fight.

At the local level, television stations sometimes staged their own bouts. To grab the attention of as many viewers as possible, the stations rarely resisted the temptation to transform the traditional sporting experience into a mere spectacle. In New Orleans, for example, where sports had always held its own in a culture that had mothered jazz, Creole cooking, and the Mardi Gras, WDSU-TV and the local Pepsi-Cola Bottling Company inaugurated a weekly series of local boxing shows. The bouts, which featured the flailings of inept amateur teenagers, won the plaudits of the city's civic and religious leaders. WDSU explained to skeptical parents and community leaders that a carefully regulated boxing program would curb juvenile delinquency. To simulate an arena-like atmosphere, the station set up seats for 500 spectators, employed a professional ring announcer, and built a regulation-size ring. The "authentic" surroundings and the omnipresent television cameras stimulated the youngsters to fight with an unrelenting intensity that belied their tender years. A New York station even staged bouts between five- and six-year-old boys, and in Los Angeles a station carried fights between women.

Old-time fight fans bitterly complained that television had created a monster, an entirely new form of entertainment which bore only a faint resemblance to traditional boxing. Veteran fans of pugilism understood and appreciated the intricacies and aesthetics of a boxer's defensive finesse, of biding one's time until a proper opening occurred, and of softening up an opponent early in the match with nonlethal blows. When displayed on the tiny screen, however, the older style seemed almost unmanly. To television spectators, accustomed to the violence of cowboy shows, televised fights often seemed to be tame fare indeed—or so said Archie Moore, who had once been an old-style fighter himself. (In actuality, television could never capture the startling reality of splashing blood and sweat as blows landed; the medium softened the brutality of the sport.) In response to the demands of television, Moore changed his style from that of a classic boxer to that of a television slugger. So did many others. Television viewers, in the words of sportswriter John Lardner, were "punch hungry." And the boxers most in demand were those who won an appellation for having what promoters called a "good TV style." The traditional aesthetic of the ring was sacrificed to spectacle, to the demand by television viewers for more brutality.

Television transformed traditional fighting in other ways. The busy schedule of bouts on television required a never-ending supply of winning fighters. "The big thing you were up against is that there had to be a loser, you know? And you couldn't bring a loser back on TV," explained Chris Dundee, a prominent fight manager from Miami, Florida. "The sponsors didn't want losers, just winners. And let's face it, the sponsors called the shots during the TV age in boxing." Consequently, sponsors and managers rushed young fighters into main event bouts long before they had acquired the necessary skills to do well.

A clear instance was Chuck Davey, a handsome "television product" fresh off the campus of Michigan State University. Davey's career served as a grim omen of the future of televised boxing. Pitted against a series of abject journeymen on television, Davey skyrocketed to the top. Television fight audiences loved him; he became an instant "parlor hero." But then disaster struck. In 1953 Davey met the much more experienced Kid Gavilan for the welterweight crown. Some 35 million television fans watched Gavilan utterly embarrass the overmatched Davey. Davey could never come back. "One bad fight on TV would kill a guy," recalled Dundee. "Because everybody—I mean everybody—could see it." By 1956, according to Nat Fleischer, the editor of *Ring* magazine, the bible of boxing, television had depleted the ranks of professional fighters by a whopping 50 percent.

The voracious, insatiable demand by television for fighters encouraged the monopolization of fight promotion by the International Boxing Club (IBC). By controlling the key arenas, and indirectly through the underworld a large stable of fighters, Jim Norris, the president of the IBC, drove independent promoters out of the fight game. Between 1949 and 1953, Norris promoted all but two of the twenty-one championship bouts held in the United States. With Norris as the overlord of fight promotion, underworld figures Blinky Palermo and Frankie Carbo used the new fight market created by television to gain control of most of the nation's best fighters. In 1952 the Justice Department began antitrust proceedings against the IBC, which culminated in the dissolution of the organization in 1959. Carbo, Palermo, and Norris all eventually served short prison terms for income tax evasion. The antitrust actions and convictions for income tax fraud, along with televised hearings by the Kefauver Committee on organized crime (which included its dealings with boxing), darkened the reputation of a sport that had always had difficulty establishing an image of integrity.

The collapse of the romance between television and prize fighting came quickly. Television and other at-home activities drove down live attendance and destroyed the once-prospering small fight clubs, which were responsible for the nurture of future fighters. In 1948–49, ten to twelve thousand fans regularly watched the Friday night card at Madison Square Garden; by 1957, when the Garden had become little more than an oversized television studio, attendance averaged a mere 1,200. By 1958, along "Cauliflower Row," as the local "fight mob" dubbed Eighth Avenue in New York City, nearly all of the fight clubs and gyms had closed. In the early 1950s, over 300 fighters had worked out of Stillman's Gym; by 1958, only some 90 boxers used the famous fight factory. Television also wiped out the small-city circuit. The total number of fight clubs in the country declined from about 300 in 1952 to less than fifty by the end of the decade.

Television ratings told the same grim story. In 1952, 31 percent of all households watching television had their sets regularly tuned in to prime time fights; by 1959, the figure had fallen to only 10.6 percent. Apart from the other problems that beset the romance between television and boxing, by the late 1950s boxing simply could not compete head-on with the new prime time forms of programming. By 1960 only the Gillette Friday night bouts (cancelled in 1961, revived in 1963–64, but again dropped in 1964) appeared regularly on network television. Not even such a compelling media figure as Muhammad Ali could revive the sport as it once had been. Never again would the tiny arenas in Tacoma, Washington, Lincoln, Nebraska, and Bangor, Maine, nor the big arenas in Chicago, Detroit, and New York be filled regularly with ring patrons. Television had spelled disaster for the sport.

To seize and hold the attention of a maximum number of viewers, then, television had induced changes in the traditional modes of wrestling, Roller Derby, and prize fighting. In all three, physical motions took on more exaggerated forms: in wrestling, aerial moves; in Roller Derby, faked violence; and in prize fighting, slugging. Promoters and television producers added a larger array of extraneous entertainment: colorful announcers, gesturing athletes, and catchy music. But such measures ultimately reduced whatever authenticity these "sports" had once enjoyed. And in the long run the public simply lost interest in them. What remains to be examined is whether television and the privatization of leisure in the 1950s would prove equally disastrous to the National Game—baseball.

4

Major Minor Troubles

The American infatuation with baseball, like the attachment to many of the world's religions, arose in part from the myth of its creation. The myth that Abner Doubleday invented baseball at Cooperstown, New York, in the summer of 1839 apparently got underway some fifty years later. In 1889, Albert G. Spalding, a former big-league pitcher with an underhanded curve ball that baffled the hitters, then president of the Chicago baseball club and a pioneering sporting goods manufacturer, organized a world tour of professional ball players. Spalding had hoped to convert foreigners to the "American National Game" and (though he did not publicly admit it) to promote the sale of his sporting goods abroad. By and large, the foreigners remained unimpressed with Spalding, his ball players, and the American National Game.

Nonetheless, to welcome the return of Spalding and his players to American shores, National Baseball League authorities threw a huge banquet at Delmonico's restaurant in New York City. Some 300 celebrities, including Mark Twain, came. At the conclusion of a sumptuous meal, Abraham G. Mills, the fourth president of the National League, arose to speak. Carried away perhaps by the momentous nature of the occasion, or perhaps by too many toasts of red wine, Mills exclaimed that both "patriotism and research" revealed that baseball was an original American game. The audience responded warmly. "No rounders! No rounders!" they shouted. The assertion of Mills, according to the *New*

York Clipper, the leading sports sheet of the day, "forever squelched" the insidious rumor that baseball had foreign origins; in other words, that it had evolved from the English boys' game of rounders.

The *Clipper* was wrong. No doubt old-timers, if they heard Mills's claim or read the *Clipper* account, smiled, for they knew well enough that the game of baseball played in 1889 had gradually developed from various kinds of informal ball games played by boys on empty lots and village greens early in the nineteenth century. In 1903, Henry Chadwick, one of the most knowledgeable historians of the sport, reasserted the obvious, that baseball had arisen most directly from rounders. Even the rules of the two sports were nearly identical, Chadwick wrote.

Yet baseball leaders thought the dispute important enough to appoint a special commission of seven men of "high repute and undoubted knowledge of Base Ball" to resolve it for all time. Except for sending out letters of inquiry to old-time ball players associated with the sport, the commission engaged in no research, and unfortunately, a fire destroyed the letters from the old-timers. Undeterred, the commission (in 1907) published a report anyway. It concluded that "according to the best evidence obtainable to date," General Abner Doubleday, a Civil War hero, conceived baseball at Cooperstown in 1839. To support the Doubleday theory, the commission relied upon but one source, the recollections of Abner Graves, a former resident of Cooperstown. Graves, 68 years after the alleged event, recalled that in the spring of 1839 Doubleday "designed the game to be played by definite teams or sides. Doubleday called the game Base Ball, for there were four bases in it."

But the evidence against the Doubleday story is overwhelming. If Doubleday was at Cooperstown in 1839 (as claimed by Graves), then he must have been absent without leave from West Point, where, at the time, he was a cadet. Unfortunately, or perhaps fortunately for the myth, Doubleday had passed away before the commission began its investigation. At any rate, in his memoirs Doubleday never once even mentioned the sport of baseball. Furthermore, Abraham G. Mills, the chairman of the 1907 commission, was a long-time acquaintance of Doubleday, dating from the time they had served together in the Civil War. Yet prior to 1907 Mills had never asserted the Doubleday thesis, not even at the opportune moment of the Delmonico's feast in 1889. In 1937, a librarian, Robert W. Henderson, destroyed the myth; he carefully documented the thesis that baseball had gradually evolved from English rounders.

Despite the contrary evidence, the myth has remained alive and well. In 1939 the major leagues celebrated the "centennial" of baseball with impressive ceremonies at Cooperstown. That year they dedicated the Hall of Fame, presented a pageant revealing the Doubleday contribution, and staged an all-star game between teams of former all-time great players. The United States Government joined the festivities by issuing a commemorative stamp, marking 1839 as the date of the birth of the "national game." Even today, long after the Doubleday myth has been thoroughly discredited by several scholarly studies, the tale is often repeated by sportswriters and, more circumspectly, by Hall of Fame publicists.

Why the myth? The acceptance and perpetuation of the Doubleday myth suggests that it satisfied profoundly felt national needs. Albert Spalding, a member of the 1907 commission, surely doubted the Doubleday story, for his own history of baseball, published in 1911, included accounts of games played prior to 1839! Yet the purpose of Spalding's history was to show how baseball epitomized American character. Baseball, "as no other form of sport . . . is the exponent of American Courage, Confidence, Combativeness; American Dash, Discipline, Determination; American Energy, Eagerness, Enthusiasm." Baseball was "free from the trammels of English traditions, customs, and conventionalities"—in short, free from the artificiality and decadence of the Old World and imbued with the independence, authenticity, and vitality of the new.

The identification of baseball as a sport exemplifying American character helped to establish its unique position in the minds and hearts of the people. As Mohammedans have their Mecca and Jews and Christians their Jerusalem, baseball followers have their Cooperstown. Each year thousands of Americans "pilgrimage" to the "shrine," Baseball's Hall of Fame and Museum. There they can see statues and pictures of their former heroes and observe the "relics" used by them—old, discolored bats, balls, and uniforms. They can visit the "hallowed ground" of Doubleday Field, where young Doubleday "immaculately conceived" the game. Each year sportswriters dutifully select great players of the past for "enshrinement," after which those players become "immortals." Baseball has enjoyed a special position in the national heritage that no other American sport has quite equaled.

But the appeal of baseball rests on more than the myth of its national origins. "Ask a question about the arts and you cannot help but get a lot of round, imprecise words that are hard to sort into a pattern," Heywood Hale Broun has written in *Tumultuous Merriment*; "ask about politics and you will get sonorous abstractions; ask about life and you get a subjective lecture from someone who probably hasn't lived enough of it to be worth listening to; ask about baseball and there it is, crystal clear." No ambiguities, no greed, no artifice resides in the world of baseball. Baseball's clarity springs in part from its accessibility to measurement—batting averages, earned run averages, runs batted in, and a host of other statistics.

Baseball echoes an older America, a leisurely paced past of farms and small towns. Baseball's spatial organization, as Murray Ross has imaginatively argued, suggests an "artificial rural environment, one removed from the toil of an urban life, which spectators could be admitted to and temporarily breathe in." In the ball park the fan could find acres of green grass and clean, white boundaries—far from the noise, dirt, and squalor of the city. The early ball parks even had pastoral-sounding names: Ebbets Field, Sportsman's Park, the Polo Grounds. (In more recent years, rustic names have given way to urban names: Shea Stadium, the Astrodome, the Superdome.) Most of the action revolves around the hitter and the pitcher in one corner of the playing field. From this "urban corner," the field opens up to less busy, rural-like vistas. Compared with football, baseball is an individualistic sport; the batter confronts the pitcher in utter solitude.

Baseball is bound by its own sense of time. Released from the tempo of the clock, each team has equal opportunities (innings) to score. A team is never beaten until the last batter is retired. A team might be down eight runs, like the Philadelphia Athletics in the fourth game of the 1929 World Series, and still come back to win (as the A's did, 10–8). Finally, baseball seems to capture the slow rhythms of the seasons. "Is there anything that can evoke spring . . . better than the sound of the bat as it hits the horsehide?" asked novelist Thomas Wolfe.

Though baseball had become a commercial venture as long ago as the 1860s, the athletes and the owners were able to project an aura of pristine purity. Rather than playing for money, fans believed, the athletes played for the joy they found in the game itself. Likewise, the fans usually accepted the claims of the owners to be public-spirited men who served as trustees of "The Game." "With them baseball is an avocation," declared Commissioner Ford Frick. "They are primarily in baseball because they are interested in baseball as a game." At the apex of the sport stood the Commissioner of Baseball. With the reign of Judge Kenesaw Mountain Landis (1921–44), the commissioner became baseball's ultimate watchdog. Known for his fearless rectitude, Landis acted as policeman, prosecutor, and judge. His stern but benevolent rule had ensured the game's continued integrity.

The popularity of baseball had never been greater than it was at mid–twentieth century. The immediate post–World War II era saw the breaking of all attendance records for both major and minor league baseball. Even hamlets as small as 8,000 sometimes hosted professional baseball teams. The professional entity known as Organized Baseball consisted of an elaborate hierarchical structure. After the big leagues, at the apex, came three Triple A leagues, then Double A Leagues, then A, B, and C leagues, until finally one reached D leagues such as the Nebraska State League. As in a Horatio Alger story, an aspiring player began his career in a lowly league, and if he performed well he ascended the ladder to the major leagues. When Jackie Robinson broke the "color barrier" in professional baseball in 1946, the game had finally opened its portals to deserving men of all races. Its claim to being "the" National Game more closely approximated reality.

Yet at the very apogee of Organized Baseball's success, the sport came under a heavy siege. When in 1954 Gerald Holland, in the first issue of the new journal *Sports Illustrated*, tried to make a case for the 1950s being a new Golden Age of Sports, he deliberately or otherwise neglected to furnish a detailed discussion of the state of baseball. Buried deep in a table presenting the estimated attendance at various sports, Holland reported that baseball games at all levels were expected to attract 85 million fans in 1954. But he furnished no comparative data for earlier years, thus leaving the implicit impression that the figure represented a banner year for the National Game. In truth, baseball suffered severely from the Great Sports Slump of the 1950s.

Attendance at professional baseball games fell so suddenly that it caught even the most prescient observers by surprise. By 1956 major league attendance had dropped a third from 1948 levels; had it not been for franchise switches from Boston to Milwaukee and from St. Louis to Baltimore, the decline would have been even more drastic. By mid-decade, venerable parks like the 50,000-seat Polo Grounds would sometimes be nearly deserted; on one warm May afternoon in 1957, for example, only 1,604 fans showed up for a game against the St. Louis Cardinals. The skid was not a temporary aberration; it was permanent. Average game attendance did not reach the mark achieved in the 1948–52 era until 1978, and even then total attendance lagged far behind the population growth of the metropolitan areas served by major league franchises.

In the 1960s, regular season television ratings for big-league games also fell behind those for regular season games of professional football; by the mid-1970s they stood at less than half of those for pro football. Furthermore, the once-thriving system of minor league baseball nearly collapsed. Only the most sanguine observer would disagree with Bill Veeck, the former owner of the Cleveland Indians and St. Louis Browns, who concluded in 1958 that baseball is no longer "America's only game in town."

As was the case with prize fighting in the 1950s, baseball's attendance problems stemmed principally from the twin but closely related phenomena of the increasing privatization of leisure and the growth of television. The exodus to the suburbs left the inner city with larger numbers of lower-income residents who simply could not afford tickets to big-league games. Or to put it another way, the nonwhite proportion of the population of the central cities grew from 39 percent in 1950 to 51 percent in 1960. In 1958, through a hotel air vent, Bill Furlong of the *Chicago Daily News* secretly heard Calvin Griffith, president of the Washington Senators, explain why he wanted to move his team to Minneapolis. "The trend in Washington is getting to be all colored," Griffith bluntly told his fellow American League owners. However tactless Griffith's remarks, they revealed a valid short-hand explanation of why support for professional baseball had declined among inner-city residents.

More and more suburbanites chose to spend their spare time in ways other than watching professional baseball games. Being a summer sport, baseball had to compete directly for the attention of the suburban husband/father with home repairs, lawn care, and the family whom he might be seeing only on weekends. Moreover, "Why should a guy with a boat in the driveway, golf clubs in the car, bowling ball and tennis racket in the closet, a trunkful of camping equipment, two boys in the Little League and a body full of energy left over from shorter working hours pay to sit and do nothing but watch a mediocre game?" asked W. Travis Walton of Abilene, Texas, in a letter published in *Sports Illustrated* in 1958.

After World War II, massive infusions of new money made it possible for classes of people whose patterns of leisure had earlier been practically invisible to cultivate new life-styles. One of the most startling results was the amazing growth of what might be called a "car culture." In the postwar years, customized cars and hot rods became the art objects of millions of teenagers; high-speed auto racing became a male mania cutting across all age brackets. In the South, baseball had once been far and away the favorite sport; in 1948, North Carolina alone had forty-four professional minor league baseball teams. By 1964 the number had shrunk to six. The Southern Association, a once-prospering minor league composed of some of the South's largest cities (Atlanta, New Orleans, Memphis) saw attendance fall by half between 1947 and 1953.

By the 1950s, stock car racing had replaced baseball as the rage of much of the South. Southern heroes were now men like Junior Johnson, who learned his driving skills by eluding federal revenue agents as he delivered moonshine whiskey from the Carolina hills to the coastal cities. Unlike many of the "imported" professional ball players, Junior Johnson was "a good old boy," who shared many of the personal characteristics of his admirers. Stock car racing fans could even drive the same model car as Johnson, and they could see their cars as extensions of themselves, as supreme instruments of power, liberation, and glamour.

In the 1950s, those fans who did venture downtown to the ball parks, at least those in the major league cities, confronted a series of possible adversities. Multi-lane, limited-access thoroughfares had not yet been cut into the heart of the cities; thus one needed a Job-like patience to fight the creeping traffic. Upon arrival downtown, there was the problem of parking. All of the stadiums had been built long before the automobile had become a family necessity; to get to the parks in earlier times, fans had used trolleys. The teams had made few if any provisions for the car revolution of the postwar years. When one found a parking place on a street within easy walking distance of the ball park, he might encounter street urchins who would demand "protection money" to safeguard one's car. If one refused to pay, he might find his car vandalized.

Finally, there was the ballpark itself. All but three of the parks had been built before 1926. In 1957, Robert Creamer called the Polo Grounds (built in 1891) an "antiquated museum"; a year earlier James Murray had described Pittsburgh's Forbes Field (built in 1913) as a "museum decorated with pigeon droppings." In many parks, support posts obstructed a clear view of the field; often the parks were dirty; all were without lounges. Instead of being a pastoral retreat, the rickety old stadiums might remind fans of the generally squalid conditions of the inner city. By contrast, James Murray noted that the recently built horse racing tracks featured escalators, courteous personnel, restaurants, cocktail lounges, and cushioned seats. Baseball franchise-holders, resting on the belief that Americans would remain loyal to the sport of their fathers, were slow to provide modern facilities for the spectators.

While in the long run television drove down live attendance at all levels of baseball, it was less the cause of baseball's tribulations than has been commonly supposed. Nearly all lovers of baseball, unlike their football counterparts, found watching a game on television far inferior to being physically present at the game. In short, the game was poorly suited to the requirements of the new medium. As in the case of the puck in hockey, a baseball was too small to follow easily on the tiny screen. Whereas in wrestling and prize fighting the action could be easily distilled, the essence of baseball involved an acute awareness of the entire playing area. The baseball fan not only enjoyed the isolated instances of action—the pitch, hit, catch, or throw; he also wanted to see the runner leading off base, the signals of the third-base coach, and the positions taken by the fielders. The relationship of the hit ball to the playing area was a vital part of observing a baseball game.

Only the fan in the stands, not the television viewer, could command all these perspectives. Unlike football fans, few baseball fans claimed that watching a televised game was superior to watching the game live.

Televised baseball failed to hold the attention of the casual viewer. Just as the performance of a piece of music sets up a pattern of sound which must be resolved by its completion (otherwise tension remains with the listener), a true fan must watch a baseball game to its completion (otherwise the fan is left with a sense of irresolution). Thus, regardless of the score, to the fan, the ninth inning is as valid as the first. Television, on the other hand, tried to reach both fans and casual viewers. To attract the casual viewer, it ingrained in the viewer a different norm, or value: That value was simply observing which team won the game. If one team scored five runs in the first inning, casual television viewers were likely to turn off the set or switch to a golf match. The importance of the score thus replaced the integrity of completing the triads of strikes and innings. "People can't learn to watch baseball that way," exclaimed Oakland Athletics owner Roy Eisenhardt in 1983; "they're just learning to watch television."

Nonetheless, to fill the yawning craters in summer schedules, early television passionately pursued the National Game. In both the 1940 and 1941 seasons, Larry MacPhail, Dodger president, allowed the telecast of about one game a week from Ebbets Field. The war halted this experiment, but in 1946, when MacPhail headed the Yankees, he sold the team's season television rights to the DuMont network for $75,000. As the number of stations and sets grew, most teams did not hesitate to sell rights to local stations. Some owners believed television might actually generate more interest in the team and thereby increase attendance. The cost of video rights multiplied rapidly for teams in the larger cities and for the annual World Series. In 1950 Commissioner Chandler sold the rights to the World Series from 1951 through 1956 for $6 million. (By 1951, some fifty million fans witnessed the Series on television—far more fans than had seen the Series live over its entire forty-eight-year history.) For the 1957–62 period, the cost of these rights leaped to $15 million. By the 1960s, the World Series television contract alone almost paid for the premiums on the players' pension fund.

While Organized Baseball recognized quite early that embracing the new medium might spell trouble for both the major and minor leagues, the big-league magnates were unable to devise a satisfactory television policy. The cooperation essential to joint action had always been difficult to achieve among the faction-prone holders of big-league franchises. "I found out a long time ago that there is no charity in baseball," Jacob Ruppert, owner of the New York Yankees, explained in the 1930s, "and every club owner must make his own fight for existence." In the instance of television, each club sought to maximize its revenues without worrying about the consequences for baseball as a whole.

At the very time that television and baseball were beginning their courtship, the governing structure of the sport was in turmoil. After the death of Judge Kenesaw Mountain Landis in 1944, the owners had appointed Senator A. B. "Happy" Chandler as Commissioner. To the chagrin of the owners, Chandler showed signs of trying to exert leadership; he even had the temerity to lecture his bosses. "You don't own the game," he once said. "The game belongs to the American people." In 1951, the owners refused to renew his contract. Then, after a brief interregnum with no commissioner, the owners appointed Ford Frick, a harmless and agreeable former sportswriter, to the post.

Until 1961, when Congress passed the Sports Broadcasting Act, major league baseball was unable to develop a national television package for regular season games that included all the franchises. In 1954 the majors submitted to the Department of Justice a plan for a "Game of the Week" in which the Commissioner of Baseball would negotiate with the networks for the sale of the national television rights of the member franchises. The Justice Department advised that the proposal would violate federal antitrust laws; Organized Baseball acquiesced without taking the issue to the federal courts. A Congressional investigation in 1951 of baseball's exemption from the antitrust laws plus a pending suit in the federal courts challenging the legality of the reserve clause may have accounted for the timidity of the owners in challenging the Justice Department. In short, the owners may have feared the possible loss of baseball's unique legal status.

Given these circumstances, the networks negotiated contracts with individual clubs for national telecasts. Those franchises located in larger cities received higher rights payments, thus increasing the disparities in income between big-league clubs. By 1958, on each weekend, fans had a bonanza of network baseball telecasts available at their fingertips. The CBS network, with Dizzy Dean and Buddy Blattner doing the play-by-play, carried games on both Saturday and Sunday. NBC countered with a weekly game featuring Lindsey Nelson and Leo Durocher. Local television stations joined the parade. Perhaps the saturation point was reached in 1958, when television stations WFIL of Philadelphia, WOR of New York, WLW of Cincinnati, WLW-D of Dayton, and the CBS network all carried a single game from Philadelphia. Altogether, in 1958, *TV Guide* estimated that 800 major league games appeared on television.

For baseball aficionados across the country, watching and listening to Jay Hanna "Dizzy" Dean on the CBS Game of the Week became virtually a weekend ritual. Apparently sensing that the game could not always hold the viewer's attention, Dean himself took center stage, letting the game provide background images for the spell of his personality. A former pitching star for the St. Louis Cardinals in the 1930s, Dean began his broadcasting career in 1940 as a radio commentator for the St. Louis Browns. In 1950 he moved to New York to do Yankee pregame shows on WBAD, the flagship station of the DuMont radio and television network. He was an "instant success" in New York, and in 1955 he joined Buddy Blattner, another ex–big leaguer, to do the Game of the Week.

Dean, who claimed to have attended a one-room school in Chickalah, Oklahoma, only long enough to get into the "Second Reader," enthralled viewers with his country drawl, unusual verbal conjugations, uninhibited anecdotes, and "corn pone idiom." (When Dean heard that the school teachers in St. Louis had complained about his syntax, he shot back: "Sin Tax. Are them jokers in Washington puttin' a tax on that too?") He mixed descriptions of the game with lengthy discourses on the marvels of eating black-eyed peas and hunting "possums" in persimmon trees. When the game became unusually boring, he might bawl out an impromptu version of the "Wabash Cannonball."

Some observers feared that the blatant mix of colorful announcers, television, and advertising endangered the traditional baseball drama. Extraneous experiences distracted the fan from the game itself. Larry MacPhail, ironically a pioneer in baseball promotional gimmicks while the general manager at Cincinnati and Brooklyn, declared in a 1958 issue of *TV Guide* that television was changing baseball from a sport to "mere entertainment. The way things are going, baseball soon will be at the mercy of a push-button audience." Manufacturers of men's products, particularly cigarettes and beer, found in televised baseball a wonderful opportunity to move their goods. "Let's face it:" exclaimed Red Smith, "The sport of Father Chadwick and Al G. Spalding has been taken over by John Barleycorn and Lady Nicotine, who are not going to let it go as long as it sells products."

In large part, minor league baseball was a victim of big-league greed or perhaps ineptness in dealing with television. The return of general prosperity in the 1940s had stimulated a boom in minor league ball, one that exceeded even that of the pre–World War I era. Annual attendance increased nearly three-fold between 1939 and 1949, from fifteen million to forty-two million. Then came the invasion of commercial television. Alone, the minor leagues could do nothing to stem the intrusion of big-league telecasts into their home territories. In 1940 the major leagues had adopted a rule—"1-D"—which essentially prohibited radio broadcasts and telecasts of their games to the home territories of minor league clubs. But threatened with antitrust action by the Justice Department and greedily seeking to maximize their own broadcast revenues, the owners repealed the rule in 1951.

During the 1950s, Organized Baseball, including official spokesmen for the major leagues, regularly attempted to get Congress to pass a special broadcasting bill that would have made it possible for the big leagues to adopt a rule prohibiting telecasts in minor league territories without running afoul of the nation's antitrust laws. Yet the big-league owners apparently only paid lip-service to the proposal. Franchise holders could have individually blacked out big-league games, but to have done so would have meant a reduction in their television revenues. Eavesdropping through the Detroit hotel air vent in 1958, Bill Furlong overheard Ford Frick make some revealing remarks to the big-league owners. The minor league leaders "have asked me to tell you if you are going into a minor league city [with television], please don't go in on the day they're playing a home game," the commissioner said. "They can stand it on Saturday, but feel that Sunday will kill them. There now, I've delivered the message.'' With that, Frick, and needless to say, the big-league owners, dropped the subject.

For the minor leagues, the repeal of the blackout rule appeared to be disastrous. Television from nearby New York City quickly killed baseball in both Jersey City and Newark, New Jersey. Both cities dropped out of the International League in 1950. After 1950, nearly everyone who owned a television set could see the big-leaguers play for nothing. The local minor league heroes seemed to pale before such big-league stars as Henry Aaron, Stan Musial, Willie Mays, Warren Spahn, Ted Williams, Bob Feller, and Mickey Mantle. ''The fan listened to major league ball on radio, watched it on television and just wasn't hungry enough to go out and watch the comparative humpty dumpties in the local park,'' explained Robert Creamer in *Sports Illustrated*.

The attendance at minor league games fell from 42 million in 1949 (before the advent of nationally televised major league games) to 15 million in 1957 and 10 million in 1969. In 1949 there had been fifty-one minor leagues; that number fell to thirty-six in 1954 and, by 1970, to only twenty. In the 1970s, in order to survive, almost all minor league clubs had to receive substantial subsidies from major league affiliates. By then, college baseball teams began to replace the minor league franchises as a major source of big-league recruits.

Yet it was not simply the deluge of big-league telecasts into minor league territories that caused the minor league catastrophe. The trend toward private leisure-time activities adversely affected baseball attendance at all levels. Many people turned to stock car racing, or engaged in water sports, golf, or tennis. They watched non-sports forms of television programming. Shows like ''My Friend Irma'' provided ''the real competition that the minor leagues have to meet,'' according to Gordon McLendon, president of the Trinity Broadcasting Company of Dallas, Texas.

The collapse of minor league baseball left a gap in the lives of many Americans. (Television probably destroyed even more local semi-professional teams.) Countless men and boys no longer had direct access to the professional baseball system, which to many of them constituted a sort of transcendent world populated by demigods. Unlike the players on television, those on the local teams, when observed only from the stands, were neither too close to nor too far from their admirers to tarnish their heroism. An important source of communal experience had also been demolished; no longer could minor league baseball teams serve as rallying points for local communities.

Determining the precise impact of television upon attendance at big-league games is fraught with difficulties. The television history of the Braves (Boston, Milwaukee, and now Atlanta) dramatically illustrated the apparent effects of the cool medium. In 1948 the Boston Braves won the National League pennant and drew nearly one and a half million fans to their home games. For the paltry sum of $40,000 the management then sold the rights to telecast all Braves games for the 1951 and 1952 seasons as well as most of the 1953 and 1954 seasons. Although the Braves finished in the first division of the National League in three of these four years, their home attendance fell to an abysmal 281,278 in 1952, a loss of 81 percent. Faced with financial disaster, the Braves owner, Lou Perini, moved his club to Milwaukee in 1953. At first he allowed no telecasts; he relented only when Milwaukee played in the 1957 and 1958 World Series. Then, beginning in 1962, he permitted limited telecasts of road games.

Although attendance at Milwaukee was consistently above the major league median for all franchises—the Braves drew over two million fans for four straight years and had the highest home attendance in the National League for six consecutive years—a new set of owners transferred the franchise to Atlanta in 1966. Television and radio revenues, rather than attendance, dictated the move. Milwaukee, the new owners reasoned, had a media market circumscribed by Chicago to the south, Lake Michigan to the east, Canada to the north, and Minneapolis–St. Paul to the west. While the Braves had garnered $525,000 from broadcast rights in Milwaukee, Atlanta offered them $1.5 million for their television-radio rights. "We moved south in the first place because of TV," explained Thomas Bennett of the Braves public relations office. "We filled that gap in eight states which had been without a big league team." In the future, potential broadcast revenues rather than population concentrations often would play a determining role in the location of major league baseball franchises.

Several owners of big-league clubs hoped to solve media and attendance problems simply by shifting their franchises to other cities. The astonishing success of the transfer of the Braves from Boston to Milwaukee in 1953 touched off a mini-stampede by club owners seeking more lucrative markets. The St. Louis Browns, who perennially lost money in competition with the St. Louis Cardinals, moved to Baltimore in 1954, and the Philadelphia Athletics transferred to Kansas City in 1955. But after the euphoria of the first year of major league baseball in the two cities had worn off, both clubs suffered from a combined 28 percent loss in attendance. The willingness of Arnold Johnson, the owner of the Kansas City team, to trade or sell some of his best players to the powerful Yankees (including Roger Maris, who was destined to break Babe Ruth's single-season home run record) did nothing to encourage the success of major league baseball in Kansas City. Yet the apparent failures of big-league baseball in Baltimore and Kansas City did not stop the transfer of franchises.

The decisions of Walter O'Malley, owner of the Brooklyn Dodgers, and Horace Stoneham, owner of the New York Giants, to abandon New York for the West Coast in 1958 revealed the complex dynamics of franchise hopping. In the previous five years, according to Congressional testimony, Brooklyn had been the most prosperous franchise in the major leagues, but O'Malley claimed that Ebbets Field, the home of the "Bums," was beyond hope. It seated only 35,000 fans, had parking space for only 700 cars, and was located in a decaying neighborhood. The Polo Grounds, except for its 50,000-plus seating capacity, suffered from similar liabilities. Publicly, O'Malley claimed that the future of baseball in New York depended on the construction of new parks easily reachable by cars and with plenty of parking space. But O'Malley, a buccaneer determined to maximize his personal wealth from baseball and the most powerful single person in Organized Baseball from the mid-1950s until his death in 1979, disliked the necessity of competing with both the Yankees and the Giants in greater New York City. Brooklynites saw too much baseball on television. "Our people were TV-sated," O'Malley once said.

O'Malley dreamed of locating the Dodgers in an uncontested media market; he was especially enamored with the potentialities of pay television. Apparently both O'Malley and Stoneham had engaged in secret negotiations with Skiatron TV, a pay-cable company. In 1957 Congressional hearings, O'Malley estimated that pay television could double his income in New York. In Los Angeles, without the competition of another big-league club, the rewards might be astronomical. Unfortunately for O'Malley, an initiative petition in Los Angeles blocked the awarding of a franchise to Skiatron. Yet by blacking out home games and televising only road games, the Los Angeles Dodgers would receive more money from the media than any other franchise except the Yankees.

O'Malley's move to Los Angeles spawned a much more bitter reaction among fans than had the carpetbagging of the Braves and the Browns. Brooklyn had supported the Dodgers well. In the 1950s, the team had been the most profitable in baseball. The Dodgers had long been a source of the borough's separate identity within New York City. Taking their name from the "trolley dodgers" of the early twentieth century, the team had become Brooklyn's most unifying force. Brooklyn residents felt a deep sense of loss and betrayal. "When the Dodgers left Brooklyn," recalled Jim Kaplan in *Sports Illustrated* (1983), "we lost our innocence forever. Love and loyalty, we were shattered to hear, were only so much mush to the people in power." Certainly, O'Malley's decision gave the "big lie" to owner claims of being gentlemen-sportsmen who simply served as trustees of sports franchises for the benefit of a city's fans.

Initially, the Dodgers played in the Los Angeles Coliseum, a structure designed for track and football. The 250-feet left field and 320-feet left-centerfield fences made a travesty of the game. Cheap home runs came in record numbers. "These performers dress like ball players," wrote Red Smith in *Sports Illustrated*, "look like ball players, wolf sirloins and pinch waitresses like ball players, but that story about Walter O'Malley bringing big league ball to Southern California is pure fiction, the greatest hoax since Orson Welles' Martians." Perhaps the short fence damaged the mystique of the home run, but the Dodgers led the major leagues in attendance, a position they would continue to hold for many years to come. Others criticized the city of Los Angeles for providing the Dodgers with Chavez Ravine, 300 acres in downtown Los Angeles with easy access to several freeways, as a site for the construction of a new stadium. Originally the site had been scheduled for a public housing project for the poor; a 1958 referendum to block the use of the land by the Dodgers narrowly failed.

For O'Malley, the move to Los Angeles proved to be a financial bonanza. He had obtained the exclusive right to move his franchise into the nation's third largest metropolitan area, which promised not only an increase in attendance but a large television market as well. While O'Malley bore the costs of the actual stadium building, the city and county of Los Angeles spent some $5 million preparing the site for construction. The new stadium, completed in 1962, held 53,000 spectators, had parking space for 24,000 cars, and cost $18 million. Dodger Stadium included a fashionable Stadium Club, where a fan could obtain black caviar, pâté de foie gras, and drinks of his or her choice. The stadium also featured an electric scoreboard that could flash up in an instant Stan Musial's lifetime batting average or the closing Wall Street averages.

In the meantime, Stoneham, who had been persuaded by O'Malley to move to San Francisco in order to reduce traveling costs and continue the popular rivalry between the two clubs, was not so fortunate. Candlestick Park, built by the city, was poorly located for the use of cars and was buffeted regularly by high bay winds that sometimes turned baseball games into survival contests.

The construction of Candlestick Park and Dodger Stadium initiated a wave of stadium building for both professional baseball and football teams. Just as the cathedral represented the spirit of the Middle Ages and the great railroad terminals that of the nineteenth century, the sports stadium seemed to express the civic pride of urban America in the 1960s and 1970s. Of the twenty-eight teams in the National Football League, for example, twenty-six played in city, county, or state facilities. Never before had local governments furnished such massive subsidies to professional sports teams. The stadiums carried high price tags. A modest stadium cost about $30 million, but Houston's Astrodome, the first stadium equipped with a roof for all-season play, cost $45 million to complete in 1965. The cost of the Astrodome paled before that of the New Orleans Superdome, which mounted to at least $350 million before it was finished in 1975.

Baseball paid a price in more than money for its new parks. While the new stadiums could be reached by car far more easily than the older ones, had no columns blocking the vision of the fans, and were usually located in safer neighborhoods, they lacked "personality." All of the new stadiums were nearly identical; a fan could wake up in the middle of a stadium in Cincinnati, Pittsburgh, St. Louis, or Philadelphia and not know where he was. The older parks, on the other hand, were picturesque. Since they had been built to conform to the available space, each had a distinctive character. Some had short fences in right field, some deep; some were double-deckers, some single-deckers. Moreover, the older parks were far more intimate; fans could sit much closer to the players than in the new parks. The fans near the field could hear the infield chatter, could hear the manager yelling to an outfielder to change his position, could hear the umpires calling balls and strikes. Fans could also yell at the players and sometimes be heard; on occasion, the players delighted fans by responding to specific comments.

Yet none of these measures produced a full-scale recovery of baseball's former ascendancy as "The National Pastime." In the years to come, the baseball magnates would take other steps to restructure the game more closely to the requirements of television and the national mood. In the meantime, college authorities also had to wrestle with falling attendance and determine how they would manage the new electronic medium.

5

Reining in the Medium

While college football did not enjoy the benefits of an "immaculate conception," it did have its own special niche in American life. Football's distinctive appeal flowed from the combination of its violent character and college setting. The origins of the game can be traced back into the Middle Ages, when villagers engaged in savage brawls with the ostensible purpose of moving an inflated animal bladder across a previously defined goal line. There were no referees or standardized rules: The players kicked, wrestled, struck with their fists, and sometimes bit their opponents. Damaged property, bloodied bodies, broken limbs, and sometimes even death accompanied the contests. Between 1314 and 1617, English monarchs and local magistrates banned football on at least thirty separate occasions, but the game's popularity survived undiminished. Apparently football offered the villagers the opportunity to channel their violent tendencies and aggressions into a form of ritualized combat.

But in the United States, the sport seems to have disappeared until it was revived by the young in the early nineteenth century. By then American college students had begun to use hazing and interclass football matches as a way of initiating freshmen into the rigors of college life, and perhaps as a kind of rite of passage from childhood into adulthood. As early as 1827, freshmen at Harvard began to square off on the first Monday—"Bloody Monday"—of each school year. In 1840, Yale also took up the practice.

Like the medieval game, these class matches were nothing less than unregulated melees. Students came out of the contests with black eyes, bruised bodies, sprained limbs, and shredded clothes. But the ferocious games apparently fostered class unity. According to a Brown periodical, "The result of it all is that one class is *beaten* collectively, each class individually. It affords talk for the winter; and the bruised limbs, black eyes and cracked heads are carefully treasured up by the Freshmen as spoils of the battlefield, to be du(al)ly handed down to the incoming class the following year." Perhaps the contests also provided a much-needed respite from the intellectual and spiritual side of the college experience. At any rate, college officials generally frowned upon the violence, so that by 1860 football had been abolished on most campuses.

When football became a full-fledged intercollegiate spectacle in the late nineteenth century, violence continued to be central to the game's appeal. The student players took a special delight in their wounds, nourishing them for many years after having played the game. In preparation for the Harvard game of 1878, Yale player Frederic W. Remington, who was later to become a renowned illustrator, took his football jacket to a local slaughterhouse and dipped it in blood to "make it more businesslike." The antics, cheering, and enthusiasm of the young ladies at football games led G. Stanley Hall, the psychologist-president of Clark University, to conclude in 1900 that "while the human female does not as in the case of many animal species look on complacently and reward the victor with her [sexual] favor, military prowess has a strange fascination for the weaker sex, perhaps ultimately and biologically because it demonstrates the power to protect and defend."

For many students, football—not professors, classrooms, or chapel—was the very essence of their college experience. "You do not remember whether Thorpwright was a valedictorian or not," wrote a college alumnus in 1890, "but you can never forget that glorious run of his in the football game." As early as the 1890s, during the week of the "Big Game," students decorated their houses with banners, perhaps built floats, and prepared for a round of weekend parties. On the Friday night before the game, they might hold a parade and a pep rally, climaxed by a huge bonfire. At the game (unlike at a baseball game), one found vivid displays of school colors, vociferous school cheers led by "yell captains,'' and boisterous singing. In the 1890s one could also see Yale's indomitable mascot, a prize English bulldog who had cost the students the princely sum of $300. After the game students, alumni, and others who wished to be identified with the college often embarked on a busy round of bacchanalian feasting.

College football bound alumni to their alma maters. When autumn leaves began to change color, alumni everywhere turned their attention to the fate of their college's football team. Alumni remote from their college campuses sponsored elaborate homecoming events and printed bulletins listing the latest achievements of their classmates and the latest exploits of their football team. "The feeling of solidarity and loyalty in the student body that intercollegiate contests develop is a good thing,'' said ex-President William Howard Taft in 1915. "It outlasts every contest, and continues in the heart and soul of every graduate as long as he lives.'' Taft was right about binding loyalties. Even conservative pundit William F. Buckley, Jr.—who claims never to follow the scores of his alma mater (Yale) in the newspapers—admits that, when he happens to attend a Yale football game, he cheers "lustily'' for the Bulldogs.

At mid-century the appeal of college football had never been more potent, but like baseball, the college sport faced trying times ahead. It did not escape the Great Sports Slump of the 1950s. Television, falling student enrollments, and the growth of private forms of leisure produced a sharp drop in attendance, but unlike boxing and baseball, the colleges tried to take steps to counter the calamitous effects of the new medium. In 1951, the National Collegiate Athletic Association formulated a controversial "package'' television plan that, with revisions over the years, kept an uneasy truce within the college ranks. In the 1960s, college football attendance rebounded and television ratings ascended to new heights. No longer a socially exclusive sport, college football directly entered the world of big-time entertainment. And television pumped millions of new dollars into the coffers of the larger football-playing schools, thereby expediting the professionalization and nationalization of the sport.

Nonetheless, at the very time that television was making its debut on the college scene, the colleges faced the darkest hour in their athletic histories. Reports of corruption surfaced from campuses across the country. First came the basketball fixes of 1950–51. In 1951, New York District Attorney Frank Hogan revealed that thirty-two players from seven colleges, including players from the strongest teams in the nation, had been involved in fixing point spreads. Madison Square Garden was not only the mecca of college basketball; it was the clearinghouse for a large sports gambling establishment. Rather than picking a winning team or giving odds on favorites, the bettors wagered on how many points a particular team would win by. The system invited fixes, for the fixed team did not have to lose the game; it merely had to win by less than the quoted spread. The revelations of corruption shocked the entire nation. Coinciding as it did with the "fall" of China, the commencement of the Korean War, the Soviet detonation of an atomic bomb, and charges of treason in high governmental places, the basketball scandal contributed to a general climate of suspicion and mistrust.

The scandal revealed a sordid underside to the world of college sports. Apart from the apparent widespread immorality of college players, the scandal disclosed that many colleges, in their mad scramble for opportunities to play in the big city arenas, to win national renown, and to generate more revenues, engaged in illicit forms of recruitment and subsidization. The Catskill Mountain hotel resort leagues represented notorious examples. As many as 500 college players "worked" for munificent salaries in the Catskill resorts, where they "incidentally" played basketball in organized leagues.

Close on the heels of the basketball scandal came shocking revelations of corruption in college football. In 1950 the United States Military Academy acknowledged that all but two members of its varsity football team had been dismissed for cheating on examinations. The guilty cadets stained the image of the great Army teams that had dominated college football for a decade. A highly publicized educational survey in 1952 suggested that the University of Maryland had become virtually a "football factory"; according to the survey, 54 percent of Maryland's total scholarship funds went to football players. And in 1953 the NCAA reported that Michigan State, which had fielded the nation's top team in 1952, had operated a huge "slush fund" from which "needy" football players could draw assistance.

But if all of this was not enough to shatter the confidence of college officials, they merely had to look at attendance figures for college football games. In 1950 alone, attendance at college games dropped 1,403,000 below 1948 totals.

The scandals in college sports had a far-reaching impact. To counter the corruption and establish approximately equal conditions of competition among college athletic teams, the colleges eventually abandoned their laissez-faire stance of the past. At the 1950 NCAA convention, the delegates narrowly failed to suspend seven colleges cited for violating the association's rules; "the sinful seven" had been accused of offering full-ride athletic scholarships without regard to the athlete's financial need. Rather than continue the apparently unenforceable "need" test, the 1952 convention decided to permit full-ride scholarships based only on athletic promise. This action represented a fundamental reversal of a time-honored tradition in college sports: namely, that a college athlete should not receive any kind of financial remuneration for play. College sports had taken an official step away from its genteel, amateur origins.

The 1952 convention extended to the NCAA additional weapons for enforcement of the association's legislation. Earlier, colleges, considering themselves to be honorable institutions, had tried to police themselves, but the corruption of mid-century had revealed the utter inadequacy of self-imposed restraints. For the 1952–53 season, the NCAA took the historic step of placing two colleges—Kentucky and Bradley—on probation. The convention also adopted legislation governing post-season bowls, named a full-time executive director (Walter Byers), and established a national headquarters in Kansas City, Missouri (later moved to a suburb, Shawnee Mission, Kansas). With these actions, the colleges had taken the first steps toward the conversion of the NCAA into a major athletic regulatory body. But before the colleges could take any comfort in their efforts to clean their Augean stables, they had to deal with the new medium of television.

Eager for the publicity springing from televised contests and in some instances eager to seize the meager revenues offered by the new medium, the colleges at first placed no restrictions on telecasts. Each college negotiated as best it could its own contract with television stations or, if it could command a larger audience, with a national network. By 1950 both the University of Pennsylvania (with ABC) and Notre Dame (with DuMont) enjoyed contracts with national networks. And by 1950 televised college football games virtually flooded those areas of the country in which television stations had been built. In September, the *New York Times* reported that "TV football coverage will offer New York fans a choice of five different games every Saturday afternoon during most of the season and three night games in addition."

Yet as early as 1948 the colleges had begun to take notice of the possible ill effects of television on attendance. A pilot study conducted by the Crossley Corporation for the NCAA in New Haven, New York, Philadelphia, and Baltimore revealed one especially disturbing fact: 50 percent of those interviewed rated viewing games on television to be equal or superior to watching from the stands. In 1950 the Big Ten Conference banned televised games entirely; attendance dropped less in that conference than nationwide. In the same year the NCAA set up a special television committee and authorized a systematic study, by the National Opinion Research Center (NORC) of the University of Chicago, of the impact of television on attendance in the fall 1950 season. That fall, ticket sales tumbled to an all-time postwar low.

Alarmed delegates gathered at the NCAA convention in Dallas in January, 1951. The NORC report on the 1950 season did nothing to relieve their anxieties. If there had been no televised games in 1950, the NORC concluded, attendance at college games would have been 40 percent higher than it actually was. The stunned delegates voted overwhelmingly for a moratorium on the wholesale telecasts of football games in the 1951 season. They instructed their television committee to establish an experimental program of total and partial blackouts so that the NORC could make a comparative study of the impact of television on the gate. In signing a season contract for all college games with the Westinghouse Corporation as sponsor (Westinghouse chose NBC to carry the games), the NCAA permitted the telecast of only seven regular season games in each region of the country. Apart from a small portion kept by the NCAA to defray expenses, the participating colleges shared the $700,000 paid by Westinghouse.

This collusive action by the NCAA touched off a heated five-year controversy. The trade associations of the broadcasting industry, the large advertising agencies, politicians courting angry television viewers who now found their favorite games blacked out, and certain of the larger football powers within the NCAA all attacked the strictures. All of these groups (except the fans, of course) had a direct financial stake in the NCAA's television policy. But for public consumption, the critics invariably took the high road. They argued that the NCAA strictures violated the principles of American free trade and, in any case, would fail to restore attendance to pre-1950 levels.

So long as the NCAA banned the telecasts of any games, it inevitably enraged some football fans. When the fans discovered in 1951 that certain of the classic contests would not be on television, they angrily turned to their political spokesmen. In 1951, legislators in Oklahoma and Illinois introduced bills requiring that the games of their respective state universities be televised. But to force telecasts might lead to boycotts by other colleges, and so the bills got nowhere. Kentucky governor Lawrence Weatherby wired the Justice Department, charging the NCAA with engaging in an "illegal conspiracy" in open defiance of the nation's antitrust laws. Buffeted by conflicting political pressures, the Justice Department reported that it had the NCAA policy "under investigation." Again nothing happened. Treading a delicate path between antagonizing the NCAA and its member colleges on the one hand and assuring irate fans that they were doing something about the blackouts on the other, most politicians continued to attack the bans publicly but avoid any substantive action against the colleges or the NCAA.

When faced with a sufficiently serious challenge, the NCAA television committee revealed a keen sense of the art of compromise. For example, in the fall of 1951 the committee decided to permit the telecast of the Notre Dame–Michigan State game after Representative Gerald Ford of Michigan (a former Michigan player) attacked the policy as being "extremely arbitrary." "I feel strongly," said Ford, "that an inflexible program such as that now enforced by the NCAA inevitably will lead to state or federal legislation which in the long run will be undesirable and certainly costly." In other instances throughout the 1950s, the NCAA selectively acquiesced to public pressure.

But the advertising and broadcasting industries represented a more serious threat to NCAA policy than the politicians. The Radio-Television Manufacturers Association and the National Association of Broadcasters set up a special Sports Committee to launch an all-out campaign against the NCAA bans. Spokesmen for the organizations addressed civic groups, gave radio and press interviews, participated in public debates with NCAA officials, and on one occasion even addressed an NCAA convention.

As their principal artillery, the broadcasting groups subsidized and publicized a master's thesis in psychology prepared by Jerry Jordan at the University of Pennsylvania. (Probably not coincidentally, Jordan's father was C. L. Jordan, executive vice-president of N.W. Ayer & Son, an advertising agency which handled several large sports accounts.) Jordan claimed to refute "scientifically" the NCAA's NORC study. Sampling television owners and nonowners in the Philadelphia area, Jordan found that during the first year of ownership, those who had access to television did indeed stay away from college games more often than nonviewers. But once the novelty of television had worn off—in about a year, according to Jordan—the fans returned to the stadiums. The broadcasters distributed Jordan's booklet, which included color bar graphs, cartoons, and lavish photographs, free to broadcast stations, libraries, and sports organizations throughout the country. They hoped to convince the public that the NCAA action was a "misguided and illegal boycott," which not only denied the public access to televised football games but also failed to increase the live attendance at college games.

In response, the NCAA continued to publicize the NORC findings. Much more elaborately than was done in Jordan's investigation, the NORC each year examined a number of variables in an effort to determine the saliency of each in accounting for football attendance. They repeatedly concluded that television—not student enrollments, the weather, prosperity, or even a team's won-lost record—was principally responsible for the great slump in attendance at college football games. According to the NORC, only the NCAA restrictions on telecasts prevented a total calamity. Yet, even with the strictures of the NCAA, college football attendance would not reach 1948 totals until ten years later.

Neither the media industry nor political leaders, however, posed the most serious challenge to the NCAA television policy; the biggest threat came from within the NCAA ranks themselves. For the cool medium divided the colleges into warring factions. On one side stood the big-time football-playing colleges, who were most concerned about maximizing video revenues. Pitted against them were the small football-playing colleges, who wanted both to protect their attendance from the menace of television and to receive some share of the ascending television revenues. Only the most carefully drawn compromises prevented television from driving the NCAA asunder.

Two big-time football schools, the University of Pennsylvania and Notre Dame, mounted the first tests of NCAA authority. In 1951, officials at Notre Dame, a university with an enormous national constituency, accused the NCAA of exercising "dictatorial powers." Even though Notre Dame had televised all of its games during the past three years, Father John J. Cavenaugh, the president of Notre Dame, told delegates to the NCAA convention, nearly all of the Irish games had been sellouts. Rather than acknowledging their financial stake in a laissez-faire television policy—the Irish stood to lose at least half a million dollars in television revenues annually—Notre Dame insisted throughout the 1950s that the public had a right to see unlimited telecasts and that televising games actually created additional fans.

The University of Pennsylvania took a more serious step. Like Notre Dame, Penn had a rather lucrative television contract, reportedly worth $75,000 annually. In the spring of 1951, Penn announced that it would defy the NCAA by televising all eight of its home football games. Acting more decisively than in the past, the NCAA responded swiftly; in a fashion similar to that of other powerful economic cartels, the NCAA immediately suspended Penn and asked that the schools on Penn's fall schedule boycott the "truant eleven." Half of Penn's opponents promptly announced that they would comply with the NCAA boycott. Confronted with a football schedule in ruins, Penn reluctantly retreated. By successfully resisting Penn's efforts to establish an independent television schedule, the NCAA temporarily weathered an important challenge to its existence and also strengthened its hegemony over college sports.

In 1955 the regional football powers in the Big Ten and Pacific Coast conference posed an equally serious threat to the NCAA. Straightjacketed by the right to telecast only one game per season under the NCAA strictures, the colleges in these conferences could have generated far more television revenues for themselves by remaining outside the NCAA package. According to a press report, the Big Ten had been offered $1 million for television rights to its 1955 games; the entire NCAA package paid only $1.33 million. Furthermore, legislatures in seven states considered bills to force the telecasting of all games.

Herbert "Fritz" Crisler, the University of Michigan athletic director, succinctly put the case for the position of the regional schools before the 1955 NCAA convention. The Big Ten schools did not want to pull out of the package, he explained in his typically disarming tone of voice. To televise all games of the Big Ten schools, he admitted, would damage the attendance of all the colleges in the Midwest. Yet the "economic force of television is tremendous, the political opinion staggering, the political overtones frightening." The Big Ten had no choice, he implied. Either the NCAA must make major concessions or the conference would be forced to pull out. Faced with the genuine prospect of a Big Ten withdrawal and the destruction of the NCAA itself, the historic 1955 convention gave the television committee a "blank check" to compromise with the Big Ten. The committee devised a regional-national plan which permitted the telecasting of more regional games. Under the new plan a school might appear on television three times (counting regional games) rather than once, as in the past. This plan set the basic pattern for NCAA telecasts for the next seventeen years.

While at first the college authorities had been concerned mainly with the effects of television on attendance, always lurking in the background was the issue of who was to receive the increasing revenues—both real and potential—that might arise from television. Initially, except for a small sum taken by the NCAA to defray administrative costs and the NORC studies, those schools appearing on the package telecasts received all of the funds from the networks. By 1953 this amounted to about $100,000 per game, no mean sum in that day. (The total package owned by NBC increased from $700,000 in 1952 to about $3 million in 1960.) Those schools who failed to be chosen for network television coverage received nothing—and, in fact, probably experienced a drop in attendance because of television.

In 1952 the television committee of the NCAA suggested that television monies from the national package contract might be split equally among the football playing-colleges, or at least that those colleges not appearing on television receive some of the package. The existing plan, as Asa Bushnell, Eastern Conference athletic director and long-time administrator of the NCAA's television program, noted, resulted in the "monopolization of the network by a few major colleges—the putative aristocracy . . . [who received most of the] financial and publicity rewards." Ed "Moose" Krause, Notre Dame delegate to the convention, responded that the so-called "share-the-wealth" plan of the smaller colleges was "un-American," "socialistic," and "communistic."

In the end, the smaller colleges capitulated. Had a majority of the delegates voted for the share-the-wealth plan, the larger football schools might have walked out of the NCAA. In that event, the smaller schools feared they would be faced with another flood of telecasts, as in 1950. Gradually a compromise evolved in which the NCAA forced the network holding the package to televise a few "unattractive" games each season. Yet the big-time schools benefited far more than the small-time schools from the package.

When, in 1962, CBS upped the ante for annual television rights from $3 million to $5.1 million, the smaller colleges reintroduced the idea of sharing the wealth. After exhaustive discussions, on two separate occasions the television committee voted by large majorities in favor of such a plan. Yet the argument of NCAA counsel that such a plan would probably violate antitrust law and the adamant opposition of the larger colleges crushed all efforts to more nearly equalize the revenues from television. As the national television contracts continued to increase, the more successful football schools got richer while the less successful ones became relatively poorer.

The turbulent marriage of television and college football in the 1950s gave way to a state of protracted bliss—at least for the successful big-time schools—in the 1960s and 1970s. Annual attendance soared from twenty to thirty million in the 1960s and jumped another five million in the 1970s. While television ratings of college games lagged slightly behind those for professional football games, they exceeded those of regular season major league baseball games. And the televised bowl games at the conclusion of the season became spectacles almost as significant as the World Series, the professional football league playoffs, and the Olympic Games.

Partly in response to television, the colleges introduced a new, more wide-open style of offense to the college game. Clockstopping rule changes allowed college teams to execute twenty-seven more plays per game in 1968 than in 1964, and a study of the 1970 season found that the colleges averaged forty more plays per game than their pro counterparts. The full adoption of two-platoon football in the 1960s permitted the coaches to perfect more complicated offensive systems. It also resulted in the disappearance of one of the last pretensions of player-centeredness in the sport: the tradition of the players rather than the coaches calling offensive and defensive signals.

The 1960s produced record highs in scoring, passing, rushing, receiving, and kicking. Coaches with fleet split ends or flankers frequently went for the "bomb." Quarterbacks sometimes filled the air with fifty or more passes per game, figures that would have astonished football fans in the 1920s and 1930s. The "I" formation, a popular offensive system developed by Tom Nugent at Maryland in the 1950s, permitted a team to combine both potent running and passing attacks. Perhaps even more remarkable were triple-option formations, which featured the quarterback as an integral part of the running attack. Oklahoma's wishbone (invented by a Texas high school coach and adopted first at the college level by Darrell Royal at Texas) and Bill Yeoman's veer at Houston regularly produced more than 400 yards rushing per game. Many fans found the college game, with its explosive action, more exciting than the pros.

Weekly football telecasts enhanced the importance that fans attributed to the weekly press polls for determining the top teams of the nation. Individual journalists had named national champions since the 1890s, but it was not until 1936 that the Associated Press invented the weekly press poll. To name the top twenty teams, the Associated Press polled about fifty writers and broadcasters nationwide. By establishing a board of college coaches to name the top teams in 1950, United Press International joined the polling game. The absence of a system for determining a national champion or the relative strength of teams made the polls a powerful symbolic substitute. Many fans echoed the feelings of Dan Jenkins, a feature writer for *Sports Illustrated*: "I . . . will assure anyone who is uncertain about it that there is no drama, no suspense, excitement, thrill or feeling of necessity in sport that can equal the countdown to an opening kickoff between two great teams or contenders for that elusive, cantankerous, agonizing, dreadful and wonderful thing called No. 1.'' A college's standing in the weekly press polls was often more important to the fans, players, and coaches alike than the defeat of a traditional rival or a conference championship.

Bowl games, though late arrivals on the college football scene, eventually furnished an exciting climax to the regular season. The parent of college bowls, the Tournament of Roses or Rose Bowl, traces its origins back to 1902. In the depressed 1930s, boosters in Southern cities hoped to attract tourists and outside investors by founding the Orange (1933), Sugar (1935), Sun (1936), and Cotton (1937) bowls. Initially, the bowls offered little financial inducement to the top football-playing schools; the inaugural Orange Bowl, for example, paid each team a mere $1000 to make the New Year's day trek to Miami. The Orange Bowl officials even had to pay ABC to get the network to carry the event on nationwide radio.

Television changed all of that. With snow blanketing much of the North and few people working on New Year's Day, televised football soon enjoyed a huge captive audience. Sponsors scrambled for an opportunity to display their wares, and the cost of television rights soared. In 1960 NBC paid the Rose Bowl half a million dollars for rights; in 1983 the figure had escalated to $7 million. Even minor bowls that scheduled their games prior to New Year's Day benefited from the largesse of television; in 1980, the Bluebonnet, Gator, and Liberty bowls received about half a million dollars each from television.

Until the early 1960s, NBC, the early leader in sports television, held the rights to the ''housewife's delight''—three consecutive football games lasting from noon to nearly midnight on New Year's Day. On NBC, the viewer could begin the new year with the Sugar Bowl; as the final whistle ended the Sugar Bowl, the Rose Bowl began; and the Rose Bowl then led into the Orange Bowl. NBC's happy monopoly on the housewife's delight ended in 1961. As Carl Lindemann, then the head of NBC Sports, explained, ''We went down to New Orleans one year to renew the Sugar Bowl, and at a dinner—this nice lady said: 'Mr. Lindemann, you folks up North are all so charming. We had some down from up North just last week. You know . . . a Mr. Moore.' '' Lindemann gulped, for Tom Moore was the president of ABC. "All of a sudden the Sugar Bowl wasn't returning our calls," Lindemann recalled.

In the 1960s, for those teams aspiring to big-time status, regular bowl appearances became mandatory. A team could earn up to a million dollars, as much as one-third of its total athletic budget, by agreeing to play in a single bowl game. Play in bowl games also assisted in recruiting. By using bowl games as lures, universities in the Big Eight and Southeastern conferences snatched recruits from the home grounds of the Big Ten colleges. (Until 1969, the Big Ten permitted only one institution each year to participate in a bowl game.) Given the stakes involved, the determination of matchups in the bowls generated almost as much national excitement as the games themselves. Several bowls were contractually bound to invite specific conference champions. Those not tied to conference commitments tried to attract the highest-ranking teams or the teams that had the largest followings. The fact that the bowl games often determined the mythical national championship added to the interest in the contests.

"Pseudoevents"—those created largely or solely by the media—also generated interest in the college game. Walter Camp, the architect of American football, had named mythical "All-America" teams as early as the 1890s, but in the 1960s the selection of all-star teams of college football players became something of a national ritual. The press services, magazines, broadcasters, and organizations of football fans chose not only all-American teams and all-conference teams but participants in East-West, North-South, Blue-Gray, and other all-star bowl games.

The biggest individual prize became the Heisman Trophy, which had been awarded each year since 1936 by the Downtown Athletic Club of New York City in honor of a former coach and athletic director. A group of sportswriters and sportscasters chose for the award the "outstanding" intercollegiate player of the year. That the winner of the award was (with but one exception) an offensive back, nearly always played on a nationally ranked team, usually appeared in nationally televised games, and was the beneficiary of an intensive selling campaign by his college's athletic department did not seem to tarnish the glamour of the award. And the recipient welcomed the publicity, the potential commercial endorsements, and the likelihood of a better professional contract.

Apart from the drama transpiring on the field and the pseudoevents, television encouraged the colleges to add larger doses of entertainment to accompany the games. Each game featured half-time shows complete with large marching bands, baton twirlers, and card sections. (Elaborate, animated card sections apparently began at Oregon State in 1924, but became the standard fare of football games only in the 1950s.) The most remarkable change came in cheerleading. Until the post–World War II years, most colleges had used only male "yell captains." In most parts of the country, for a female to have led cheers would have been considered indelicate at best. But in the 1950s fans began to regularly witness not only the spectacle of briefly clad coeds leading cheers but lines of girls doing fast and leggy cancans. As Broadway-like chorus-line routines swept the country, the girls became first and foremost entertainers rather than cheerleaders. To be successful as a "cheerleader" now required expert coaching and hours of grueling practice. In 1954, Lawrence Herkimer of Dallas founded the National Cheerleaders Association, which eventually supervised the training of some 16,000 fledglings each year.

Televised college football took on a life apart from the action on the field. Like baseball's Dizzy Dean and Monday Night Football's cast of Howard Cosell, Don Meredith, and Frank Gifford, college football announcers sometimes became celebrities in their own right. In the 1950s Lindsey Nelson won some renown for his straightforward, reliable play-by-play accounts on NBC; in 1962 he assumed the same role with CBS. In the 1960s and early 1970s Chris Schenkel, who touted the college game from the opening kickoff until the final gun, and ebullient Charles "Bud" Wilkinson, former Oklahoma head coach, led the ABC television team. When Schenkel's cheerleading began to seem out-of-touch with the popular realism—if not iconoclasm—of the 1970s, Roone Arledge, head of ABC Sports, replaced the network's main broadcast team with Keith Jackson and Frank Broyles. Some viewers found Broyles's Ozark twang grating, while others found it easy to listen to; regardless, Broyles was unusually insightful and almost never resorted to the jargon and hackneyed expressions so typical of most commentators. Viewers also liked Jackson's blend of knowledge and "down-home" folksiness.

Until the 1980s, ABC had shamelessly shilled college football, which, according to the ABC announcers, constituted an island of the pure bracketed off from the evil outside world. It was a sport of ancient rivalries, coaches who embodied the highest plateaus of morality, and "student athletes" who sought nothing more than good, clean fun and victory for their school. But in the 1980s ABC, as it had already done in its coverage of NFL football and the Wide World of Sports, began to combine traditional show-biz with a fast-breaking news-story approach to the sport. In 1981, for example, the network aired Jim Lampley's controversial interview of two athletes who claimed recruiters had offered them substantial bribes to play for Clemson University, and in 1982, in a half-time special, Lampley probed the absence of black head coaches in the college ranks. Both shows suggested an uglier dimension of college sports never before revealed on television.

Gradually, the NCAA retreated from the television policy worked out in the 1950s. The fifties policy had been designed to maximize the number of schools which appeared on network television while simultaneously protecting the others from competition with televised games. But the public, the sponsors, and the television networks wanted telecasts of only the games featuring top-ranked teams. "The quality of football is the key to the success of the package," declared Donn R. Bernstein, ABC's media director of college sports. "We can't sell a game between two teams nobody has heard of." Under mounting pressure from ABC, which had lost some $4 million on the 1970 package, and the big-time schools, the NCAA in 1971 decided to permit ABC to add a full minute of advertising to each game, to select the last nine dates of the television schedule just twelve days before kickoff, and to nationally telecast the games of any college a maximum of five times rather than three over a two-year period. The 1971 policy represented a step away from the ideal of maximizing the number of colleges that would have their games televised. Between 1966 and 1974, a mere sixteen schools appeared in 74 of the 84 regular season national telecasts; however, many more of the smaller schools did have their games televised regionally.

Despite the compromise of 1971, the big-time football schools (which consisted of some 70 colleges of over 100 schools in Division I of the NCAA) continued to chafe under NCAA television restrictions. In 1976 they (excluding the Big Ten and the Pacific Coast conferences) formed the College Football Association

(CFA), complete with an executive director, to represent their interests within the NCAA. As the 1970s closed and the 1980s began, a rupture within NCAA ranks appeared possible, for the CFA schools insisted on exercising firm control over big-time college football. As it was, Appalachian State, with a stadium holding 18,500 spectators, had as much of a voice within the NCAA as Pennsylvania State, with an 83,770-seat stadium and a $9 million athletic budget. "Too many of the matters that affect us are voted on by people who have no empathy for us," said Joe Paterno, Penn State's football coach and athletic director. Television furnished the wedge for forcing reforms within the NCAA. In 1982 the CFA forced a showdown by signing a separate (tentative) television package with NBC. Hurriedly, NCAA officials worked out a compromise. Central to the compromise was a commitment to the larger schools to reduce the number of schools in Division I, the division committed to big-time college sports. The larger athletic institutions could thereby have more power to determine their own television policies, the number of coaches, and recruiting regulations. The compromise also entailed an entirely new television package.

The new policy maximized television revenues for the big-time schools. In 1977 CBS had tried to obtain a piece of the college football pie, but Roone Arledge had come up with a staggering $120 million over four years to keep ABC's exclusive rights through 1981. In 1981 the NCAA signed a contract with ABC and CBS to do the traditional Saturday afternoon games and with the Turner Broadcasting System to handle special Saturday night games. The new package brought a soaring increase in revenues. The colleges were to receive $74.3 million annually from television rights, more than twice as much as they had obtained only two years earlier.

In exchange for such generosity, the colleges made some major concessions to the networks. The NCAA increased the number of appearances a school could make in a single season to six. One could see on television at least a third more games than under the old ABC package. The bad news: The NCAA also hiked the number of commercials per telecast, from twenty-one to twenty-six. While the new package produced enormous increases in revenues, nearly all of the money continued to go to the large schools. Unless a school appeared on television (or belonged to a conference

that shared television payments), it received no television revenues, and the increased number of televised college football games
probably reduced the attendance at the games of the smaller
schools.

In 1984 the United States Supreme Court struck down the
package contracts of the NCAA, declaring them to be in violation
of federal antitrust law. Each college could now negotiate its own
television rights free of the authority of the NCAA. The immediate effects of the decision remained unclear: It might lead to the
television chaos prevalent in college basketball and/or to a CFA
contract of the bigger schools with one or more of the major networks. Regardless, the Court's action represented a stunning set-
back for the NCAA as a regulatory cartel. Not only did the NCAA
lose its control over television football, but it could no longer use
television to discipline member institutions. Furthermore, the decision of the Court appeared to benefit most (even more than the
NCAA package had done) the football programs of the big-time
colleges in high-density population centers or with national followings.

The turbulent marriage of college football to television
yielded mixed results. The NCAA television package apparently
prevented even more disastrous drops in attendance in the 1950s
and encouraged the growth of the sport in the 1960s and 1970s.
But the colleges paid a price. The issue of television dollars divided
the college ranks, threatening to drive the NCAA apart. Big-time
college football became more commercialized and professional-
ized than ever, thereby further eroding the special amateur aura of
college athletics. And televised college football contributed to the
nationalization of American sports. Now on Saturdays, spectators
tuned in to the matchups of the big-time universities on television
rather than going out to the local college or high school stadium to
watch a football game.

The marriages of the electronic medium to boxing, professional baseball, and college football had been far from blissful or
problem-free; yet at least one marriage, that of the medium to a
mere youngster—professional football—resulted in the transfor-
mation of a secondary sport into a phenomenally successful form
of entertainment.

6

The Making of a Sport

"When I became commissioner of the [National Football] League in 1960," recalled Pete Rozelle some years later, "the office was in Philadelphia and there was a staff of two guys and an eighty-year-old Kelly girl." By 1970 the NFL office took up the entire twelfth and thirteenth floors (in 1984, five floors) of a skyscraper on Park Avenue in Manhattan. Plush carpets of crimson and green, burnished walnut desks, and deep leather chairs reflected the opulence of the league. The two guys and the eighty-year-old Kelly girl had been replaced by some forty employees. And by 1970, televised Sunday afternoon professional football had become firmly entrenched in the schedules of over eleven million American families—or, at least, the adult male members of eleven million American families. Having eased past the television perils that had beset boxing and baseball, pro football, by skillfully wedding itself to the new medium, had become the darling of the American sports fan.

For over half a century, pro football had languished in the backwoods of the nation's sporting landscape. Former New York Giants halfback Frank Gifford, who did not come into the NFL until 1952, remembered returning home to California after the season was over and having his friends ask: "Where have *you* been?" The game had a narrow following. "The pros are potbellies," a sportswriter said in the 1930s. "A bunch of beer swizzlers playing lazy football. And the only thing worse is the bunch of beer swizzlers watching.''

Unlike the college game, with its alumni supporters, the pro game had never enjoyed the luxury of a built-in constituency. Instead of college campuses, the cradle of the pro game had been the tough mine and mill towns of Ohio and western Pennsylvania. As early as the 1890s, local clubs (often formed by the players themselves) began to pay some men a few dollars to risk life and limb on Sunday afternoons. Eventually, after expenses and perhaps a modest profit to the promoters had been paid, the clubs divided all of the game receipts among the players.

The Panhandlers, a team representing the Panhandle Shops of the Pennsylvania Railroad in Columbus, Ohio, may have been typical of the pre-1920 teams. As recalled by Harry Marsh in *Pro Football*, "The boys worked in the shop until four Saturday afternoon, ate their suppers at home, grabbed the rattlers to any point within a twelve-hours ride of Columbus, played the Sunday game, took another train to Columbus and punched the time clock at seven Monday morning." No leagues existed in the pre-1920 era, and each team scheduled its own matches. Finally, in 1920, teams representing mostly small towns from Ohio formed the National Football League in the showroom of the Hupmobile automobile agency in Canton, Ohio.

Until the mid-1950s, NFL teams rarely made profits. In its first thirty-five years, some forty franchises joined the league, struggled for survival, and then expired. Major college games invariably outdrew the pro games. To many Americans, at least those with a college background, play for pay continued to carry the stigma of ungentlemanly behavior; it violated the principles of amateur sports. Thus in the early days the pros had to appeal largely to noncollege audiences unfamiliar with the delights of football. The newspapers all but ignored the pros. Even in the daily papers located in the larger cities, readers could find pages of speculation and reports about college games, but no mention at all of pro games.

The NFL shared some of the general prosperity of sports in the immediate post–World War II era, but now confronted an expensive war with a rival, the All-America Conference, organized in 1946. Competition for player talent cost the two leagues an estimated $6 million. In 1949 the All-America Conference finally surrendered to the NFL, though the Cleveland, San Francisco, and Baltimore franchises were allowed to enter the NFL on favorable terms.

From the earliest days of television, professional football was more successful in managing the medium than were most other sports. Unlike the savagely independent barons of baseball, the owners of football franchises were willing to delegate much of their authority to the office of the commissioner. Their willingness to relinquish power stemmed in large part from the fact that most of them shared common Irish-Catholic origins and had shared the long history of financial tribulations that had beset their sport. Through the many years of shoestring operations, George Halas, Arthur Rooney, Jr., Timothy Mara, de Bennville "Bert" Bell, and George Preston Marshall had worked closely together. Thus, the NFL owners, unlike the more prosperous baseball magnates, had developed a "clubby" relationship. And unlike the barons of baseball, they chose as commissioners men who had experience in the business side of the sport.

The astute leadership of commissioners Bert Bell and Alvin "Pete" Rozelle contributed greatly to the success of the NFL's marriage to television. Although from a Philadelphia Main Line family, Bell had been something of a playboy as a youth; he married a chorus line girl. Rejecting the family tradition of law, he had muddled for years in the slough of pro football as the owner-coach of the Philadelphia Eagles. In 1946, his fellow owners appointed him commissioner. Working in shirt-sleeves and out of his own home, Bell soon exhibited a flair for dealing with fellow owners, players, and the United States Congress. Unlike the timid, impotent commissioners of the other professional sports, Bell united his strong-willed owners into what was essentially a single economic cartel, one far stronger than Organized Baseball or pro basketball.

In 1952 Bell began to build the NFL's prosperous relationship with television. As finally consummated after the Sports Broadcasting Act of 1961, it rested on the blackout of home games, the blackout of other NFL games in the home city when a team was playing at home, and the negotiation by the league with a television network of a single "package" contract for all the franchises rather than having each franchise arrange its own television deal.

Unlike the college football package, each team would share
equally in the television receipts, regardless of whether they appeared on television.

The experience of the Los Angeles Rams convinced Bell of
the need for restricting telecasts. In 1949 the Rams drew 205,109
fans to their home games; in 1950, when for the first time the club
televised all of its home games, attendance fell to 110,162. In 1951
the Rams again blacked out home games, and attendance
promptly doubled. Bell concluded that, when dealing with the new
medium, the league had to act as a single economic unit. He
rammed through the 1952 owners meeting amendments to the
NFL bylaws that made him virtual dictator of the league's television policies.

But then the United States Justice Department intervened; it
insisted that the new bylaws constituted a restraint of trade and
thereby violated American antitrust laws. Bell rallied the owners
to fight the order in the federal courts. In a ninety-two-page brief,
the NFL contended that football telecasts afforded the viewer "a
spectacle as attractive as that which he sees when he visits the stadium, minus the discomforts of the trip." Unrestricted telecasts
would destroy live attendance. In 1953, Federal District Judge
Alan K. Grim ruled that professional football was indeed a
"unique kind of business" in which the classic forms of economic
competition could be disastrous for the entire league. Although
Grim rejected the commissioner's assumption of sweeping powers
to control the telecasts of member franchises, he implicitly upheld
the home-game blackouts. Bert Bell was elated.

At first the television industry itself approached pro football
warily, for the sport still ranked below baseball, college football,
and boxing in popularity. Teams that wished to have their games
televised often had to devise their own networks. The 1951 Chicago Bears, for example, had an eleven-city network—and actually had to pay two of the television stations (in St. Louis and Louisville) to carry their games. They suffered a $1,750 loss from the
1951 television project. Both NBC and CBS, the Big Two of the
broadcasting industry at the time, totally ignored the NFL. However, in 1951, the DuMont network televised five regular season
games; by 1954 the network had increased its regular season coverage to twelve games. DuMont also carried the NFL championship

games from 1951 through 1955, for which the network paid a mere $95,000 annually. In the early 1950s, according to Bert Bell's testimony before a congressional committee, broadcast revenues from both radio and television made up less than 15 percent of the gross income of NFL franchises.

Yet, by the mid-1950s major advertisers and the big networks had begun to take notice of the NFL. Before DuMont had made pro football available, sports fans had faced grim options on blustery fall Sunday afternoons: They might take the family dog for a walk, go to a downtown movie, or join the high brows by watching serious drama, special news programs, or concerts from Carnegie Hall on television. When DuMont's average audience rating rose in 1954 to nearly 37 percent of all households that had sets turned on, even the most skeptical network executives were impressed. By then, television was carrying pro football far beyond the franchised cities, to such remote outposts as Bippus, Indiana, Portland, Oregon, and Bangor, Maine. In 1956, *TV Guide*, which would soon become the nation's largest-circulation magazine, began to feature easy-to-make "Gridiron Gourmets" to be eaten from lap-held trays while watching the games. And housewives increasingly took note, sometimes angrily, of the retreat of their husbands into the dimly lit world of televised pro football. In that same year, 1956, NBC seized the rights to televise the NFL title game from DuMont, and CBS began to air regular season games. For their rights, CBS paid slightly over a million dollars annually.

Television created millions of new fans for pro football. It helped the novice to understand and appreciate the intricacies of the sport. As one fan put it: "You watched a game on television and, suddenly, the wool was stripped from your eyes. What had appeared to be an incomprehensible tangle of milling bodies from the grandstand, made sense. [Television] created a nation of instant experts in no time." The central requirement of the game—that the offense must move the ball ten yards in four plays or give it up to the opposing team—set up recurring crisis points that kept the viewer's attention riveted to the little silver screen. The twenty-second or so pause between plays permitted the viewer to savor the drama. If the situation were third down and long yardage, would the linebackers blitz? Would the quarterback throw or call a draw play? Viewers could second-guess the coach or the quarterback.

And instant replays and slow motion shots—perfected in the 1960s—allowed the fans to experience an entirely different game from that of the spectator in the stands. While the fans' attention might be diffused or centered on extraneous action during the original play, replay and slow motion shots could pinpoint the receiver running his pattern, the vicious blocking of the interior linemen, or the balletlike steps of a running back eluding would-be tacklers. More than one viewer shared the judgment of critic Richard Kostelanetz, who declared that, compared with telecast games, "live games now seem peculiarly inept, lethargic, and pedestrian."

Other technological breakthroughs aided pro football's rapid spurt in popularity. Apart from replay and slow motion shots which permitted the viewer to concentrate on individual matchups (the struggle between offensive and defensive linemen for domination of the line of scrimmage, for example), color television and artificial playing surfaces radically altered the appearance of the games. Whereas in the mid-1950s viewers watched tiny black and white figures do battle, often indistinguishable by team when covered with mud, by the mid-1960s larger color television sets (combined with artificial grass) projected the differences between teams in sharp relief. Teams themselves donned brightly colored uniforms with logos on their helmets, and had the names of individual players (in addition to the traditional numerals) placed on the backs of uniforms.

One game, the 1958 championship tilt between the Baltimore Colts and the New York Giants, helped to trigger the national mania for pro football that would reach unprecedented proportions in the 1960s. With only seven seconds left in the game, Steve Myhra of the Colts calmly kicked a twenty-yard field goal to tie the game, 17–17. For the first time in NFL history, the title game went into a "sudden death" overtime. Some thirty million fans watched their screens intently as Johnny Unitas, the Baltimore quarterback, took "the Thirteen Steps to Glory," marching the Colts down the field for the winning touchdown. The 1958 title game, declared Tom Gallery, the director of NBC Sports, "gave pro football a tremendous impetus," for it had enabled millions to share the excitement of a classic sporting contest. And perhaps even more importantly, the game converted New York's advertising community into pro football fans.

Television also played a key role in the making of a new league, the American Football League, or AFL. Rebuffed in their efforts to obtain franchises in the NFL, in 1959 two millionaire Texans, Lamar Hunt of Dallas and K. S. "Bud" Adams of Houston, announced the formation of the new league, which began play in 1960. The NFL immediately retaliated by placing a competing franchise in Dallas and a franchise in Minnesota before the AFL could plant one there. The AFL nearly went down at the outset; it lost an estimated $3 million in its first year, and the undercapitalized New York franchise, essential to the AFL's potential success, threatened to drive the entire league into bankruptcy. In 1960 Harry Wismer, former sportscaster and eccentric owner of the New York team, persuaded the AFL owners to sell the league's national television rights to ABC as a package, each franchise sharing equally in the receipts. Even before the teams had yet played a single game, Wismer himself, in order to get a commitment from the ABC network, had to hustle some $2 million from wary sponsors. While the AFL television contract was modest, it temporarily kept the league afloat.

In the meantime, the NFL inaugurated its own new era. In 1959, while he was watching his beloved Philadelphia Eagles play, a heart attack struck down Bert Bell. In 1960, the owners, after nine days of heated discussion, made the surprise choice of thirty-three-year-old Pete Rozelle as their new commissioner. Unlike Bell, who had played and coached football, Rozelle had learned the game from the vantage point of advertising—or, in more polite terms, the public relations industry. At the tender age of twenty-six he became the chief publicity man for the Los Angeles Rams; in 1957 he became the Rams' general manager. Affable, smiling easily, shrewd, and always tanned, his very appearance reflected a new style of sports leadership. Trained in the skills of marketing a product, he understood better than anyone in the world of sports management how to sell sports and manage the tricky medium of television. In due time, he so won the admiration of the owners that they delegated to him nearly complete authority to handle television negotiations, relations with the Federal government, and controversies among themselves.

The "Boy Czar" soon got an opportunity to test his skills—not so much along New York's Broadcast Row as in the halls of the United States Congress. In 1961 the NFL had signed a television pact with CBS similar to the one that the AFL had with ABC, but in this instance the Justice Department immediately intervened. Since pooled television contracts eliminated competition between franchises for network television revenues, Judge Alan K. Grim concluded that the NFL's 1961 contract with CBS was a restraint of trade and therefore violated federal antitrust law.

Aroused by this adverse decision, the professional sports leagues (including major league baseball) turned to Congress for a bill to exempt package contracts from the nation's antitrust laws. Package or pooled contracts, the sports magnates argued in the congressional hearings, were essential to the very existence of modern sports leagues. Since each team would receive equal revenues from the package contracts, clubs in small television markets, like the Green Bay Packers, could more easily compete with teams in large market areas, like the New York Giants. The absence of such contracts, Rozelle testified, would "seriously impede the league's effort to maintain a balanced league." On condition that the pro football magnates leave Friday and Saturday playing times exclusively to the high schools and colleges, the NCAA lent its support to a bill authored by Representative Emanuel Celler of New York that would exempt the package media contracts of the pro sports leagues from antitrust law.

Only the Justice Department and the National Association of Broadcasters actively opposed the bill. In a letter to the congressional committee, a Justice Department official noted that in 1960 CBS paid $1.5 million to televise the games of all but four of the NFL franchises. But under the contract struck down by Judge Grim, which included all NFL teams, the network would have paid $4.65 million. Thus, he concluded, "to hold exclusive telecasting rights . . . CBS was willing to pay 200%" more than it had paid in 1960. "This is, to us, a striking example of the evils of monopoly." The television networks, apparently recognizing the futility of opposing the bill and not wanting to offend the sports leagues, remained discreetly silent. "In record time," according to *Broadcasting* magazine, Congress passed by voice vote and President John F. Kennedy signed the Sports Broadcasting Act of 1961. The act, which permitted professional sports franchises to negotiate as a single economic unit the sale of national broadcast rights, clearly displayed the clout of professional sports on Capitol Hill.

The Sports Broadcasting Act of 1961 and the mounting enthusiasm for pro football opened the door to skyrocketing television contracts and an open war between the two professional football leagues. Rozelle ignited the spiraling inflation in television contracts by negotiating an annual $4.5 million contract with CBS in 1962, but the real turning point came in 1964. Since Nielsen ratings had jumped a whopping 50 percent between 1961 and 1963 for NFL games, Rozelle held a strong bargaining hand. All three national networks—CBS, NBC, and ABC—decided to do battle for the NFL rights. As the bidding day drew near, rumors of an astronomical hike in rights flew around the hallways of Broadcast Row in Manhattan. Aboard the commuter trains of the New Haven Railroad, "the Greenwich Jets," as the media employees along the Row were known, started making book and organized a pool to pick the winning bid. "As I started hearing those reports toward the end," recalled Rozelle, "my hopes were climbing a million dollars a day. Toward the end, based on the stuff passed on from the Greenwich Jets, I thought we might even be getting as much as $10 million a year for the package." But the final figure far surpassed Rozelle's fondest dreams. CBS submitted a bid of $14 million a year.

Later that day, Rozelle placed a long distance call to Cleveland Browns owner Art Modell in Florida. The conversation, according to the recollection of Rozelle as reported by William O. Johnson, Jr., allegedly went along the following lines:

> ROZELLE: Art? Art, CBS got it. For fourteen million.
> MODELL: How much?
> ROZELLE:: Fourteen million, Art.
> MODELL (long pause): We-e-ell, it could be worse. I did expect a little better, but, hell, Pete, seven million a year isn't half bad. We can make it.
> ROZELLE: Art—Art—FOURTEEN MILLION A YEAR. Twenty-eight million for two years.
> MODELL (longer pause): Pete, you gotta stop drinking at breakfast.

Little wonder that Arthur Rooney, Jr., veteran owner of the Pittsburgh Steelers, exclaimed: "Pete Rozelle is a gift from the hand of Providence." Under the 1964 contract, each NFL franchise received over $1 million a year. "What Rozelle did with television receipts probably saved football at Green Bay," commented Vince Lombardi, the head coach of the Packers, who many thought had saved football at Green Bay himself.

Within only two hours of learning that CBS had won the NFL rights, Carl Lindemann, head of NBC Sports, sat down in the offices of the American Football League. NBC decided to retaliate by gambling on the new loop. To provide enough funds for the AFL to compete for top players, NBC agreed to pay the league $42 million over five years, five times what ABC had been paying. Under a new contract signed in 1964, each AFL franchise received about $850,000 annually from television. Fully aware that the venture would be unprofitable, NBC hoped the losses would be offset by an increase in public goodwill and would satisfy their affiliates' hunger for more sports programming.

Suddenly, overnight, NBC had wiped out the bush-league image of the AFL. The new contract permitted the AFL to engage in all-out "Battle of the Paychecks" with the NFL for college stars. Carl Lindemann even sent letters to leading college players assuring them that the "Seal of Sarnoff stood rock-ribbed behind the league"; in some instances NBC even advanced cash to needy franchises. Both leagues resorted to clandestine operations to sign college stars, but in 1965 the AFL signed the biggest prize of all, a slope-shouldered quarterback from the University of Alabama, Joe Willie Namath, for the astonishing sum of $420,000 for three years, a figure far in excess of any contract then granted to an athlete in either pro football or basketball. Art Modell of the rival NFL hooted that the signing of Namath was merely a "theatrical stunt." But the high command of the New York Jets, now headed by David "Sonny" Werblin, recognized that the value of a player, especially in the nation's media capital, could encompass both talent and charisma. Namath had both. In their first season with Namath at the helm, Jets ticket sales jumped from an average of 22,000 to 40,000 per game. Soon other players received even higher contracts, so that Namath's salary proved to be one of the best bargains in pro sports.

In 1966 Rozelle pulled off an even bigger coup for the NFL than the 1964 deal. In 1964 Rozelle had enjoyed the luxury of having three suitors, but when the NFL contract expired in 1966 he had only one, CBS. NBC still had its contract with the AFL, and ABC was committed to NCAA football. Rozelle's approach to CBS combined the proverbial carrot and stick. As a stick, he threatened to have the NFL form its own network; the league even went so far as to commission a full-scale study of the feasability of creating a pro football television network. As a carrot, he promised to drop the NFL's long-standing ban on telecasting out-of-town games when a team was playing at home. Bluff, threat, and concessions worked; CBS upped its annual ante to $18.5 million.

If not for the continuing Battle of the Paychecks, owners in both leagues could envision a world of ever escalating profits. Consequently, in the spring of 1966 the owners hammered out a peace settlement. Under the terms of the agreement, Rozelle became the sole commissioner, the league established a common player draft to end the bidding war, and the two leagues (or conferences, as they were to be called after 1969) agreed to a championship game to begin in 1967. Despite the requirement that the AFL pay the NFL $18 million for their territorial "invasions" of the New York and San Francisco areas, "the two things we wanted we got—the championship game and the pre-season games," declared Lamar Hunt of the AFL.

Congress promptly added an antitrust exemption for the merger as a rider to an unrelated anti-inflation bill sought by President Lyndon Johnson; in 1966 the President signed the Football Merger Act into law. Senate Whip Russell Long and House Whip Hale Boggs, both from Louisiana, were chiefly responsible for guiding the legislation through Congress. Perhaps not coincidentally, only nine days after the bill became law the NFL awarded New Orleans an expansion franchise.

One thorny problem remained—the disparity in television markets between the two leagues. To reduce the difference, in 1970 Pete Rozelle arranged (by paying the teams an indemnity) for the transfer of the Cleveland, Baltimore, and Pittsburgh franchises from the National Football Conference (the old NFL) to the American Football Conference (the old AFL). The realignment reduced the NFC's 2–1 television market advantage to 7–5.

Initially the AFL fared poorly in the championship games. In the first year, 1967, Vince Lombardi's Green Bay Packers whipped the Kansas City Chiefs, 35–10; in 1968 the Packers defeated the Oakland Raiders, 33–14. But Super Bowl III in 1969 symbolically established the AFL's parity with the senior loop. That year Joe Namath, leading the New York Jets of the AFL against the Baltimore Colts, confidently predicted: "We'll win. I guarantee it.'' And the Jets did, 16–7. In the 1970s, AFC teams dominated NFC rivals in interleague games.

By the mid-1960s, the cool medium had made pro football into a major spectacle. After 1964, from about noon to six or seven o'clock on every Sunday afternoon during the fall, CBS and NBC presented two nationally televised games each. No longer was football a sport which attracted only "outsiders"; rather, televised professional football seemed to be perfectly suited to the needs of the growing white-collar and professional classes in the United States. According to national public opinion polls, the game appealed most to the "successful," to those who had the benefit of a college education, who lived in the suburbs, held jobs in the professions, and enjoyed higher incomes than the national average.

Pro football, while not offering the same hoary mystique as baseball, reflected its fans' work experiences. Most Americans now worked in large corporations, bureaucracies, universities, or institutes, and football was very much a corporate or bureaucratic sport; eleven men acted in unison against eleven opponents. Football was time-bound; the ever-present clock dictated the pace and intensity of each game. Teams worked "with" or "against" the clock. Like modern work, football embodied rationality, specialization, and coordination; the game required careful planning and preparation. Football exemplified the way many Americans lived: their "strategies" and "tactics"; their crushing disappointments and joyful triumphs.

Yet football suggested that committees, systems, bureaucracies, and technologies were still only the tools of men, not their masters. The long completed pass and the breakaway run reflected not only careful planning and long hours of practice, but human potency, natural skill, and grace under pressure. But as in all sports, fate or luck could often be decisive. Even the best made plans and the best of human performance might fall victim to the unpredictable bounce of the oblong ball.

Beyond the appeal of televised football as a microcosm of the bureaucratic world, the popularity of the sport reflected a wide-ranging quest among the "successful" in the 1960s and 1970s for individual power and fulfillment in activities apart from their jobs. As the society had become more rationalized and systematized and more people worked in bureaucracies, the importance of the individual seemed to diminish. In the 1960s corporations discovered a pervasive problem of morale among executives. Rising absenteeism and declining rates of productivity, especially among the "middle managers," reflected a growing dissatisfaction with the anonymity and impotence entailed in being an "organization man." According to one study, white-collar employees, on the average, devoted only about 50 percent of their potential labor to the job. Many sought fulfillment elsewhere. They streamed to seashores, lakes, and rivers; they took up bridge, tennis, golf, and do-it-yourself projects in record numbers. A few dropped out to become "hippies," experiment with hallucinogenic drugs, or live in communes.

The nation seemed obsessed with the exercise of power, perhaps because of widespread feelings of individual impotence. Historians and political scientists praised strong Presidents—at least until opposition to the Vietnam War mounted in the late 1960s. Manufacturers designed cars with horsepower far beyond the requirements of everyday driving; their cars, as standing symbols of power, were embellished with ferocious-looking grills and bore such power-evoking names as Cougar, Thunderbird, Stingray, and Mustang. High-speed auto racing became the nation's fastest growing sport. Advertisers, ever-sensitive to the national mood, suffused their products with promises of power. Using a certain perfume made a woman irresistible to men; eating a certain breakfast food transformed a frail youngster into a sure-fire athletic champion. The nudity and four-letter words now found in the movies shocked millions, but perhaps more significant was the rising amount of brutality, murder, mutilation, and rape shown in commercial films. Even the Saturday morning children's cartoons featured an unending array of violence in technicolor. Basketball produced the "slam dunk," hockey the "power play," and tennis the "big game." Even the staid game of baseball took steps in the 1960s to bring more offense to the sport.

But no sport in the 1960s exceeded the capacity of the bone-crunching game of pro football to compensate for feelings of individual powerlessness. Television marketed football as a ceaseless struggle between cartoon primitives. "Games are won or lost in the trenches," repeatedly intoned the play-by-play announcers. Accompanied by a "Did you see that?" style of narration, the cameras gave viewers incessant close-ups of the powerful "mastodons" at work—Mean Joe Greene, Conrad Dobler, Merlin Olsen, Sam Huff. The size of the players reached surrealistic proportions. Linemen weighing a mere 225 pounds were thought to be suffering from conclusive malnutrition; coaches either promptly released them or put them on a weight-lifting program and a regimen of high caloric intake.

In fact, the game was violent beyond the comprehension of those who did not directly engage in it. Because the players were swathed in padding, their faces obscured by visored helmets, and the action was limited to a nineteen-inch television screen, the intensity of the violence was reduced to more tolerable dimensions. In 1972, psychiatrist Arnold Mandell, who that year became a consultant for the San Diego Chargers, described in *Nightmare Season* the first play he witnessed close up from the sidelines:

> Crunch . . . slap . . . snap . . . groan . . . scream . . . thud . . . Shit! Fuck! Motherfucker! I have to admit it, I closed my eyes. When I got up the courage to open them, I saw the result of my first on-the-field NFL play. Banaszack was down on his back in front of me. His mouth was twitching peculiarly. His eyes were closed. Rick Redman, our linebacker who got Banaszack, was down, too. On his right side and holding his left shoulder and whimpering quietly. . . . They had actually accelerated into each other before the hit. Two hundred and twenty pounds hitting two hundred and twenty pounds while accelerating.

The Green Bay Packers and their coach, Vince Lombardi, epitomized the importance of brute power in pro football. Lombardi, the most successful coach in the NFL in the 1960s, taught old-fashioned football. "Don't give me any fancy offenses or tricks on defense," he snapped. "You block better, you tackle better than the other guy, you win the football game." The success of the Lombardi system achieved a kind of immortality when the Packers defeated the Dallas Cowboys in the 1967 NFL playoff game, a game thought by many to be the greatest ever played. On Green Bay's frozen Lambeau Field, with the temperature hovering at thirteen degrees below zero, the Packers trailed 17–14, with thirteen seconds left to play. Then the Packers quarterback, Bart Starr, went over on a one-yard sneak behind a tremendous block thrown by Jerry Kramer on Dallas defensive tackle Jethro Pugh.

In countless replays, television vividly recaptured the explosive power of the block, and Kramer used the play to help turn his account of the 1967 season, *Instant Replay*, into a best seller.

Perhaps it was little wonder that President Richard M. Nixon was the nation's number-one football fan. To Nixon, a man obsessed with winning and losing, football was a miniature school of life, but without life's everyday ambiguities and moral dilemmas. Nixon believed football furnished a healthy antidote to the excessive individual freedom and lawlessness of the 1960s and 1970s.

Nixon regularly placed long distance telephone calls to stadium locker rooms to congratulate winning college and professional football teams. On three occasions he personally presented the annual award to the number-one-ranked college team in the nation. The strategy and tactics of the game intrigued Nixon. He even gave unsolicited suggestions of pass plays, including diagrams, to George Allen, coach of the Washington Redskins, and Don Shula, coach of the Miami Dolphins, for big games. He used the term "game plan" to describe his proposals for ending the Vietnam War and for dealing with the nation's economic problems.

The annual Super Bowl, a product of the 1966 NFL-AFL merger, climaxed Americans' season-long infatuation with professional football on television. No one at first expected the Super Bowl to far exceed all other sports spectacles in the size of its television audience and the national audience it generated. Within only half a dozen years, it overtook the 100-year-old Kentucky Derby and the 70-year-old World Series in popularity. "Super Bowl Sunday" became a national holiday, one far more rigorously observed than Washington's Birthday, Independence Day, or even tippling on New Year's Eve.

Television made it so. From the outset, both NBC and CBS, who alternated coverage of the event after 1968 (and ABC after 1982), used the game as a major "promo"—network jargon for advertisement—for their respective networks. For example, when NBC carried the game, the network began an exhaustive campaign during their weekly summer baseball games to remind viewers that the network of the peacock had exclusive rights to telecast a football game held in mid-January of the next year. The promotion continued during the World Series in October, during weekly NFL games in the fall, and on talk shows the week before the game. In addition, the network purchased space in newspapers and magazines to "hype" their exclusive coverage.

The Super Bowl promoters exploited the modern fascination with numbers. With everyone wrestling with 1040 tax forms, counting calories, and watching the dizzying performance of Dow Jones Industrial Averages, only the Super Bowl, of all the world's big sporting events, had a number after its name. And not just any number, but a Roman numeral. It all began in 1971, with Super Bowl V. Super Bowl V then gave birth to its predecessors, Super Bowls I, II, III, and IV. Attaching Roman numerals was perhaps more appropriate than even its promoters dreamed, for it helped to link the pageant with the spectacles of ancient Rome.

Other numbers helped to sell the Super Bowl while simultaneously numbing one's comprehension of the event. In the 1980s, over 130 million people, over half the nation's population, watched the game on television. No other American sports event and only an occasional television special approached that number. Unofficial Las Vegas estimates placed legal and illegal betting on the game at $260 million, or two dollars for each viewer. A half-minute commercial in 1983 cost $400,000, nearly half a million dollars for only thirty seconds of television time. (The Equitable Life Assurance Society reported that its sponsorship of family tennis tournaments in every state in the union, including all expenses paid for sixty-four finalists to attend the United States Open, cost less than a single commercial on the Super Bowl.) The same half-minute for Super Bowl I, in 1967, had cost a mere $35,000. Each player on the winning team at the 1983 Super Bowl received $70,000 for his services. At each Super Bowl, the NFL lavished upon the 2,000 members of the media courtesy cars, reams of canned interviews, hospitality rooms stocked with free drinks, and free bottles of perfume for their wives or lady friends.

The hype and hoopla surrounding the event came to overshadow the game itself. Cabinet members, corporate executives, and celebrities of all sorts vied for tickets. Upon arriving at the game site, they often embarked on several days of an "orgy of corporate excess." The Super Bowl "is for the royalty to attend," wrote John Jeansonne in *Newsday*, "and for the peasants to watch on TV, a situation that does not cause the NFL . . . any guilt feelings." By the mid-1970s the networks devoted up to five hours to the spectacle, including endless background reports on the two teams and on past Super Bowls. As in all NFL games, the actual playing time, interspersed between commercials, the half-time intermission, players getting back to the huddle, and quarterbacks calling the signals, consisted of less than ten minutes per game.

Furthermore, with but few exceptions, the games themselves turned out to be excruciatingly boring. Apprehensive lest errors lose the game before an audience of half the country, the coaches devised game plans even more conservative than the regular season ones. Up through the 1974 Super Bowl, quarterbacks had thrown an average of one-third fewer passes than in regular season, the teams had scored an average of only one touchdown for each seventeen minutes of play, in 443 attempts runners had gained twenty or more yards on only four occasions, and there had been only one long pass thrown for a touchdown. But little did it matter, for the game itself was only a backdrop to the total television "spectacular."

By the mid-1960s, some of the effects of television on specific sports had become manifest. Prize fighting and minor league baseball nearly failed to survive the new medium. Major league baseball attendance dropped; the sport never regained its former ascendancy in the hearts of Americans. On the other hand, after a turbulent relationship with television in the 1950s, college football became a growth sport in the 1960s while television and professional football were locked in a marriage so mutually beneficial that observers had to wonder if it had been made by mere mortals. While television had assisted in making pro football a major sport, sports could also help make a major television network.

7

The Making of a
Network Sports Division

On the evening of May 17, 1976, the lobby of the lush Century
Plaza in Los Angeles overflowed with television executives and
well-wishers. They had gathered at the Plaza after the conclusion
of the annual Emmy ceremonies, which had been held across the
street in the Shubert Theatre. Everyone seemed to be congratulat-
ing everyone else. Except, that is, in one category—sports—where
ABC nearly ran away with the honors. At the annual television
awards show, the ABC network had captured thirty-two of the
thirty-four statuettes granted in the sports area. Nearly twenty
minutes of precious network prime time had been consumed while
the National Academy of Television Arts and Sciences presented
the awards to Roone Pickney Arledge, the head of ABC Sports.
Grant Tinker (then husband of Mary Tyler Moore), producer of
the MTM properties—a CBS program supplier—and a future executive of NBC grumbled: "We really have got to do something
about this Roone Arledge. He's embarrassing. We either have to
get rid of him, get him over to CBS, or get the sports awards put
on with the technical awards the day before so they won't be on
prime time."

The story behind ABC's virtual sweep of the sports awards in
1976 reveals a unique approach to the intricate collaboration between the medium and sports. In the 1950s, none of the networks
(including the DuMont network, which folded in 1956) considered
sports programming critical to their success; they put far more of

their resources and talent into news, musicals, comedies, Westerns, and popular dramas. None of the networks even had a separate sports division; on the corporate organizational charts, sports came under the umbrella of the news division. Consequently, those responsible for sports had to battle the personnel in news for announcers, equipment, and network time. Neither did the networks develop most of their sports programming. Advertisers and advertising agencies purchased most of the rights to sporting events; the advertising men then sought a network to carry the events.

In the 1960s, ABC decided to break with this pattern. Lagging far behind CBS and NBC in ratings and advertising, the ABC network gambled that increased sports programming would give the network greater visibility, bring in new local television stations as affiliates, and improve overall audience ratings. The decision paid spectacular dividends. Sports contributed in no small part to the sudden leap of ABC from a weak third place in the broadcasting industry in the 1950s to the very top in the 1970s. ABC's reliance on the latest technical innovations and its "show biz" approach to sports touched off the process by which television hastened the trivialization of the traditional sports experience.

In the 1950s, ABC had neither an adequate number of affiliates nor the financial wherewithal to engage in serious competition for sports programs. In that decade, NBC justly claimed to be the frontrunner in sports coverage. NBC televised the World Series, the Friday night boxing card from Madison Square Garden, the regular season telecasts of NCAA football (except for 1954), the Rose Bowl, and the Orange Bowl. CBS beamed the Kentucky Derby, and after 1954 both regular season pro football and baseball's Game of the Week with Dizzy Dean. Only twice had ABC ventured into the perilous waters of big-time sports telecasts—to telecast the baseball Game of the Week in 1953 and 1954 and NCAA football in 1954. Both experiments had cost the network dearly. When the decade of the 1950s closed, ABC did not own the rights to a single major sporting event. Furthermore, the network fell far behind CBS and NBC in prime time ratings.

The major turning point for ABC came with a flurry of critical decisions made between 1959 and 1961. In 1959 the network appointed Tom Moore as head of programming. "Tom Moore is most responsible for ABC going into sports with both feet," declared Jim McKay. "Somebody said he's crazy about two things—sports and shooting craps. When he's shooting craps with a sports show he's in seventh heaven." Moore soon began to collaborate with Edgar Scherick, a veteran in televised sports programming. While employed with the Dancer, Fitzgerald & Dancer advertising agency in the 1950s, Scherick had put together "Baseball's Game of the Week" with Dizzy Dean and the "NFL Game of the Week" for the Falstaff Brewing Company. He had also worked for CBS and owned Sports Programming, Inc., a sports program supply company, which ABC purchased in 1961. Scherick's experience and bravado was indispensable to the growth of ABC Sports. Most important of all, in 1959, ABC landed a large account from the Gillette Safety Razor Company.

Unknown to the ABC high command, NBC wanted to get rid of its Friday night fights, sponsored by Gillette. In the wake of the great quiz show scandals, revelations of sleaziness in boxing, and falling Nielsen ratings for boxing, NBC decided to develop a new image of staunch integrity and dignity. To do so, the network decided to dissociate itself entirely from boxing. But Gillette saw the famed Friday night fights as the linchpin of its vast advertising campaign aimed at American men. Thus they asked their ad agency, Maxon, to explore ways of keeping the fights on the air.

In November of 1959, Tom Moore received a surprise phone call from Lou Maxon, head of the Maxon agency. Maxon and Moore quickly arranged a meeting with Gillette officials. In exchange for ABC's carrying Gillette's weekly fights, the razor company promised to give the network all of its television advertising dollars except those already committed to NBC for the World Series. "How much money is it?" tentatively asked Moore. "About $8.5 million," replied the Gillette advertising manager. Moore could hardly disguise his astonishment. That was more money than ABC had spent on sports during the network's entire history. The $8.5 million suddenly placed ABC in a position to bid for the rights to big-league baseball, pro football, and college football.

In short, Gillette furnished the seed money with which ABC worked its way up to the championship in sports ratings. First, Gillette dollars allowed ABC to obtain the biennial NCAA football contract for 1960–61. Although the network lost the contract for the next five years, it reacquired the rights for the 1966 season. Second, Gillette initially financed the "Wide World of Sports" series, which became the longest-running sports series on television. The success of Wide World, in turn, helped ABC develop its close relationship to the Olympic Games. Of the major milestones in the history of ABC Sports, only "Monday Night Football" (begun in 1970) owed nothing directly to Gillette money.

ABC first went after the NCAA football contract. To keep the cost of the rights from soaring, ABC kept the news of the newly acquired windfall from Gillette a top secret. Edgar Scherick, in charge of ABC's bidding, concocted an elaborate scheme designed to fool NBC. Since CBS was already tied up with an NFL contract, Scherick correctly assumed that they would not bid for the NCAA rights. He further surmised that Tom Gallery of NBC would have two bids available. If ABC and/or CBS sent representatives, then he would submit an envelope containing a higher bid. If no other network had a person at the bid letting, then Gallery would submit an envelope with the lower bid. Scherick commissioned Stan Frankle, an innocuous-looking assistant comptroller at ABC—a man unknown to NBC officials— to present ABC's bid.

The ruse went off as planned. As the members of the press, NCAA officials, and bystanders gathered, no one noticed or spoke to Stan Frankle. Promptly at one o'clock, Asa Bushnell, the head of the NCAA television committee, stood up and said: "We're ready to start the bidding." Gallery stared around the room, looking for familiar faces. He saw none. Bushnell spoke directly to Gallery: "Tom, we're ready." After quickly glancing around the room once more, Gallery placed one of his envelopes on the table in front of Bushnell. Immediately, Stan Frankle walked up to the table and delivered ABC's surprise bid. Stunned silence fell over the room; faces turned ashen. "The NCAA would as soon have had a Martian descend and bid as give their games to ABC," Scherick recalled. "ABC was a guttersnipe operation to them, third ranked. Hell, maybe fourth, behind DuMont." Finally, James Corbett, Louisiana State University athletic director, moved that the NCAA group adjourn to a nearby room to discuss the unforeseen turn of events. Behind closed doors, the committee discussed how they might still make the award to NBC, but they could hardly pass up the additional million dollars offered by ABC. After forty minutes, they returned to the room and announced that the NCAA rights now belonged to ABC.

The acquisition of the NCAA rights with the new dollars extended by Gillette led directly to the employment of Roone Arledge, an appointment that was to have far-reaching consequences for television sports. Graduating from Columbia in 1952 after having served as president of his class, president of his fraternity, and editor of his college yearbook, Arledge had hoped to become a writer. Instead, he took a job with the old DuMont network as a "gofer." After a stint in the armed services, he returned to television to produce shows for NBC's local station in New York. "No one would have predicted at the time," recalled a contemporary of Arledge's at NBC, "that Roone would become the greatest son of a bitch to ever sit in the control room of a sports telecast." In 1959, he won an Emmy for "Hi Mom," a children's program. After previewing Arledge's "For Men Only," which had been turned down by NBC, Scherick hired the highly personable redhead to produce ABC's NCAA games for a salary of $10,000 annually.

In due time Arledge became a television sports impresario without peer. He exhibited exceptional skills in all phases of his work, including the hiring of personnel, administration, packaging, promotion, and the acquisition of rights. Having climbed the same treacherous corporate ladder as his subordinates, Arledge enjoyed the respect and loyalty of his staff. "Roone's greatest asset, which very few people know, is people," Tom Moore once exclaimed. "Listen, he's got the goddamndest troop of people over there you've ever seen!" In an industry known for the intensity of its insecurities and the absence of stability, somehow Arledge built an exceptionally high esprit de corps among the staff of ABC Sports. From the early 1960s to the late 1970s, ABC Sports lost only one top person in the sports division. Contrast this record with CBS; in the 1970s, the network sports division suffered through eight presidents in nine years.

With the Gillette money in hand in 1960, Moore, Scherick, and Arledge set out to acquire the rights to as many prestigious sports events as the network could afford. Moore first sent Arledge after the big college bowls. While Arledge failed to capture either the Rose, Cotton, or the Orange Bowls, his active bidding wildly inflated the prices that the other networks had to pay. And ABC did win the rights to the Sugar Bowl. The network followed this triumph by capturing the rights to the Professional Golfer's Association championship from CBS, and the U.S. Open, the U.S. Women's Open, and the U.S. Men's Amateur from NBC. Rather than negotiating with the Amateur Athletic Union himself for the rights to the AAU's annual track and field meet, Scherick sent Arledge, because, as Scherick put it, "a Jew didn't go in to talk to the AAU at that time and Arledge had a much nicer name than I did." To the delight of ABC officials, Arledge, for a rather modest fee, returned with the television rights to all AAU events. The AAU package then became the centerpiece of ABC's new Wide World of Sports program.

Some negotiations proved to be simpler than others. When the ABC crew for Wide World of Sports appeared at Acapulco, Mexico, to tape the International Water Ski Championship in 1962, Paul Garcia, representative of the water skiers, approached Arledge with a proposal for televising some local divers who jumped off a nearby 87-foot cliff for the benefit of tourists. "How much?" Arledge asked. "$100,000," Garcia replied. "Out of the question," responded Arledge. Garcia then conferred with his clients. He countered with an offer of $10 per dive. Arledge promptly accepted.

No one equaled Arledge's skills in obtaining television rights to the Olympic Games. Winning Olympic rights required the knowledge and capacity to cut through the thickets of the Olympic organizational jungle, for the official Olympic structure often obscured the real loci of power. To accomplish this feat, Arledge carefully cultivated friendships among the leaders of international sport. Several years before an Olympic bid was to be let, Arledge would begin to make regular visits to the men in charge of the event. But he did not rely on fostering goodwill alone; Arledge and the ABC Sports staff always prepared for the local organizing committees an elaborate case for the network's capacity to put on a much better show than its rivals. For this presentation, the technical experience gained from Wide World of Sports in televising Olympic-type events usually impressed Olympic officials.

Sometimes such presentations had a humorous side. Minutes after ABC had won television rights to the 1968 Winter Games, to be held in Grenoble, France, the chairman of the Grenoble Organizing Committee approached Arledge. "I want to offer my congratulations and please could you also help me?" he said in halting English. "I want to know why NBC kept talking of their 'Bowel Games.' It was in very questionable taste."

The skill required to win the biennial NCAA football package may have equaled that needed to master the intricacies of Olympic politics. Even though ABC, in the 1960–61 seasons, had used twice as many cameras as NBC to produce its college game telecasts, the NCAA turned to CBS for the biennial contract of 1962–63 and returned to NBC for the 1964–65 seasons. Initially, ABC could not keep up with the escalation of rights costs, for between 1961 and 1964 they more than doubled, from $3 million to $6.52 million. But in 1964 both CBS (with the National Football League) and NBC (with the American Football League) had committed themselves heavily to pro football. By then the ownership of pro football rights involved a larger investment by the networks than the college package. Arledge went directly to Walter Byers, the head of the NCAA, with a proposition. ABC promised that it would not enter the pro television arena if awarded the exclusive rights to the college games. Byers responded favorably. Without asking for open bids from NBC and CBS, the NCAA awarded the 1966–67 contract to ABC, with an option to renew the contract for two more years. NBC was apoplectic. "Legally they didn't have to give us a shot at renewal, but morally, by God, they sure had an obligation," NBC's head of sports, Carl Lindemann, told the press. Although Byers was furious when ABC signed a contract to do Monday Night Football with the pros in 1970, ABC continued to hold the exclusive rights to NCAA football until 1982, when it began to share rights with CBS and the Turner Broadcasting System.

Arledge brought the full panoply of his production skills to the telecast of all ABC sporting events. In college football, Arledge was determined, as he put it, "to get the audience involved emotionally. If they didn't give a damn about the game, they still might enjoy the program." To obtain more audience involvement, Arledge attempted to capture the full ambience of the game setting. He used cranes, blimps, and helicopters to furnish better views of the stadium, the campus, and the town; hand-held cameras and close-up shots of cheerleaders, pretty coeds, band members, eccentric spectators, and nervous coaches; the rifle-type microphones to pick up the roar of the crowd, the thud of a punt, or the crunch of a hard tackle.

Arledge made the spectators and even the referees part of the performance. Coin-tossing ceremonies, once reserved for the locker rooms, now took place in the center of the field before the ever-present television cameras. The referees instructed the players to speak up so they could be heard on the microphones. The officials themselves began to give signals with artful flourishes. Melvin Durslag in *TV Guide* even suggested that the officials, since they had become actors, ought to join the American Federation of Television and Radio Artists.

Once the fans perceived themselves as potential performers, they began to carry banners, run onto the playing field, and engage in unseemly antics to grab the attention of the television cameras. Arledge exercised few restraints. During one game in the first season of ABC's college coverage, the cameras repeatedly turned to a young couple in the stands who embraced and kissed passionately each time Texas A & M gained more than three yards. In the early 1970s, on Monday Night Football, shots in the stands of women removing their clothes all the way down to their bras and panties—usually local strippers seeking free publicity—aroused enough protest that ABC cut back its coverage of some of the more bizarre forms of off-the-field behavior.

Without a contract for major league baseball, ABC decided to try to fill the gaps in Saturday afternoon summer schedules of its affiliates with a television sports anthology based upon the magazine formulas used so successfully by *Life* and *Look*, two mass-circulation magazines of the time. As producer of the new show, Arledge tried to treat sports both as entertainment and as fast-breaking news events. If the contest could not be carried live on the afternoon of the telecast, Wide World used videotape-delayed telecasts. Nonetheless, Jim McKay, the long-time host of the program, and his fellow commentators treated the videotaped events as though they were live. Each "sport," no matter how trivial, was also treated with all the solemnity of the British Open Golf Tournament. Wide World coined one of the most compelling clichés in sports history: "The thrill of victory . . . the agony of defeat."

Wide World gave Arledge unusual opportunities to develop

the latest production techniques and hone an experienced sports staff. He spared few expenses. Barred from baseball at home, Arledge often turned for program material to foreign playing fields. Wide World crews, with up to forty tons of equipment, literally flew to all parts of the world. This was the first program to use satellites for the transmission of international sporting events to viewers in the United States. Always a jump ahead of competitors in the use and refinement of shooting techniques, Wide World pioneered in the use of slow motion, stop action, and split-screen shots. In San Juan, Puerto Rico, Arledge even had a special 168-foot tower built to televise a golf match. Wide World used underwater cameramen equipped with aqualungs to film swimming meets. And Wide World created such successful spinoffs as "The American Sportsman," "The Superstars," and a second Wide World program beamed on Sunday afternoons.

Winner of numerous Emmys—more than any other sports series—Wide World consisted of a potpourri of feats and games, including (among others) boxing matches, track meets, ski races, surfing, cliff diving, barrel jumping, wrist wrestling, and demolition derbies. The program was especially effective in stimulating interest in winter sports and gymnastics. While the series spawned several imitations on the other networks, none quite equaled the technical finesse and lively pace of Wide World.

To grab the attention of viewers for Wide World, Arledge was quite willing to label any kind of contest a sport. He fully exploited the widespread feelings of individual impotence that somehow found compensation for many Americans in their love affair with cars. To sate the preoccupation with cars, Wide World beamed everything from demolition derbies to the Indianapolis 500, leading Melvin Durslag to label ABC "your friendly muffler network." "Does anybody really watch those racing cars chasing each other around and around every Saturday on ABC's increasingly 'Narrow World of Sports'?" asked sportswriter Dick Young. Yes, they did. In the 1960s and 1970s, some 49 million people annually went to auto races, more persons than watched live any other "sport." Furthermore, auto racing consistently drew higher television ratings than NBC's baseball Game of the Week.

The popularity of demolition derbies revealed that for every purist who came to the track—or watched on television—to see the finer points of racing, there were probably several others waiting to see a wreck, perhaps garnished with a death or at least a maiming. For many racing fans the excitement of two cars, perhaps three or four, going into a turn, tangling, spinning, splattering all over, bursting at the seams, spewing out oil and gas, crumpling in baroque shapes, and then spiraling blue smoke from the ruins equaled that experienced by the Romans at their bloody gladiatorial contests. But why should fans have to put up with the monotony between crashes? In 1958, Lawrence Mendelsohn, a former driver and owner of the Islip Speedway on Long Island, had a vision of an auto sport that would be all crashes. He put 100 old cars into an arena doing nothing but trying to smash each other out of commission. The lone survivor took the prize money. By the mid-1960s, Demolition Derby had become a staple of Wide World. It even spawned a number of imitators: football demolition, which used a red Volkswagen as a ball to be smashed across the goal line, and figure 8 racing, which had cars criss-crossing from opposite directions at the center in what amounted to a game of "chicken" at fifty miles per hour. If Demolition Derby "is sport . . .," wrote Roger Kahn, "so is lapidation, which is stoning people to unconsciousness or death." Regardless, by the 1970s up to 25 million people watched each Demolition Derby, or what William Leggett once cynically described as "the ultimate in televised corn."

An equally good case for being the ultimate in televised corn might be made for "The American Sportsman," one of the spinoffs of Wide World. Beginning in 1964, some 18 million viewers each weekend watched celebrity "sportsmen" fish, engage in he-man exchanges, and employ .458 magnum Winchesters, which looked like anti-tank guns, to shoot down elephants. According to Curt Gowdy, the narrator of the show, everything the hunters killed on their African safaris was for the safety of the "fear-maddened natives." Thus actor Robert Stack, from over one hundred yards away, gunned down a mangy lion that was billed as a "killer," and Joe Foss, the former governor of South Dakota and Commissioner of the American Football League, shot down what appeared to be an elderly, single-tusked elephant. The announcer asserted that Foss bravely stood "in the way of a thundering charge of a rogue elephant." Amidst protests from the "bow-

wows''—as one ABC official described the critics of the show—
and a decline in ratings, in the late 1960s the network replaced
hunting episodes with shows featuring ecological themes.

While in a broad sense a case could be made for Demolition
Derby and even the activities on American Sportsman being sports
events, the stunts of motorcyclist Robert Craig ''Evel'' Knievel,
could hardly be described as such even by the most tolerant word-
smith. Beginning in 1967, Wide World built Knievel into a living
legend; he appeared on the show sixteen times. The main appeal of
Knievel was the ever-present possibility that his latest stunt might
be his last—or, at the least, that he would severely injure himself.
His series of failures began in 1968 when he attempted to jump the
fountains in front of Caesar's Palace in Las Vegas and lost control
of his motorcycle as it hit the pavement at the end of the 108-foot
ramp. Knievel bounced off the pavement like a rag doll, breaking
both his back and his pelvis. Suddenly he had a daredevil image
equaled by no other person in the twentieth century.

It was the good fortune of Knievel to be performing in the age
of television, so that his mishaps could be captured in all their
slow motion glory. Some thirty years earlier, only a handful of
witnesses had watched stuntman Captain Joe Montford roar off
the lip of the Grand Canyon on a motorcycle bearing only a para-
chute, but when Knievel blasted off on his motorcycle in a vain effort to jump the Snake River Canyon, television beamed in gory
detail each snapping bone and each agonizing grimace. Before the
Snake River debacle, ABC had made Knievel the subject of two
prime time shows—one a feature film, the other an in-depth docu-
mentary. Knievel's success as a television personality led to people
all over the world volunteering to engage in death-defying stunts.
In 1974, over drinks, the Greenwich Jets grimly mused about the
possibility of televising the execution of convicted murderer Gary
Gilmore. Perhaps Howard Cosell could handle the commentary.
''I guess the definition of sports has gotten very fuzzy,'' admitted
Kevin O'Malley, director of CBS programming.

For most of the late 1960s and early 1970s, Wide World
scheduled the only boxing matches available on network television. After having flooded the airwaves with matches in the 1950s,
during the next decade the networks had almost completely pulled
away from boxing. After the cancellation of Gillette's Friday
night fights in 1964, Wide World filled some of the slack. In 1965

Wide World showed three delayed telecasts of championship fights and in 1966 its first live heavyweight championship fight—Cassius Clay versus Henry Cooper. In the 1970s boxing became the second most popular segment of Wide World—ranking just behind auto racing.

Central to the revival of interest in boxing on Wide World was the almost simultaneous rise of two remarkable TV sports celebrities: Muhammad Ali, a.k.a. Cassius Clay, and Howard Cosell, a.k.a. Howard Cohen. In 1964 Ali shocked the followers of pugilism by renouncing his "slave name" of Clay and announcing his conversion to the Black Muslim faith. Another shock followed when Ali became one of the most publicized opponents of the Vietnam War. He refused to step forward for induction into the army, an act that quickly led to his title being stripped from him.

Howard Cosell, a Brooklyn-born lawyer who had worked his way up through the ranks of ABC largely as a radio fight announcer, championed the cause of Ali. On Wide World, Cosell argued that Ali, as a conscientious objector, should have been exempted from military service and that the boxing associations who had deprived him of his title had acted unfairly. Cosell's stance attracted an enormous amount of attention to Wide World and ABC. Arledge set up a series of interviews between Cosell and Ali that approached high burlesque. Some fans loved the repartee, especially Ali's poetic threats against Cosell: "When I'm finished and at the bell, I'll jump over the ropes and take on Howard Cosell." Others despised both Ali and Cosell. Letters arrived at ABC describing Cosell as a "nigger-loving Jew bastard" and Ali as a "traitor" who ought to be shot or subjected to even more drastic horrors. But Arledge, perhaps conscious that bigotry begat higher ratings and more press attention, never flinched. He continued to feature the Ali–Cosell show.

With the technical wizardry he acquired doing the Wide World of Sports, Arledge turned the Olympic Games into marvelous television extravaganzas. Prior to ABC's acquisition of the 1968 rights to the Winter Games in Grenoble and the Summer Games in Mexico City, the television networks had given little attention in the quadriennial spectacle. At Grenoble, as Abby Rand of *TV Guide* described it, ABC put on a "27-hour Olympic orgy." The network even turned over one prime-time evening to the Winter Games. Arledge sent over a 250-man crew with forty color cameras and used the Early Bird satellite to instantly convey the action to viewers in the United States. From the cold mountainsides of Grenoble, the ABC crew moved to even higher altitudes in Mexico City to do the Summer Games. Since the high altitude led to the shattering of numerous world records in track and field, the Games enjoyed an unusually high built-in drama. But ABC Sports did not sidestep the intrusion into the Games of the deep racial divisions in the world. They televised Tommie Smith and John Carlos, the black American sprinters, as they stood on the victory platform during the playing of the National Anthem with black-gloved fists raised defiantly in the air and heads bowed to protest racism in the United States. Howard Cosell quickly obtained interviews with Smith, Carlos, and other American athletes.

To the world, the Munich Games of 1972 appeared to take place in a gigantic television studio. As one wag put it, the United States sent two teams to Munich: the 470 American athletes and the 330 men and women bearing the banner of ABC Sports. To make detailed information on every athlete and event instantly available, ABC installed a bank of computers. Arledge, who personally directed the games, deftly switched back and forth from one event to another as he peered at some forty television monitors.

Unexpectedly and tragically, the invasion of the Israeli compound by Arab terrorists transformed the games into a genuine news story. Immediately ABC Sports became a news system. As negotiations lingered on and the terrorists postponed their deadline for the execution of the hostages, television cameras positioned near the compound zoomed in on the hangmanlike-visage of a terrorist with a stocking cap pulled down over his head. West Germany and Israeli officials finally settled on a desperate plan which was to culminate in an ambush of the terrorists at an airport near Munich. The plan failed. The terrorists killed the Israeli hostages, though German authorities seized three of the guerillas and killed the others. Captured by television in all of its grotesqueness, the surrealistic spectacle was reminiscent of the assassinations of President John F. Kennedy and Lee Harvey Oswald in 1963.

The secret of ABC's success sometimes lay in more than well-made plans. As Arledge was about to switch to a battle for third place in team gymnastic exercises at the 1972 Olympics, Gordon Maddux, ABC's expert commentator, tugged at the sleeve of Jim McKay. ''Jim, that little girl did something I've never seen before,'' exclaimed an excited Maddux. Maddux thought he had just seen a backward flip dismount on the uneven bars. Both McKay and Maddux quickly flipped through the ABC biographical "playbook." Nothing on Olga Korbut. Sensing a story in the making, Arledge, despite the astonishment of those near him in the control booth, decided to abandon the planned script and follow the instincts of Maddux and McKay. This one decision, seemingly small at the time, had enormous repercussions. For it not only transformed tiny, sixteen-year-old Olga Korbut into an instant celebrity, but attracted more attention to gymnastics than the sport had received in its entire history. In 1976 ABC made gymnastics the centerpiece of its coverage of the Montreal Olympics.

So successful were Arledge's productions of the 1968, 1972, and 1976 Games that Pete Axthelm suggested in 1976, perhaps with tongue in cheek, that Arledge ought to be put in charge of the entire management of the Games. The elaborate equipment needed for the telecast of the Games and the experience acquired from the Games gave ABC an advantage over its rivals in sports television that lasted well into the 1980s. ABC Sports helped push the network to the top; in the fall of 1976, ABC passed CBS in the Nielsen ratings for all shows.

Monday Night Football constituted the final milestone in ABC's ascension to the top of the sports world. The initiative for the program came from Pete Rozelle, commissioner of the National Football League, rather than from the television networks. Rozelle, fearing that televised Sunday doubleheaders had reached their maximum potential audience, had tried in the mid-1960s to interest the networks in a prime time telecast. Only by entering the prime time market, Rozelle reasoned, could the NFL make new converts. In the 1966 negotiations with CBS, Rozelle had forced the network to telecast four preseason games and one regular season tilt at night. When Rozelle put the proposal up for bids in 1970, none of the networks wanted to jeopardize their more profitable Monday night programming of sitcoms and variety shows. But Howard Hughes's newly acquired Sports Network Incorporated (SNI) was prepared to seize the opportunity to join in big-time sports television. Threatened with the prospect of several of its affiliates switching to Hughes on Monday night, ABC reluctantly submitted a bid. Arledge insisted that Rozelle let him have total control over the selection of announcers and a share of the better games on the NFL schedule. Although SNI offered a higher bid, the NFL awarded the contract to ABC, since ABC had more prestige and a larger number of affiliates. For the initial contract ABC paid $8 million for thirteen games, less than half the rate paid by CBS for its Sunday afternoon NFL games.

With the Monday night program ABC brought a new production standard to the telecasting of professional football games. Unlike NBC and CBS, ABC employed a two-unit production team, one of which (headed by Chet Forte) dealt with the play-by-play while the other (under the direction of Don Ohlmeyer) handled only isolated coverage. Nine cameras (with sometimes as many as five devoted to isolated matchups of players) and two videotape machines furnished the ABC crew with unequaled technical capacity. Taking his cues partly from the play-by-play announcers but relying as well on his own knowledge of the game, Ohlmeyer seemed to enjoy a prescient capacity for anticipating plays. "What it is, basically, is a matter of guessing right," Ohlmeyer modestly said. "It's like playing quarterback and middle linebacker at the same time."

Yet more important to the success of Monday Night Football than the technical quality was the drama created by Arledge in the announcer's booth. Pro football had never enjoyed a rich set of traditions equivalent to baseball, but Arledge was quite willing to abandon whatever traditions the sport possessed in favor of sheer entertainment. "We wanted to feature the personalities of Howard [Cosell] and Don Meredith and not just caption pictures," asserted Arledge. "I thought people were tired of the religious approach to football," he said, "treating everything like the Second Coming."

Arledge began with Howard Cosell, already the most controversial announcer in the country, as a "color man." From the first telecast, Cosell sparked controversy. Offsetting Cosell, the streetwise, abrasive New Yorker, Arledge hired Don Meredith, former Dallas Cowboy quarterback. Meredith embodied "Middle America," but he was also gently irreverent toward the sport. The eventual combination of Cosell, Meredith, and Frank Gifford offered a perfect chemistry for making the telecast into a form of show business that could compete successfully with prime time shows on Monday night.

Nothing could stem the success of Monday Night Football. For thirteen weeks each season during the 1970s and 1980s, the ABC television crew paraded from one city to another, turning each game into an immensely exciting spectacle. As when circuses arrived at small tank towns in an earlier era, each city turned out en masse to see the ABC television team at work. Governors, mayors, and businessmen threw parties. It was, to quote Frank Gifford, "one big cocktail party." At the stadium, the fans often exhibited more interest in the announcers and the accompanying fanfare than in the game itself. Fans wondered aloud, "What did Howard think about that play?" and "I wonder what Meredith said?" Everyone clamored for the attention of the cameras: Fans, politicians, and celebrities of all sorts wanted in on the action. One night at a game in Los Angeles, Ernest Borgnine, Lee Majors, Glenn Ford, and Richard Anderson all crowded outside the television booth; they looked like a set piece from *The Godfather*. Players also quickly got into the spirit of the occasion, flexing their muscles and hamming it up for national television.

"The traveling freak show," as it was labeled by Don Meredith, altered the Monday night habits of a large portion of the American people. As husbands deployed their sixpacks, wives across the country shuddered. "Oh no, surely not another football game!" they implored. Movie attendance nose-dived, hookers left the streets, restaurants closed their doors, and bowlers rescheduled their leagues. But gamblers and bookies rejoiced. For Monday Night Football offered the addicted sports gambler yet another opportunity to recoup his weekend indulgences. "The people at ABC," exclaimed one New York bookie, "are the best friends our industry has this side of the Jersey City police department."

Eventually, even many wives joined their husbands to hear the orotund pronouncements of Cosell, listen to the refreshing wit of Meredith—perhaps "Dandy Don" would finally "put Cosell in his place"—and, above all, enjoy the liquid intonations and handsome profile of Gifford. Indeed, for many Americans Monday Night Football became one of the most important family rituals.

For the two decades following the 1960s, ABC determined the overall shape of television sportscasts. Armed with an arsenal of new technology and innovative production methods, ABC tried, as Arledge put it, "to bring the viewer to the game rather than the game to the viewer." In other words, ABC attempted to duplicate the sensations that fans would experience if they were actually present at the event. In reality, the sports telecasts perfected by ABC brought the viewers a completely new experience of sports. Multiple cameras, slow motion capabilities, and "personality" announcers permitted television directors to produce original creations of sports events. In this new form of televised sports drama, the director sought above all else to avoid lapses in excitement, for he strove to keep the viewer glued to the television set. Thus the director broadened and intensified the visual and aural range of the event. He employed controversial announcers, catchy music, and graphics. By telling viewers of past heroes and past records, and of how the event related to the past, the announcers established the historical context of the drama. During the game, they kept the viewer apprised of key events as they transpired. Presumably keen students of the game, they described and interpreted the action for the viewer. They often attempted to convince the viewer that the contest was an exciting game even though the viewer might, on his own, have found it otherwise. And when all else failed, the announcers attempted to generate drama in the broadcast booth itself.

The new sports drama created by television inexorably threatened the authenticity of the traditional sporting experience. To keep a maximum number of viewers watching the event, the temptation—conscious or unconscious—for television to exaggerate or magnify sensations arising from the contest and to introduce sensations extrinsic to the contest was irresistible. It was precisely at this point that the original sports drama began to degenerate into spectacle or simply entertainment. But in so doing it appealed to those ignorant of the nuances of the genuine sports drama, who watched the televised performance only to be "entertained." Simultaneously, the new drama tended to delude the true sports fan into being satisfied with an endless array of crude forms of sensationalism.

8

The Networks Slug It Out

Nothing revealed the importance of sports programming to the networks more dramatically than the bizarre negotiations for the 1980 Moscow Olympics. When in 1974 Moscow had been awarded the 1980 Summer Games, only ABC, of the Big Three television networks, was certain to offer a bid for the television rights. That changed in 1976–77, when ABC burst to the top of the Nielsen ratings; a leap that had been partly a consequence of its spectacular coverage of the 1976 Games in Montreal. CBS had long revealed a disdain for sports, but decided it could ignore the Games in the future only by imperiling the stature of the network. Under the tutelage of Robert Wussler, the new head of CBS Sports (1975), and with the encouragement of William Paley, the chairman of the board, CBS determined to increase its sports coverage; above all, the network wanted the contract for the 1980 Moscow Games. Of the Big Three, only NBC hung back, fearful that it did not have the resources to engage in all-out war with its fellow giants of the broadcasting industry.

The war starred a classic, if somewhat comic, cast of adversaries. On one side stood the network chiefs, who represented in sharp relief the glory, glamour, and wealth of American capitalism. Lean, tanned, quick-witted, supersophisticated, fond of Gucci shoes, they resided in a universe of Manhattan skyscrapers and chauffeured limousines. They looked and talked much alike but viewed each other with a profound mistrust. On the other side stood the burly, pallid, somewhat grim bureaucrats who composed the Soviet negotiating team. Having won and then held power in the cold corridors of the Kremlin, they had demonstrated a keen instinct for survival in the land of the purge. In this, they shared something with the network chiefs, for the television executives were no less vulnerable to swift turns in fortune that might send them reeling back to the Siberias of American broadcasting.

Both CBS and ABC shamelessly courted the Moscow negotiating team. For instance, during the fall of 1975, ABC's morning show, "A.M. America," presented a week of reports on life in the Soviet Union. "We made Moscow look like Cypress Gardens without the water skiers," admitted one embarrassed ABC man. CBS followed with a prime-time bomb in 1976 featuring a shivering Mary Tyler Moore standing on a street corner in Moscow, where she hosted a show about the Bolshoi Ballet. Asked if the show was part of the CBS Olympic campaign, Robert Wussler snapped, "No question about it." Yet, when Russian officials suggested that the Soviet Union should receive more favorable treatment by the news divisions of the respective networks, both networks balked.

Then entered the mysterious West German theatrical impresario, Lothar Bock. Because of his past bookings of Soviet entertainment troupes in the West, Bock enjoyed the trust of the Soviet negotiators. In 1976 Bock began serving as an intermediary for CBS. At the urging of Bock, William Paley himself, one of the patriarchs of American television, visited Moscow. (In an unprecedented show of goodwill, the Soviets even permitted Paley to fly in his private jet to Moscow.) Paley and Igor Novikov, the head Soviet negotiator, got along well. For over four hours, they dined and drank *tête-à-tête*. CBS officials were confident that the private meeting had resolved all the major issues and that the network had a lock on the Moscow Olympics.

But then the Soviet committee suddenly changed the rules of the game. The Soviets decided to hold an auction, an unending series of bids until one victor emerged and the other two networks dropped out. (By this time, NBC had also decided to join the fray.) "They want us to be like three scorpions fighting in a bottle," exclaimed Roone Arledge. "When it's over, two will be dead and the winner will be exhausted." Apparently the minions of the

Kremlin had a far better understanding of the American economic system than anyone had supposed. They seemed to know precisely how to maximize their revenues by fully exploiting the battle between the American networks.

Subsequent negotiations became incredibly complicated. After the Soviets announced the auction plan, angry American television representatives broke off further talks. So that the networks could bargain as a single pool, the moguls on Sixth Avenue asked the Justice Department to waive the relevant federal antitrust laws. Upon learning that the American networks hoped to obtain approval of the federal government for abandoning the principles of the free enterprise system, the Soviets quickly backed off from their scorpions-in-the-bottle strategy.

Lothar Bock tried to salve the wounds of both parties. He told Wussler that the Soviets wanted to renew negotiations with CBS, but Wussler, angered by the change in Soviet strategy, refused and the proposed pool disintegrated. The wily Bock then went to NBC. For $1 million plus a promise to buy fifteen programs produced by Bock, he delivered the Olympics to NBC at a cost of $85 million. Unfortunately for NBC, the network had paid some $50 million to the Soviets when, because of the Soviet invasion of Afghanistan, President Jimmy Carter ordered a boycott of the 1980 Olympics.

The fight for the rights to the 1980 Olympics was only one of the arenas in which the networks locked in ferocious combat. The cost of rights to all the major sports events escalated at an astonishing rate. While the grand old game of baseball suffered from many ills, the 1983 television contract made them seem like only minor irritants. The networks agreed to pay the big leagues $1 billion—an amazing $810 million increase over the existing four-year contract. Likewise, in 1982 the three big networks signed pacts with the National Football League that boosted the income of each of the twenty-eight teams in the league from about $5.8 million to $14.2 million per season. In 1982, ABC also paid the United States Football League—a new loop which had not yet played a single game—$22 million for television rights. The cost of television rights to the summer Olympic Games soared from $85 million in 1980 to $225 million in 1984; that of college football and basketball rights multiplied at a similar pace. Suddenly, in the late

1970s and in the 1980s the quantities of money being transfused into sports by television were increasing at a rate far surpassing the general rate of inflation.

Rather than reflecting a new surge of interest on the part of Americans in sports, the abrupt escalation of the stakes was part of an all-out war between the Big Three television networks for supremacy in the ratings. Before the 1970s, CBS and NBC had been far ahead of ABC in financial resources and ratings; they had more or less divided the major sports packages between them—NBC beaming big-league baseball and CBS the National Football League. Neither network had considered successful sports telecasts to be essential to their overall Nielsen position. But after ABC's ratings leapt upward in the 1970s, sports became a prime concern in the executive suites of all three networks. The network chiefs came to believe that the sports division might well be the key to a network's overall prosperity. Sports telecasts reinforced the loyalties of affiliates, they reasoned, thus preventing their defection to competing networks. Furthermore, an attractive summer sports lineup was essential to the successful launching of the all-important fall schedule of new shows.

Inevitably, the unprecedented sums of money from television altered and distorted the entire fabric of American sports. The players demanded a larger share of the new dollars; assisted by court rulings and their player associations, they became far more militant than they had been in the past. Their image began to change; they often seemed more concerned with their salaries than with performance or team loyalty. To make their games more attractive to television and thus hopefully grab the largest possible share of the new-found riches, the existing major sports experimented with radical changes in the rules and scheduling of their contests. The networks created highly popular synthetic games, or "trashsports," as they were dubbed by their critics. Augmented in the late 1970s by cable television systems, the quantity of sports available via the cool medium doubled, tripled, and then expanded almost beyond belief. The sheer quantity of televised sports threatened to numb and diffuse the viewer's sensibilities.

The major team sports—pro football, college football, and big-league baseball—served as primary battle grounds for the networks. (Quadrennially, the Olympic Games joined the major team sports in the primary arena; and, in the 1980s, the networks and cable television added college basketball as a big-time television spectacle.) All of the networks believed it to be essential to own the television rights to a minimum of one and ideally to two or more of these sports. The networks no longer bid directly against one another for rights, either because the total rights package for each major team sport had become too large for a single network to handle or because one or more of the networks had other sports commitments so large that they could not bid. Thus pro football (beginning in 1970) negotiated separate contracts with all three networks, major league baseball with two networks (1976), and NCAA football and basketball also with two (1982).

Of the three major team sports leaders, Pete Rozelle, commissioner of the NFL, most successfully took advantage of the war between the networks. Before negotiations began, he carefully considered what the networks had paid for parallel kinds of programming, the ratings of NFL games, and the possible combinations of packages that could be offered to the networks. He then arrived at an ideal figure which he wanted from each network. He brought to the negotiations a carefully prepared strategy and his well-honed negotiating skills. "The negotiations with Rozelle go a little like this," explained one former network man, a veteran in dealing with Rozelle, to a congressional committee. "You walk in and he puts a sack over your head. Then in a quiet voice, a little embarrassed almost, Pete tells you how much you gotta pay. You start to say something and he asks you if you'd like a little rum-flavored tea, all the while sticking the knife a little deeper."

Rozelle was able to stick the knife in deeply because he held high cards. By the late 1970s, all three networks regarded pro football rights as absolutely essential in retaining the loyalties of their affiliates; to survive in the volatile battle with their competitors, each had to have some share of NFL television rights. Negotiating with each network separately, in 1977 "Pete the Shark," as one network negotiator dubbed Rozelle, engineered a whopping $656 million, four-year package. From the new package each pro franchise received nearly $6 million annually, six times the 1964 contract. For the first time in NFL history, television income exceeded gate receipts as a source of team income. Perhaps it was little wonder that some observers conjured up visions of pro football becoming solely a "studio sport."

Rozelle pulled off an even bigger coup in 1982. Worried lest cable television systems join them in bidding for NFL rights, observing that the Nielsen ratings of NFL games continued to climb, and obtaining from Rozelle an additional minute of advertising in each game, the networks agreed to pay the NFL the stunning figure of $2 billion over five years. This was by far the single richest contract ever signed in show business history. Each of the twenty-eight NFL teams saw their compensation suddenly increase from $5.8 million to $14.2 million annually—a huge windfall for each franchise. To put the contract in perspective, the annual television share of the Washington Redskins under the new contract exceeded the team's *gross* revenues in 1981. Indeed, in 1980 the entire Denver Bronco franchise was sold for $20 million; the new owners would receive nearly two-thirds of the sale price from a single year of the new contract. Few disagreed with Al Davis, managing partner of the Oakland/Los Angeles Raiders, when he exclaimed that "any dummy can make money operating a pro football team."

Large as the price was, the networks apparently lost no money. The reason was simple enough: NFL football attracted a disproportionately large segment of 18- to 49-year-old males, especially those in the higher income brackets—otherwise the most difficult group to reach on television and "a damn desirable demographic breakdown," as Carl Lindemann, the NBC Sports chief, once put it. A 1981 Simmons Market Research study found that six times as many persons in this prime target group for advertisers watched NFL football games as saw the highly rated series "Dallas." To reach these men, advertisers were willing to pay prime rates. One television insider estimated that $25 million of CBS's $300 million profit in 1981 came from pro football telecasts; such profits at NBC, according to another insider, mounted to $50 million in 1983.

Next to pro football, the networks prized most the rights to college football telecasts. In 1977 CBS sought to crack the long monopoly which ABC had enjoyed since 1966 in carrying college games, but Roone Arledge came up with the then-staggering sum of $120 million over four years to keep ABC's exclusive rights. In 1981 CBS succeeded. The NCAA signed a contract with ABC and CBS to share the traditional Saturday afternoon games and with the new Turner Broadcasting (cable) System to handle special Saturday night games. The new packages produced a sharp jump in revenues; the colleges now received $74.3 million annually from television rights, more than twice as much as they had received only two years earlier. (Remember, however, that the pros were receiving $400 million a year.)

Although the audience for televised regular season baseball games had failed to keep pace with that for football, the games remained attractive to the networks. They could be used to fill slow summer program schedules and to hype fall programming. Furthermore, the television ratings for the baseball playoffs and the World Series approximated those of the football playoffs, the Super Bowl, and the New Year's Day college bowls.

In 1975 ABC boldly challenged NBC's long domination of the television rights to major league baseball. The big leagues awarded ABC the more lucrative "Monday Night Baseball" telecasts (begun by NBC in 1972) plus alternating rights (with NBC) to the playoffs and the World Series; otherwise, NBC had to be satisfied with the less desirable Saturday afternoon telecasts. NBC cried "foul play," for the architect of the 1975 plan, John Lazarus, director of radio and television for major league baseball, had formerly been an employee of ABC. The chief beneficiary of the new package, however, was big league baseball, which now received from the two networks $92.8 million over four years—$20 million more than NBC had been paying.

In 1983 NBC retaliated. They upped their payments to a staggering $550 million for roughly half of the rights package over six years. If ABC refused the other half of the package, NBC expressed a willingness to purchase the entire baseball contract for $1 billion. By upping the stakes so high, NBC hoped to force ABC either to come up with an equally large sum or to drop out of the baseball picture entirely. Furthermore, NBC had just lost out in the bidding for NCAA football and the new United States Football League rights. It faced the prospect of a continued attrition of affilates to ABC, and, as a laggard in the ratings race, desperately needed a summer sport to trumpet its fall entertainment schedule. Don Kowet of *TV Guide* suggested an even more sinister strategy (one confirmed by a highly placed source at NBC). By opening with such a spectacular bid, NBC hoped to bleed ABC so badly that the network could not be a serious contender for the 1988 Seoul Olympics. Whatever the motives of NBC, ABC agreed to pay the $575 million required for its share of the big-league television package. The upshot of the battle of the two networks was that baseball received the stunning total of $1.1 billion from the 1983 pact. This meant $4 million per year for each club—more than three times the earlier network revenues.

In addition to negotiating the package contracts with the networks, big-league baseball also permitted each franchise to sign contracts with local stations or cable systems. Thus, in effect the networks, local stations, and cable systems might all be competing against one another for the same television rights. The cost of rights varied enormously from one city to the next; in cities with a large population and competing television stations, a baseball franchise might be able to receive handsome rewards from local television rights. In 1978, for example, the Kansas City Royals, received a mere $350,000 from local broadcast rights, while the Yankees took in $1.3 million. The Yankee contract with the Sportschannel cable network, signed in 1982, reportedly called for over $100 million to be paid out over fifteen years.

"The Greenbacking of Pete Rose" graphically illustrated the importance of local television to baseball. In 1978 Rose, an unusually popular superstar of the Cincinnati Reds, became a free agent and signed a three-year pact with the Philadelphia Phillies for $2.2 million. The Phillies could afford such generosity only because of local television station WPHL-TV. Bill Giles, the executive president of the Phillies, went to the station manager of WPHL with a proposition: If the club acquired Rose, could the station pay an additional $600,000 annually to the Phillies? Although skeptical, Gene McCurdy, the general manager of WPHL, asked the station's sales staff to find out what Rose might do for advertising sales. They discovered, said McCurdy to a *Sports Illustrated* writer in 1979, "that Pete Rose playing for the Phillies would do two things: 1) he would certainly raise viewing levels and this could be translated into an increased demand for commercial time, and, 2) his presence would have a strong emotional effect on certain clients—people who would buy time partly because they could then see themselves as being instrumental in getting Pete Rose to play for the Phillies." Never before had television ratings and revenues been so directly linked to the transfer of an athlete from one team to another. In the future, before making offers to free agents, sports tycoons would attempt to calculate the effect of such a signing on local television revenues.

The purchase of big-league clubs by organizations with television interests aroused fears that the game would be inexorably altered to serve those interests. The 1964 purchase of the New York Yankees by CBS seemed to confirm such fears. Cartoonists had a field day showing players' caps with the CBS eye in the middle, Jackie Gleason playing shortstop, and comedians stepping out on the field before the game to warm up the crowd, just as they did before "The Danny Kaye Show." Inevitable Senate hearings followed; Senators intoned that they would give the matter further study to see if CBS and baseball ought to be made subject to the nation's antitrust laws. Under the direction of CBS, Yankee performance on the field sank to the lowest point since prior to World War I, and attendance collapsed. In 1973 CBS sold the team to a syndicate headed by shipbuilding magnate George Steinbrenner. Yet by the 1980s, organizations with broadcast interests owned at least seven other big-league clubs.

The struggle for the rights to professional basketball and the revival of televised boxing reveal the intensity with which the networks tried to gain ascendancy on Saturday and Sunday afternoons. In 1965 Tom Moore, Julie Baranthan, and Roone Arledge of ABC met to discuss their Wide World of Sports series. Wide World, now in its fourth year, had not quite sold all of its ads. The reason: CBS's new "Sports Spectacular," which had moved to Saturdays opposite Wide World. Baranthan, the general manager of ABC, mused aloud, "If we could just get them down a few points . . . ." Arledge interrupted, "Why not put live sports—like basketball—opposite their taped events? Tom, you know Walter Kennedy [NBA commissioner], don't you?"

The ABC–NBA marriage was soon consummated. ABC hoped to improve their share of the audience by only 5 percent, but NBA basketball ratings did even better, dunking the CBS Sports Spectacular into oblivion. Yet, the ratings for NBA games climbed slowly, from 20.2 percent of all television sets turned on in 1965 to 27.1 percent in 1968. The expectations by ad agencies of a basketball boom in the 1970s did not materialize. The NBA owners blamed ABC, arguing that the network did not adequately promote the games. Some owners also suggested that the quiet irreverence of broadcaster Bill Russell, a former star and player–coach of the Boston Celtics, damaged the ratings. Thus, despite nine years of fruitful marriage, the NBA divorced ABC in 1973 and signed a contract with CBS.

Roone Arledge was furious. In his opinion the NBA had violated a gentleman's agreement permitting ABC an option to match any offer from another network. ABC took the matter to court and lost. Arledge then retaliated. He countered with a new Sunday Wide World of Sports program, scheduled directly opposite CBS's NBA games. Within five weeks the ratings for the Sunday Wide World show doubled those of the NBA games. To make the NBA games more "salable," CBS switched announcers several times and toyed with efforts to cover more than one game simultaneously. None of these experiments worked. Even when, in the late 1970s and 1980s, CBS featured matchups of popular stars Magic Johnson and Larry Bird, the pro basketball ratings managed only to break even with the college basketball games shown on NBC.

In the wake of the publicity surrounding Muhammad Ali, the Academy-award winning film *Rocky* (released in 1976), and the popularity of ABC's coverage of boxing in the 1976 Olympic Games (five Americans won gold medals at Montreal), both CBS and NBC joined ABC in reviving televised boxing. All three networks prepared to slug it out with the big dollars; the decision plunged the networks into the business of staging and promoting fights. NBC formed a partnership with Madison Square Garden, still the citadel of boxing, to furnish it with a series of bouts. CBS ensured its future boxing fare by signing several Olympians to exclusive contracts. The contract of Howard Davis, for example, called for him to fight six times over the next twenty months; he received fees ranging from $40,000 for a six-rounder to $200,000 for a ten-rounder.

ABC responded with a two-pronged strategy. Like CBS, the network signed several fighters to exclusive contracts. Thus, George Foreman agreed to a package deal with the network that included color commentary on boxing shows and the network's right of first refusal on any of his future television bouts. ABC also lured popular Olympian Sugar Ray Leonard into its camp. "Whereas fighters of old wore trunks bearing shamrocks, flags, initials, and Stars of David," commented Melvin Durslag in *TV Guide*, "viewers envision new ones containing the CBS eye and a portrait of Roone Arledge."

Secondly, ABC provided $1.5 million to launch the United

States Boxing Championship, a tournament designed to establish an American champion in every weight division. Orchestrating the extravaganza was Don King, who had promoted Muhammad Ali's matches in Zaire and Manila; Roone Arledge, head of ABC Sports; *Ring* magazine, which rated the worthiness of the participating boxers; and James Farley, Jr., New York State Boxing Commissioner. But four months and five elimination bouts after the inaugural match in January 1977, ABC suspended the tournament.

The trouble began in the second series of bouts, held at the United States Naval Academy in Annapolis. Heavyweight Scott LeDoux, enraged over an adverse decision by the judges, unleashed a series of kicks at the winner, Johnny Boudreaux, who was being interviewed by Howard Cosell on network television. In the subsequent melee, both Cosell's hairpiece and the tournament became unstuck. LeDoux later charged a fix, claiming that Boudreaux was part of a stable of fighters in the tournament controlled by King and that the judges were on King's payroll. Both King and ABC hotly denied the charges, but four weekends later, ABC revealed that it had learned that *Ring* had doctored the records of fighters. One boxer, Ike Fluellen, a policeman in Bellaire, Texas, who had not fought for over a year, discovered that *Ring* had awarded him two wins in bouts held in Mexico. Other fighters reported that, to be invited to compete in the tournament, they had to pay kickbacks. Arledge promptly cancelled the tournament.

But the 1977 scandal by no means stilled network interest in boxing; enthusiasm for televised boxing continued to mount to heights achieved only in the 1950s. The networks coveted fights, said NBC boxing advisor Ferdie Pacheco in 1983, "for the same reason that millions of people traveled to the Klondike and California and the Spaniards crossed oceans and deserts—gold, my friend, it's the gold rush." In the early 1980s, boxing prevailed in the Saturday afternoon ratings over every kind of sports program except football. It especially appealed to young men between 25 and 35, a group much sought after by advertisers. "Boxing has been used as the greatest counterprogramming tool in [recent] sports history," claimed Mike Cohen, a boxing promoter and former NBC Sports official. "Golf, tennis—it kills these events. Basketball and horse racing, same thing."

The voracious demand by the networks for attractive Saturday afternoon boxing cards radically transformed the sport. For the sake of the gold offered by television, the number of championship fight divisions ballooned from eight in the 1950s (under the control of a single association) to a bewilderingly complex array of twenty-eight championships in the 1980s. Unlike the 1950s, when the International Boxing Club had monopolized the promotion of televised fighting, in the 1980s the networks had to look to several promoters to supply fighters. When television had established a market for a particular fighter, his manager-promoter quickly signed him to a long-term contract. Since (as in the 1950s) one or two losses could end a boxer's career on television, managers chose their fights with the greatest of care, hoping to pit their man against a patsy. The result? Terrible mismatches. Fights in which the networks were far from candid about the relative merits of the contestants and the connections the fighters had with various promoters. But none of these considerations adversely affected the television ratings. Even the cable networks joined in the fight game.

The intense competition for the top position in sports led the networks to beam a galaxy of synthetic "sports," or "trash-sports," which blurred all distinctions between traditional sports activity and the so-called sports drama of television. "Legitimate sports, for the most part, have limited audiences," declared sportscaster Vin Scully. "But when you give it another dimension—entertainment—you capture a new breed of viewer." Hence, the multiplication of synthetic sports.

Synthetic sports came in two principal forms. One was bizarre or unusual physical activities: high-wire acts, the national logrolling championships, cliff diving at Acapulco. These were shown on television but not originally invented for television audiences. The activity need not be a contest—cliff diving, for example—and therefore was a sport only within the loose rubric employed by television. ABC's Wide World of Sports pioneered in telecasting "sports" of this kind. In the 1960s, Wide World brought viewers such spectacles as the national wrist-wrestling championships from Petalooma, California, and a rattlesnake hunt in Keane, Oklahoma.

A second form of synthetic sports was physical contests in which celebrities were the only or the principal contestants. Even in the earliest days of the medium, celebrities sometimes competed on televised programs. "Celebrity Billiards," syndicated in 1968 and featuring the renowned pool shark Minnesota Fats (Rudolph Walter Wanderone), exploited the popularity of the movie *The Hustler* (1961), starring Paul Newman and Jackie Gleason, to become a popular show. Each week the garrulous Fats brought in such guest opponents as Zsa Zsa Gabor, Phyllis Diller, Mickey Rooney, Sid Caesar, and Bill Cosby. He spotted each celebrity a handicap. The winner received $1,000, the loser $500. Although Fats was a non-tournament billiards player who based his appeal mostly on his capacity to entertain, he insisted that Celebrity Billiards was bringing "class" to billiards, just as Lili St. Cyr had transformed the "vulgar exhibitionism" of disrobing to the level of a "champagne bath."

In the 1970s, as the battle of the networks reached red-hot proportions, the quantity of synthetic sports created especially for television proliferated. ABC's "The Superstars" seemed to touch off the mania. Superstars began with Dick Button, a former Olympic figure-skating gold medalist, who had long wondered who was the best all-round athlete in the country. To find out, he tried to peddle a television series in which the nation's top athletes would compete against one another in contests outside of their specialties. Initially, all three networks showed him the door, but when ABC lost the NBA contract to CBS in 1972, leaving a scheduling hole to fill on Sunday afternoons, Barry Frank, head of Trans World International sports packagers, sold the idea of a superstars contest to his former boss, Roone Arledge. The manufactured-for-television events aired on Superstars included running, rowing, bicycling, bowling, crawling through an obstacle course, softball throwing, and weightlifting. Beginning with one show in all of 1973, Superstars had ballooned to ten annual programs by 1977.

"The Superstars" begat a progeny almost as ubiquitous as the sitcoms and the soaps. At ABC, viewers soon witnessed "The Women Superstars," "The World Superstars," and "The Superteams," which matched pro teams in such events as canoe racing and tugs-of-war for a purse of $330,000. NBC responded with "Dynamic Duos" and "US Against the World" (a celebrity Olympics). At CBS, "The Challenge of the Sexes," which pitted male versus female athletes, spawned "Celebrity Challenge of the

Sexes." One contest, a tennis match between Farrah Fawcett-Majors and Bill Cosby on Celebrity Challenge, drew a whopping 49 percent share of the television audience. Since Majors was not—to say the least—adept at tennis, Melvin Durslag concluded in *TV Guide* that the astronomical rating must have resulted from men ogling Farrah Fawcett-Majors cavorting about in shorts.

There seemed to be no end to synthetic sports. "I've got ideas for telecasts in envelopes piled as high as this building," declared Robert Wussler, the president of CBS Sports, in 1978. "I'll bet 25 percent of those ideas are good ones." "The World's Strongest Men" featured men carrying refrigerators on their backs in a footrace; others included the "World Championship Buffalo-Chip-Tossing" contest and the "Joe Garagiola/Bazooka Big League Gum Blowing Championship." One critic wondered if we would soon see Princess Grace racing go-carts with Baron de Rothschild or Golda Meir shooting pool with Anwar Sadat. "The way we are going," asserted Curt Gowdy, a spokesman for the old school of sportscasting, "we'll see Secretariat racing a Wyoming antelope."

The attraction of synthetic sports was no mystery. From the standpoint of the networks, the shows could be produced cheaply. They could be filmed well in advance and dropped into the schedule whenever convenient. Fans loved the shows, partly because of the possibility of seeing celebrities look disoriented. They took pleasure in seeing 300-pound shot-putter Brian Oldfield paddling his canoe in a circle, and former heavyweight boxing champion Joe Frazier flailing across a swimming pool like a harpooned whale. Nonetheless, in the early 1980s, the networks, led by CBS, began to cut back slightly on the quantity of synthetic sports. Perhaps the Golden Age of synthetic sports had passed; the liberties taken by the synthetic sports with the traditional sports experience had apparently gone too far. After an initial fascination, fans tired of them.

In another arena of the battle of the networks, each network experimented with ways to make their telecasts of existing sports more interesting to viewers. From the earliest days of the medium they supplemented visual images with interviews, graphics, catchy music, and the words of play-by-play announcers. They initially employed former radio broadcasters who were known for their "golden throats" and abilities to describe in abundant and vivid detail the course of a game. Even though the fans could now see the games for themselves, many of the former radio men could not curb their propensity for garrulity and hyperbole. Most of the announcers uncritically touted all aspects of the sports which they covered.

The fundamental reason for the absence of a critical stance by announcers was clear enough. They were not hired as objective reporters or critical essayists but as entertainers. To shill the products carrying the telecast and the sport itself, they had to keep the viewer watching the game. Thus television inherited from radio the practice of retaining only announcers who pleased both advertisers and the sports establishments. Even after ABC had proven with Howard Cosell that controversial announcers could enhance interest in a telecast, sports leagues continued to carefully monitor announcers. The NCAA, the most sensitive of the sport associations, routinely screened all college football telecasts and informed the networks how they might improve their telecasts. In 1982 the NCAA vetoed both Fran Tarkenton and Paul Hornung as potential announcers, claiming they had been too closely identified with professional football. The same year they turned down Pepper Rodgers as a color commentator because he was "too controversial." Rodgers had filed a $331,000 breach-of-contract suit against the Georgia Tech Athletic Association in the wake of his firing as the Yellow Jackets' head football coach in 1979.

Gradually, the television producers added "expert" analysts or celebrities to their broadcast teams; sometimes they dropped former radio play-by-play men entirely. By the 1960s, dozens of athletes, ex-athletes, and even referees began to invade broadcast booths. While the furry-tongued diction of the athlete-announcers sometimes bordered on incomprehensibility, the producers believed that their inside knowledge added to the fan's enjoyment. It was the golden age of the cliché, when the air rang with such unmemorable phrases as "a great second effort," "a game of inches," "It's anybody's game," and "They came to play." In the 1970s, announcers not only curbed their use of clichés but tended to warn the audience when one was coming. "To use an old cliché" was the way veteran sportscaster Curt Gowdy put it.

In 1970, when Roone Arledge put together the announcing team for Monday Night Football, show business considerations frankly took priority over all other concerns. Since Monday Night Football had to compete with prime time shows, Arledge began with the assumption that the announcers would furnish a large part of the drama. Cosell especially fulfilled Arledge's fondest hopes. Nearly everything Cosell said seemed to ignite controversy. Caustic, unctuous, polysyllabic, given to making even the most trivial observation sound like something profound, Cosell claimed to "tell it like it is."

With characteristic bluntness, Cosell summarized his own role as a performer and television's effort to enhance the appeal of a sporting event with extraneous entertainment. "Look, there is no damn way you can go up against Liz Taylor and Doris Day in prime-time TV and present sports as just sports or as religion." No one had stated more explicitly the willingness of the networks to adapt sports to the requirements of sheer entertainment. Ultimately, the main responsibility of the sportscaster was not that of a reporter—to accurately inform the audience—but that of an entertainer: to keep the fans glued to the television set.

Sometimes the introduction of extraneous entertainment into sports telecasts backfired. In 1973 and 1974, for example, NBC tried to duplicate the successful formula of Monday Night Football in its telecasts of Monday night baseball games. They hoped to capture women and all others not yet addicted to the National Game by inviting a celebrity guest each week to join Curt Gowdy and Tony Kubek in the broadcast booth. Dizzy Dean, Satchel Paige, Joe DiMaggio, Bobby Riggs, Dave DeBusschere, Howard Cosell, Danny Kaye, and Chuck Connors, who were among the celebrity guests, were usually only a distraction and added nothing to the game itself. Before the third inning of one game had been completed, Bobby Riggs had plugged a new tennis machine, a book, vitamin pills, a senior tennis tour, a tennis pro in Las Vegas, and a private club. Since the guests interposed themselves between the audience and the "precise and stately ballet" of the game, as *Newsweek* put it, the game became "a kind of Muzak for the eyes." In 1974 NBC cut back on the number of celebrity guests, and in 1975 they dropped entirely the use of their "designated dullards."

While no network dared even attempt to find a clone of Howard Cosell, the networks did seek approximations of Don Meredith. In 1974 NBC even lured Meredith away from ABC, but four years later he returned to the even lusher fields of ABC. While no other ex-athlete brought to the game quite the same kind of gentle and humorous irreverence as Meredith, others achieved a new level of excellence in analysis. Viewers and critics especially praised Dick Enberg, Pat Summerall, Vin Scully, Al Michaels, and Frank Gifford for their straightforward descriptions. Ex-player Merlin Olsen and former coaches Frank Broyles and John Madden received high marks for their insightful commentaries.

But intrinsic to the medium was a tendency to excess. Incessant talking and endless replays tended to subtly numb the senses. The announcers could analyze too much. In 1984, Roland Merullo, a carpenter residing in Pownal, Vermont, poignantly described in *Newsweek* a reaction shared by many football viewers:

> I watched a close game recently, the kind of seesaw battle that, 15 years ago, would have had me clutching the arms of my chair until the final seconds. But I could hardly sit through it. Every play, no matter how mundane, was shown two or three times, accompanied by volumes of analysis. By the start of the fourth quarter I felt as if I had watched three games and been through two years of coaching school.

In their battle for supremacy, the networks also experimented with the use of women and, in one instance, a professional gambler as announcers. In 1974, CBS hired veteran sportscaster Jane Chastain to do NFL games, but the network dropped her after only three games. According to CBS officials, viewers complained that "we don't need a broad on football." In 1975 CBS tried a more successful tactic. They hired former Miss America Phyllis George to co-host weekly pre-game, half-time, and post-game football shows. Eventually, George, who admitted to being ignorant of the finer points of the game, became a permanent, perhaps one should say "decorative," fixture of CBS football telecasts. In 1978, CBS boldly hired Jimmy "The Greek" Snyder, a one-time Las Vegas linemaker, as an "expert analyst" to appeal to the some 40 million Americans who bet on NFL games. NBC retaliated by employing *Newsweek* columnist Pete Axthelm as their in-house prognosticator.

In the late 1970s and in the 1980s, competition between the networks for the services of successful announcers, producers, and directors of sportscasts intensified. Many switched networks.

By luring hard-driving producer Don Ohlmeyer from ABC, for example, NBC (in 1977) rejuvenated its comatose sports division; Ohlmeyer had won seven Emmys for his producing and directing of ABC's 1976 Olympic coverage. High network personnel, like the professional athletes themselves, hired agents to represent their interests. Sometimes the agreements between the announcers and the networks restricted the flexibility of producers. Joe Garagiola's 1982 contract with NBC, for example, required that he do more play-by-play innings in the World Series than any other announcer. Salaries climbed to levels equivalent to those at the apex of the entertainment world. In 1982, an ordinary announcer received some $300,000, a senior luminary about $750,000, and a top-flight producer up to $400,000. Howard Cosell's income from television, radio, and outside work exceeded Dan Rather's $1.6 million, said to be the highest amount paid to a network newscaster. (It was still less than the $2 million per annum paid to Moses Malone, the center for the Philadelphia Seventy-Sixers.)

In the 1970s, competition between sportscasters extended to the local television stations as well. The profitability of local stations depended heavily upon the audience ratings for their local news/weather/sports shows. These shows could attract lucrative spot commercials, and slight changes in the ratings could spell the difference between a profit or loss for the station. Consequently, in the 1970s stations began to hire charismatic men and women to read the news, flamboyant weather forecasters, and sportscasters with a flair for bringing additional excitement to the sports news. Rather than simply reading the scores and showing filmed interviews with managers and the like, local sportscasters began to approach sports with less reverence, employ more humor, and express their opinions freely. In 1973, for example, Jim Bouton of WABC-TV in New York featured a segment on stickball in Manhattan, allowed himself to be knocked down by female skaters in a Roller Derby match, and roped a calf at a local rodeo. When Yankee pitchers swapped wives, Bouton predicted that Bowie Kuhn, the Commissioner of Baseball, would tell them not to do it again. (Instead, Kuhn announced that their action was "deplorable.")

Another WABC-TV sportscaster, Warner Wolf, who was at one time part of the broadcast team for ABC Monday Night Baseball telecasts, became something of a celebrity in his own right in New York. His catch phrases—like "Gimme a break!" (after a

dumb play or bad call) and "Let's go to the videotape!" (to introduce a taped highlight from a sports telecast)—became part of the
argot of New York sandlot players and television viewers alike.
When Wolf was lured to another station (WCBS-TV), WABC un-
successfully took him to court, citing the spectacular loss in advertising revenues that his defection would allegedly mean for the station.

Syndicated sports shows, cable television, and communications satellites added vast new dimensions to the fight between the
networks for supremacy in sports. From the earliest days of televised sports, independent producers had put together shows to be
aired either by one of the big networks or by a special syndicated
network of local stations, some of which might be affiliated with
one of the big networks. Initially, the special networks usually
handled telecasts of sports events of regional interest, but sometimes they carried contests of national events ignored by the big
networks. In the 1960s and 1970s, for example, two independent
networks, TVS and SNI, carried several UCLA basketball games
via national hookups.

Sometimes the independents directly threatened the interests
of the big networks. In 1983, Katz Sports syndicated a new Kickoff College Classic featuring Nebraska against Penn State, carried
over more than 175 stations. Of these, 150 were network affiliates
that had to preempt regular programming—a move that angered
network chiefs. NBC tried to discipline its errant affiliates by
scheduling the second segment of the movie *The Godfather* opposite the game. Most of the affiliates refused to give in; they carried
the football game instead.

The launching of the first communications satellite in 1974
and the end of a complex set of legal restrictions on cable television in 1977 opened the way for a new era of sports television,
which took two forms. One was the so-called superstation—
WTBS in Atlanta, WGN in Chicago, and the New Jersey–based
WOR. (WPIX in New York was expected to join the "supersta-
tions" in May of 1984.) Play-by-play coverage of sports—local
baseball, hockey, basketball, and harness racing—was reported to
be the major selling point in offering these stations' programming
to cable systems.

The other innovation was cable network systems. Sports

junkies across the nation rejoiced at the formation of two sports networks: USA Network (originally the Madison Square Garden Network) in 1975 and the Entertainment and Sports Programming Network (ESPN) in 1979.

ESPN, funded by the Getty Oil Company, began with plans to be a round-the-clock sports network. Using 625 television cable systems and a satellite for transmission, ESPN initially reached some 20 percent of the nation's television viewers. At first it concentrated on telecasting the more obscure college sports. Under its contract with the NCAA, ESPN could telecast hundreds of NCAA events in some eighteen sports. To protect ABC's, CBS's, and WTBS's exclusive rights to carry live intercollegiate games, ESPN had to restrict its telecasts of football games to a tape-delayed format. Viewers might even be treated to watching such momentous spectacles as the Clemson University spring intrasquad game on a tape-delayed basis. While skeptics wondered if there were enough sports addicts to keep the network afloat, a founder of ESPN declared that "we believe that the appetite for sports in this country is insatiable." Yet, neither the USA nor ESPN networks were able to prosper by televising sports alone. In 1982, the USA network (which was owned equally by MCA, Inc.; Time, Inc.; and Paramount Pictures Corporation) launched a new daytime schedule composed of "women's" programs to supplement its nighttime sports coverage. And ESPN widened its offerings to include a news show and morning stock market reports.

Subscription pay cable also joined the competition. In 1982, Eddie Einhorn, co-owner of the Chicago White Sox and founder of the TVS sports network, introduced pay television to Chicago. In 1980, Bill Veeck, the then-owner of the White Sox, had permitted the telecast of 140 games for a mere $2,000 per contest. Enter Einhorn as a new co-owner. Einhorn formed a sports subscription system, SportsVision, to televise games of the Sox and other professional sports teams in Chicago. Customers paid a basic fee of $21.95 per month for the service. "To me, it's un-American," said Harry Caray, former White Sox (and St. Louis Cardinals) play-by-play man, who had switched jobs to the Chicago Cubs. "Where is . . . that bartender and shut-in and that cabdriver? Well, these guys aren't going to be able to afford listening to me [on pay television]." But Einhorn made it seem like he was doing Chicagoans a favor. Only via pay television, he argued, could the

White Sox afford the free agents necessary to build a powerful club. Potentially, according to Einhorn, the White Sox could realize as much as $27 million a year from television.

Yet the wholesale replacement of network televised sports with such a system appeared to be unlikely. During the first year of SportsVision's operation, Einhorn obtained only 20,000 customers, about half of what he estimated he needed to break even. There seemed to be a definite limit on what sports spectators would be willing to pay. "If you ask people to pay enough times, they may just pick up a ball and go out and play themselves," remarked NBC executive Sean McManus. Moreover, switches of any of the major sporting events from the networks to pay systems would probably evoke the wrath of Congress.

Yet, with the cable systems, fans could now see some form of sports programming almost any time of the day. The sheer quantity of sports on television certainly reduced the uniqueness of the sports drama; with contests always present it was difficult for the viewer to get excited about who won or lost. The viewer's personal engagement in the outcome might be little more than that experienced when watching "Family Feud."

9

Packaging Sports for Television

Traditionally, the National Football League ignored most of the hoopla which had long surrounded college football. Believing its fans wanted only football, the league offered a game unaccompanied by cheerleaders, marching bands, card sections, or college boys with hip flasks. (The Washington Redskins were something of an exception. In the 1930s, George Preston Marshall, the owner of the Skins, formed a band dressed in full Indian regalia to perform during half-time at Redskins games.) In the late 1970s, all that began to change. The pro teams urged fans to bring with them banners, pennants, and towels to wave during the games; by 1980, nearly every franchise had hired "cheerleaders" to prance along the sidelines.

No team exploited sex appeal more effectively than the Dallas Cowboys. The Cowboys Cheerleaders flaunted heaving, skimpily covered breasts and short shorts which exposed some of the curvature of their posteriors. Watching a performance of the Cheerleaders, a visiting hockey coach from the Soviet Union asked his guide in halting English: "Are those fallen women?" Only a non-American would have framed such a query, for the Cheerleaders, according to Cowboy press releases, represented the "finest" young women in America. In fact, when some of the girls posed in the nude for *Playboy* magazine, the Dallas management promptly fired them.

"In their sexy, foxy way [the Cheerleaders are] a mirror image of what Cowboy football represents: entertainment dealt with as a very serious business," concluded William Oscar Johnson in *Sports Illustrated*. Suzanne Mitchell, the full-time director of the Cheerleaders held training camps and tryouts, studied films, and put the girls through three to four hours of rigorous training every camp night. Some 2,000 girls auditioned for ten spots. "It's their ultimate dream," declared Mitchell. "Where little girls used to dream of being Miss America, now they dream of becoming a cheerleader for the Cowboys instead." Some 40,000 girls between the ages of four and twelve also entered the annual "Little Miss Dallas Cowboys Cheerleaders" contest. Other spinoffs of the Cheerleaders included a line of children's clothes, costume jewelry, coloring books, trading cards, and a book entitled *The Decade of Dreams*, published in 1983 to celebrate the tenth anniversary of the Cheerleaders.

In 1974, Ted Giannoulas, dressed as "The San Diego Chicken," ushered in the age of the baseball mascot. By 1983, at least half of the twenty-six major league teams deployed mascots of one kind or another. Using classical forms of pantomime, the mascots, adorned in colorful costumes, tried to make people laugh. The Chicken himself grossed some $100,000 annually from about 250 personal appearances. He performed for the San Diego Padres only at some sixteen to twenty games; the rest of the time he worked minor league baseball parks, professional basketball games, fairs, and other public gatherings.

At the great face-off between the Chicken and "Phillie Phanatic," another popular mascot, held in 1983, the Chicken pulled off his most successful caper ever. "I spotted a beautiful blonde ball girl in left field," the Chicken told Melvin Durslag in *TV Guide*. "I took a seat near her. Slowly, I kept inching my chair towards hers. The crowd started to howl. Now I was next to her. I put my arm around her. All of a sudden, I started kissing her madly and we fell off the chairs and stumbled across the Astroturf, wrestling. The fans went nuts. The next day, a local writer voted me the nod over Phillie Phanatic, reporting that I introduced Philadelphia to the roll in the Astro-hay."

Nonetheless, there were some big-league holdouts; some clubs believed the field ought to be reserved for the players. "If we look like clowns out there," said Fred Claire, executive vice-president of the Los Angeles Dodgers, "we want it to be accidental. We don't hire clowns." Although the Kansas City Royals hired the Chicken to perform at least once a year, they otherwise banned mascots, including those of opponents. "We feel the game is the show," declared Dean Vogelaar, director of public relations for the Royals.

Likewise, in 1983, students at the University of Virginia stoutly resisted a new mascot invented for television by Todd Turner, the university's Sport's Promotion Director. A bright orange creature, " 'Hoo"—the name shortened from Wahoo, a name sometimes used to refer to University of Virginia athletes—made his debut in Virginia's opening football game with Duke on September 3. There, 'Hoo suffered showers of ice cubes from detractors and the indignity of having his tongue removed by "pie-eyed fraternity boys." The *Cavalier Daily* described 'Hoo as "a video game reject who tried out for Ms. Pac-Man and didn't make the cut." A letter to the paper put the matter in perspective. It called the 'Hoo "a bastard child born out of the incestuous relationship between the athletic department and the cash register." Finally, the athletic department of the university retreated; the student council then settled upon their traditional mascot—a student dressed as a Cavalier.

Cheerleaders and mascots represented only one facet of the effort made by sports to obtain a bigger share of the pot of gold offered by television. One sport after another packaged or repackaged itself for the new media. Sports were especially tailored to appeal to those millions of potential viewers who were not devoted followers of the games themselves; they were transformed so they could compete more successfully with other forms of entertainment. Apart from instituting cheerleaders, men dressed in chicken uniforms dancing on the top of baseball dugouts, exploding scoreboards, artificial grass, and tight-fitting uniforms, both football and baseball tinkered with the fundamental nature of their sports. The two sports reordered the delicate balance between defense and offense. To increase the interest of fans, especially television fans, both sports set up new scheduling and playoff systems. Baseball even transformed the venerable World Series into a nighttime affair. Each sport extended the length of its playing season, overlapping it with dates earlier reserved for other sports. The moguls made every effort to maximize media revenues, even if it meant sacrificing or endangering the traditional structure of their sports.

Initial efforts designed to make professional baseball a more salable media event had failed to relieve the National Game of its tribulations. The problems of the 1950s continued into the 1960s. Average attendance at big-league games lagged behind the levels achieved in the immediate postwar era, minor league baseball was only a shell of its former self, and television ratings remained far below those of professional football. The expansion of the number of major league franchises, the relocation of teams, and the building of new ball parks—many of them in the suburbs— failed to furnish the magic elixir for reviving the popularity of the game.

The first step taken by baseball in the 1960s to make the sport more attractive to television completely backfired. In the early 1960s, baseball aficionados began to ask: "Whatever became of the .300 hitter?" or, "Where did the runs go?" In the 1920s, rule changes and the "live" ball had produced higher batting averages, soaring home run totals, and record highs for runs scored. In 1930, the entire National League had hit for an average of .303. Thereafter batting averages slowly slipped downward. Then came a precipitous drop. Between the 1962 and 1963 seasons, major league run totals fell by 1,681, home runs by 297, batting averages by twelve points, and bases on balls by 1,345. Pitchers recorded 1,206 more strikeouts. The 1963 totals became the standard for the next five years. Carl Yastrzemski won the American League batting title in 1968 with an average of .301, the lowest in major league history.

Baseball observers offered a number of reasons for the decline in hitting: (1) better pitching, especially the increased use of the slider and of relief specialists; (2) efforts by more players to hit home runs rather than singles—"Home run hitters drive Cadillacs; singles hitters drive Fords," explained Pittsburgh slugger Ralph Kiner; (3) bigger and better fielders' gloves; (4) more night games; (5) more coast-to-coast air travel; and (6) larger, more symmetrical ball parks. All of these interpretations had some merit, but they essentially missed the mark. For the big-league moguls had simply instructed the umpires to enlarge the strike zone.

The baseball magnates had become acutely sensitive to the charge that baseball was too slow to sustain the interest of television audiences. "Delay, Dally, and Stall" was the way John Cashman described big-league baseball in *TV Guide*. Whereas early in the twentieth century the playing time for games averaged about an hour and a half, by the 1960s the typical game lasted over two and a half hours. Pitchers worked more slowly; batters stepped out of the box more frequently; managers held more conferences at the mound and replaced pitchers more often than in the past. To counter the slowdown, the big leagues in 1963 simply told the umpires to call pitches strikes that had formerly been called balls. By reducing the likelihood of walks and increasing the incidence of strikeouts, the change would presumably quicken the pace of the game. And indeed, pitchers quickly began to dominate the sport. But the moguls of baseball had gone too far. Not only had they damaged the integrity of the game, but television ratings continued to fall. At the very time that the nation seemed to be obsessed with power, baseball had transformed itself into a series of glorious defensive contests.

In the late 1960s and early 1970s, big-league baseball, led by the "Young Turks"—a new, less convention-bound group of owners—introduced a series of reforms designed principally to make the sport more attractive to television. Some were essentially cosmetic. For example, Charlie Finley, owner of the Oakland Athletics, dressed his team in skin-tight, Kelly-green-and-gold polyester uniforms. Soon the other teams followed suit, replacing the traditional gray-and-white flannels with brightly hued uniforms.

In 1969, in an effort to reverse the decline in offense, the Turks obtained some fundamental rule changes. The rulemakers lowered the pitching mound from fifteen to ten inches (thereby making the curve and slider less effective) and ordered the umpires to reduce the size of the strike zone. Technically, the strike zone extended from the knees to the armpits, but to be certain of obtaining a called strike, pitchers now had to throw the ball between the knees and the belt. (Moreover, the size of the strike zone differed between the two leagues.) Charlie Finley suggested even more radical innovations: the use of orange baseballs for better visibility, three balls instead of four to count as a walk, a "designated hitter" to replace the pitcher in the batting order, and the free substitution of base runners. The American League adopted the designated hitter rule in 1973, but rejected Finley's other recommendations. Traditionalists disliked the designated hitter, for it took away one of the most critical decisions for managers in game situations—whether or not to use a pinch hitter for the pitcher. The changes did produce more offense; in the 1970s, batting averages, runs, and home runs again increased.

The Young Turks also led the movement for new leadership at the top. In the fall of 1968, they dropped William D. Eckert, a former Air Force general, as commissioner; they replaced him in 1969 with Bowie Kuhn, an ex–Wall Street lawyer with connections in Washington. The owners gave Kuhn more power than any commissioner had enjoyed since the death of Landis in 1944; they hoped he would improve their relations with the federal government and the television networks. Within two years Kuhn had created the post of Director of Radio and Television (headed by Tom Dawson); signed a contract for the televising of baseball on Monday nights during prime time; scheduled part of the World Series (over the stout objections of the television networks) at night; and delayed the start of the World Series until the second Saturday in October so television could beam two weekends of games. "The [baseball] officials are very conscious of competition for broadcast time from other sports that by nature are more lively and exciting," concluded *Broadcasting* magazine in 1970. They "will no longer rest on tradition to attract viewers."

While in the 1970s and 1980s, under Kuhn's more aggressive leadership, major league baseball (though not minor league ball) showed some signs of recovery, the game continued to suffer from severe disparities in competition. More nearly equalizing the strength of teams would presumably increase fan interest. If more teams had a viable shot at winning the pennant, no single team would dominate championships over the years, and pennant races would be more closely fought. Prior to the mid-1970s, the major leagues had long argued that the "reserve clause" in player contracts and the annual "draft" of fresh talent from the minor leagues prevented the domination of pennant races by a few of the wealthier franchises. Without the right to reserve players, professional baseball argued, wealthier clubs could offer higher salaries to players on other teams and eventually corner the market on the best player talent. In theory the draft of minor league players gave each club equal access to new player talent; it negated the potential advantages of superior wealth.

But the historical record of baseball made a mockery of both these arguments. Throughout the twentieth century, franchises in the larger cities won far more pennants than those representing the smaller cities. Franchises located in New York, Chicago, and Los Angeles won over half of the total flags of the two leagues. The reason was simple enough. Disparities in population between metropolitan areas produced radical inequalities in attendance and broadcast revenues. Since baseball did not share local media income and visitors received only a small percentage of the gate, the clubs in the big cities had more income with which to purchase and develop superior talent. The substitution of free agency for the draft in the mid-1970s seemed to give an even larger advantage to the richer clubs. George Steinbrenner, the free-spending owner of the Yankees in the 1970s and 1980s, observed that "you measure the value of a ballplayer by how many fannies he puts in the seats. Reggie Jackson is worth 500,000 fannies in New York and 65,000 fannies in Baltimore." To make his statement complete, Steinbrenner should have included the amount of television revenues a player like Jackson could bring to a franchise.

Reforming big-league baseball to achieve more competitive balance proved to be a well-nigh impossible task. The "have" clubs did not want to sacrifice revenues to the "have not" clubs, and baseball's governing structure effectively blocked change. "Pete Rozelle and I are alike," Kuhn told a *New York Times* reporter in 1982. "He calls it parity in the National Football League. I call it competitive balance. But Pete can achieve parity by adjusting the schedule so the Giants, for example, can get into the playoffs easier. They arrange for weak teams to get weak opponents. If we did that, [we'd] get blown out of the water." Each league continued to act separately on most matters, and substantive decisions required the approval of three-fourths of the franchises in both leagues. In the early 1980s, Kuhn urged that the franchises share a large percentage of local television revenues, a move that encouraged those owners with lucrative local and cable television markets to block his reappointment in 1983.

Packaging hockey and basketball for television proved to be no more successful than packaging baseball. Since television officials believed American sports fans craved speed and violence in their games, they expected hockey to be a "growth" sport in the 1970s. Indeed, between 1968 and 1972, hockey's share of the Sunday afternoon television audience grew from 15 to 19 percent. But then a rapid descent began, bottoming out at only 11 percent in

1975. Network television promptly dropped weekly hockey coverage.

As a media spectacle, hockey suffered from intrinsic problems. The sport was not indigenous to the United States, and infrequent scoring tended to reduce the excitement for the novice fan. Since the sport featured continuous action, it furnished no convenient times for commercial breaks. In hockey the three-inch-diameter black rubber puck, which sometimes traveled over 100 miles per hour, often vanished from view on the television screen, leading viewers to squint, curse, and ultimately switch channels. An experiment in 1972 with tomato-red pucks failed, for the paint chipped off the hard rubber.

The enormous expansion in the number of hockey franchises also damaged the effort of the sport to become a viable media product. Expansion produced radical disparities in the quality of teams. Searching for ways to equalize competition, the weaker expansion teams resorted to a defensive and neutralizing style of play designed to slow down and intimidate the swift, more skilled teams. Action centered in the middle of the rink, where controlling the man became more important than controlling the puck, and controlling the zone became more important than both. Forechecking, body checking, strength, and toughness became more important than offensive skills. To equalize competition and furnish a better show, the hockey moguls also took a passive or permissive stance toward physical intimidation and violence. For fear of even further widening the gap between the weak and the strong teams, pro hockey took only limited steps to curb violence and none to give the offense more weapons. None of these measures tempted the networks to experiment again with weekly telecasts, but in the 1980s, the USA Network, a cable system, did begin a game-of-the-week telecast.

Until the 1950s, professional basketball dwelt in the long shadows cast by the colleges, the Amateur Athletic Union teams, and the Harlem Globetrotters (an all-black team). The emergence in the late 1940s of the powerful Minneapolis Lakers, led by towering George Mikan, and in the 1950s of the Boston Celtics dynasty, led by Bill Russell and Bob Cousy, strengthened the National Basketball Association's claim that it represented the "best of basketball." In the 1950s the NBA began to recruit the top black players, thereby reducing the strength of the Globetrotters.

Rather than presenting serious basketball, the Trotters then began to resort increasingly to showmanship. Ironically, the college basketball scandal of 1950–51 also assisted the fledgling NBA. In the wake of the scandal most of the colleges cancelled their games in the big city arenas; arena owners replaced college games with pro contests.

But in seeking to attract an audience, whether live or television, the NBA had serious problems. National television contracts, first with the DuMont network (1952–53) and then with NBC (1953–62), produced only nominal revenues. The inability of the NBA to land a lucrative television contract stemmed in part from the failure of New York to field a strong team. Ned Irish, who for many years controlled the Knickerbockers, repeatedly made ill-advised trades and drafted players for their immediate publicity value (such as stars from local colleges in New York City) rather than their future potential for the team. His abrasive personality also irritated the other franchise-holders. As something of a league outcast, Irish was unable to obtain their assistance in building a strong New York team. A winning Knickerbocker team would have increased the league's overall attendance and its capacity to negotiate more favorable television contracts.

The NBA also had a problem in coping with low scoring and a rough-and-tumble style of play. Until 1954, once a team had obtained the lead in a game, it might resort to stalling tactics. Both in order to stall effectively and to prevent stalling, the players engaged in more physical contact. "We had fouling, stalling, people leaving the arenas in the last few minutes," recalled Maurice Podoloff, the first NBA president. Then Danny Biasone, owner of the Syracuse Nets, "came up with his brainchild in 1954, the 24-second clock. If it wasn't for Danny," Podoloff continued, "the N.B.A. would not have lasted five or six more years." The twenty-four second rule required that each team had to take a shot at the basket within twenty-four seconds or relinquish the ball to the other team.

Yet experience disclosed that the time-limit rule produced subtle, unforeseen difficulties. With the new rule, it was hard for fans to get excited about the game until the middle of the last quarter. Since it was difficult for a team to build up a lead and "sit" on it, to the fans it appeared that the players did not exert themselves fully until the last quarter. On the one hand, if a team did have a large lead in the final quarter of the game, then the last portion of the game was likely to be unexciting. On the other hand, if the score was close in the middle of the last quarter, then what transpired earlier seemed, in restrospect, to have been insignificant.

Despite a sharp improvement in the quality of play and a series of titanic playoff duels between giant centers Wilt Chamberlain and Bill Russell, network television remained lukewarm toward pro basketball. In 1962, NBC even dropped its coverage of regular season games. The NBA promptly hired as commissioner Walter Kennedy, the mayor of Stamford, Connecticut, who had formerly been a publicity man for the league and for the Harlem Globetrotters, to get the league back on television. In 1964 Kennedy finally convinced ABC "to take a flyer" on a package of regular season Sunday afternoon telecasts; ABC paid a mere $650,000 for the rights. In the late 1960s and early 1970s ratings crept slightly upward, though they lagged far behind the ratings for both college and professional football. In 1974 CBS seized the contract from ABC and paid each team $535,000 annually. While the NBA's fortunes with the media had improved, the newly founded American Basketball Association (1967), which had hoped to capitalize upon television to ensure its success, was unable to land a network contract. In 1976 the ABA folded.

The promise in the early 1970s of a happy marriage between the NBA and television collapsed in the late 1970s. Ratings told the story. In 1976–77, CBS's NBA coverage attracted a 26 percent share of Sunday afternoon audiences (compared with CBS's 43 percent for pro football in the fall); by 1980–81 the numbers had fallen to 18 percent. Even the championship playoffs did poorly. For example, in 1977–78, sports events such as the Super Bowl and the World Series took six of the top nine spots on prime time television. The decisive NBA championship game, however, rated 442nd, tied with such forgettable shows as "Peter Lundy & the Medicine Hat Stallion," "The Hostage Heart," and "Country Night of the Stars." The inability of the NBA to put on an attractive media spectacle might be placed in sharper relief by observing that the "National Collegiate Cheerleading Championship" ranked 138th in prime time ratings.

The low ratings baffled aficionados of the sport. Yet critics argued that the game had basic flaws: A casual viewer could enjoy the essence of any NBA contest by merely watching the final two minutes, they said. Then there was the problem of the giant players, blessed with an almost unstoppable arsenal of offensive skills. Unlimited scoring could quickly produce ennui. To prevent a Kareem Abdul-Jabbar from scoring nearly every time he came down the floor, the NBA had to allow a large amount of physical contact. But finding the right balance between a game emphasizing physicality and one emphasizing finesse proved to be difficult.

Pro basketball failed to become a viable television spectacle for other reasons. For one thing, the regular season and playoffs seemed to be interminable. In 1983, the NBA allowed even more teams in the playoffs, extending the post-season period until as late as June 18—a date when many television fans had abandoned their sets for the outdoors. Many white fans may have found it difficult to identify with a sport in which the players were more than 75 percent black. Furthermore, teams in such major market areas as New York and Chicago performed poorly; no new dynasty arose in the 1970s and 1980s to focus the attention of unaffiliated viewers. But the most direct cause of the decline in ratings was the decision of Roone Arledge to install a Sunday afternoon version of Wide World of Sports and a synthetic sport show, "The Battle of the Superstars," directly opposite NBA telecasts. The NBA simply could not compete with Arledge's fare of car racing, boxing, and synthetic sports.

Like the baseball moguls, the NBA tried to transform their sport into a more attractive television package. They gave the networks free reign to choose which games they wanted to telecast. Unfortunately for the networks, teams from the smaller cities were too often in the playoffs and finals. (The market areas of franchises ranged from Portland, Oregon, with 398,000 people, to New York City, with a population of 7,895,000.) The networks experimented futilely with such half-time gimmicks as slam dunking and horse contests. To try to unclog the area around the basket and bring back the long-range shot, the league in 1982 adopted the three-point rule, awarding three points for shots made from beyond a perimeter drawn on the floor. The arrival of Larry Bird and Magic Johnson in the NBA produced a momentary revival of interest. But in the 1980s, NBA ratings remained abysmally low. CBS even scheduled the championship playoffs late at night, after the local news shows.

Even though the low-scoring, power football of the 1960s and the early 1970s apparently satisfied the needs of millions of spectators (especially the more economically successful), in the 1970s the moguls of the NFL began an experiment that altered the fundamental nature of the game. Since pro football, more than baseball, depended on national television ratings rather than hometown loyalties, football magnates worried lest the game become a less exciting spectacle in itself. "The product [we] provide is, of course, simply entertainment," Pete Rozelle confessed to a congressional committee. Consequently, altering the structure of the game to create excitement aroused few qualms in the inner circles of the NFL.

And critics in the 1970s frequently charged that the pro game lacked the excitement, intensity, and glamour of the college sport. The pro game had become too dull and predictable; coaches seemed determined, above all else, to avoid costly mistakes. George Allen, coach of the Washington Redskins and a prime advocate of waiting for the other team to make a mistake, took his team to the 1973 Super Bowl—where he encountered an even more mistake-proof team, the Miami Dolphins. The Dolphins, led by Don Shula, won, 14–7, to complete modern pro football's only perfect season. In the 1972 season, quarterbacks had thrown 27 fewer touchdowns than five years earlier. Rather than mount daring offensive drives that might culminate in touchdowns, coaches increasingly settled for field goals. Consequently, the diminutive soccer-style field goal kickers imported from Europe sometimes replaced the American giants struggling in the pits as Sunday afternoon's heroes.

Some of the problem apparently stemmed from more rapid improvements being made in the defense than in the offense. Since a football field consists of a rigidly defined and limited amount of space, the appearance of ever larger, speedier, and better-trained defensive players reduced offensive capabilities. Faced with better defensive players and required to keep their hands flat against the chest while pass blocking, offensive linemen, unless they violated the rules against holding, found it ever more difficult to protect the quarterback from defensive pass rushers. Defensive linemen with such appropriate labels as the Doomsday Defense, the Fearsome Foursome, and the Purple People-Eaters terrorized the lines of scrimmage. In 1975 alone, defensive players belted seventeen quarterbacks out of action. The game's "artistry," according to one critic, "has been buried under an avalanche of unnecessary brutality." Defensive coaches also borrowed from the colleges shifting "zone" and "prevent" defenses that were more effective than the traditional "man-to-man" pass coverages.

To bring more offense to the game, the NFL adopted minor rules changes in 1972 and 1974 and then a revolutionary set of changes in 1978. In 1972 the rulemakers moved the hashmarks, or inbound lines, closer to the center of the field and narrowed the distance between the goalpost crossbars. Partly in response to the challenge of the short-lived World Football League, in 1974 the NFL moved the goalposts back to the endline, changed kickoffs from the forty to the thirty-five yard line, and reduced the offensive holding penalty from fifteen to ten yards. The combined rule changes immediately reduced reliance upon the field goal, increased the number of touchdowns, and helped introduce a brief "era of the running back." In 1972, a record-breaking ten players rushed for 1,000 yards or more; the following year, O. J. Simpson of the Buffalo Bills broke the single season rushing record with 2,003 yards. But the offense enjoyed only a temporary revival. Coaches quickly developed more effective defenses against the run, and quarterbacks and receivers continued to be as vulnerable as they had been prior to 1972. By 1977 offensive statistics had again fallen, the number of long passes completed dropped to an all-time low, and injuries to quarterbacks increased.

In 1978 the NFL took more drastic action. The rule-makers permitted pass defenders to chuck, or bump, a potential receiver only once (and in 1979, only once within five yards of the line of scrimmage) and allowed offensive linemen to extend their arms and open their hands to protect the passer. The use of the hands permitted by the new rules amounted to a form of legalized holding.

Under the new rules, NFL offenses went wild. Previously blocked passing lanes suddenly opened up; quarterbacks dropped back only a few steps from the line of scrimmage and threw quicker, more closely timed patterns. Quarterback sacks fell to an all-time low. Terry Bradshaw of the Pittsburgh Steelers quickly revealed the importance of the changes in the 1979 Super Bowl, when he passed for a personal career high of 318 yards against the

Dallas Cowboys. In 1977 (the year before the drastic rules changes) the average game saw 283.8 yards gained via throwing; by 1981 that total had climbed to 408.7 yards. Scores also soared to undreamed-of heights. During the weekend of October 16–17, 1983, fourteen games produced a stunning total of 732 points, including a blockbuster 48–47 Monday night game between the Green Bay Packers and the Washington Redskins. "The league has given the offense all the weapons now," exclaimed San Francisco 49er linebacker Jack "Hacksaw" Reynolds. "It's like Great Britain against Argentina." Some games turned into aerial circuses, with both teams scoring thirty or more points in a game. "It may be track, it may be basketball," said Myron Cope, a long-time student of the sport, "but it isn't football the way it should be."

Indeed, the changes revolutionized the game. The swaggering cornerbacks, who sometimes jostled top receivers out of an entire game, suddenly became virtually obsolete. Since they could no longer repeatedly bump receivers, the defensive backs had to retreat into cautious zones. In the earlier era, receivers not only needed good hands and speed; they had to be smart enough to avoid some chucks while enduring others. But in the new era, even the most wraith-like receivers prospered.

The holding now permitted by offensive linemen negated much of the quickness that had earlier been essential to great defensive linemen. When 300-pound blockers were free to plant themselves and embrace onrushing defensive players, even the best of the pass rushers no longer seemed quite so fearsome. Linemen in the trenches now locked in "arm ball," or "wrestling matches." Pass rushers tried to get their hands inside the offensive linemen's arms and push them down or shove them aside. "The guy who has his hands inside is winning," declared George Perles, a Pittsburgh line coach. "He's got all the leverage on his side." To be effective, linemen had to develop immense upper body strength rather than quickness. Thus, linemen in the new era rushed to the weight rooms, and pumping iron became a religion for pass rushers.

Merlin Olsen, television commentator and former Los Angeles Ram star, vividly summed up the importance of the rule change. "I'd have a lot of trouble playing the game under today's rules," Olsen said in a *Sports Illustrated* (1982) interview. "My whole thrust was to try to make some initial contact with the offensive linemen, but now he'll grab you and you'll never get away. . . . The new rules have destroyed one of the finest parts of the game, the integrity of one-on-one battles on the line. You don't get that anymore. It's a wrestling match now, a joke. If you went back to the rules of five or six years ago, very few offensive linemen today could play the game. You can get any big strong guy off the street and teach him to pass-block. I'm sad. They've taken *an art form and destroyed it*. Some people are very Machiavellian. They look at the scoreboard, they look at the dollar sign. Does this mean happiness?''

Fans could also ask whether sudden death overtimes meant happiness. Principally for the benefit of television, in 1974 the NFL ordained that a sudden death overtime be played to decide the winner of games that were tied at the end of regulation play. After a team won the coin flip, it could get a good runback, move the ball forty yards or so, and kick a field goal and thereby win the game. In such a scenario, the other team did not even get a chance to score. The new rule was "like a tie game in baseball after nine innings," Warner Wolf has observed. "The visiting team scores in the top of the tenth and the game's over, with the home team never coming to bat. That's wrong."

Not only did the NFL magnates transform the games into displays of passing skills for the benefit of television audiences; they also "rigged" schedules. Pro football had long claimed that the annual draft of college talent in reverse order of a team's standing in the previous season tended to equalize competition and prevent teams from dominating championship play. But NFL history belied those claims. Despite the draft, certain teams—such as Dallas and Oakland—repeatedly participated in the playoffs. To be sure, the team with the poorest record the previous season had its choice of the top college players, but its next pick came only after all other teams had chosen a player. In other words, the only significant advantage the last-place team had over the first-place team was one man, the first pick. And one player could not reverse the fortunes of an otherwise mediocre football team.

To offset the disparities in competition, the NFL took other steps to spark interest among fans. Beginning in 1970, eight teams rather than four participated in the playoffs for the championship. The "wild card" berth in the playoffs added excitement. Under this system, one team from each conference, the team that had the best record apart from the divisional champions, joined divisional winners in the playoffs. In 1977 the NFL introduced a controversial "parity" or "position" mode of scheduling, which had the effect of pitting more of the weaker teams (according to their records in the previous season) against each other and consequently more of the stronger teams against each other for regular season play.

Pete Rozelle suggested position scheduling as a way of increasing television ratings. "Position scheduling is just another attempt to placate the television moguls," declared Jim Finks, the general manager of the Chicago Bears. Such a scheduling system, admitted a NFL spokesman, provided "better games for TV." The poor records of the New York Giants and New York Jets, teams representing the nation's largest city, especially worried Rozelle. In 1977 each club had only three wins and suffered eleven defeats. Fearing that the slightly lower NFL Nielsen ratings of 1977 stemmed from the poor performance of the New York teams, Rozelle instructed Jim Kensil, the league's executive director, to devise a more "balanced" schedule.

From the standpoint of maximizing fan interest, the new scheduling system seemed to be a dazzling success. It virtually assured that a majority of the teams would have a crack at the playoffs up to the final few weeks of the season. Attendance reached new highs, and television ratings soared. A few carpers might see the results of the "rigged" schedules as the triumph of "mediocre" teams, admitted Rozelle in 1982. "But in cities like San Francisco, Cincinnati and New York this weekend, as well as in millions of television households across the country, football fans are using terms like 'excitement' and 'entertainment.' " For Rozelle, the NFL owners, and the television magnates, entertainment rather than tradition was invariably the bottom line.

In 1983 a group of millionaires decided that the annual banquet of pro football served up by the NFL failed to sate the public appetite for the game; indeed, according to the organizers of the new United States Football League, the nation remained hungry, perhaps even starving, for more football. Rather than compete head-on with the NFL in the fall, as the ill-fated World Football League had tried to do in 1974 and 1975, the USFL scheduled its games from March to July. Now pro football fans faced the prospect of having pro football available for eleven months of each year.

Survival of the USFL depended upon television, especially the cable television explosion in the late 1970s and early 1980s. "It suddenly occurred to me that this [cable television] was going to break the NFL monopoly on pro football TV," declared David F. Dixon, the inventor of the USFL. Cable networks and local cable systems gave the fledgling league a top card to use in negotiations with the national television networks. Even before the new loop had played a single game or named a commissioner, it landed a contract with ABC which paid $9 million during the first two years and with ESPN (the sports cable network) for $4 million in 1983 and $7 million in 1984. ABC assigned Keith Jackson, one of its top commentators, to do the play-by-play for USFL games, and by the first week of the 1983 season the network had sold 90 percent (or $20 million worth) of its commercial time. In addition to the ABC and ESPN contracts, the USFL hustled some $600,000 per team in local television contracts, giving each club a starting package of about $1.5 million from television.

While the new "TV league" now had the operating funds essential to survival, it was by no means in a position to engage in an all-out bidding war with the NFL for top college talent. (Each NFL team received $14.2 million from television.) Yet the "blue ribbon high-rollers" in charge of the USFL recognized that success depended much more upon splashy media attention than on the quality of play. They hired Chet Simmons, former sports director at NBC and the head of ESPN, as their first commissioner. Simmons approved a daring foray into the college ranks. In the league's first year, 1983, the New Jersey Generals signed Herschel Walker, a University of Georgia running back and everyone's consensus to be a pro football superstar, after his junior year in college. By signing Walker, the USFL violated its own bylaws as well as a long-time understanding between the NFL and the NCAA. The college authorities fumed, yet the daring move may have done as much as television money to establish the credibility of the new loop.

In 1984 the USFL continued its invasion of the college ranks. USFL teams signed running back Marcus Dupree, another first-rate prospect, and quarterback Steve Young before the 1984 season was ten days old. The contract with Young, apparently the largest in the history of professional sports, involved some $40 million in guaranteed payments until the year 2027, including a $2.5 million signing bonus.

The moguls of professional sports were not alone in packaging and repackaging their games for television. Officials in charge of the Olympic Games and college sports likewise tried to make their games more attractive to television. For example, following the lead of the professionals, college football adopted new rules to increase offensive output. And to furnish a more attractive television package, college basketball expanded its playoff system. But the effects of television upon "amateur" sports reached far beyond these cosmetic changes. Television encouraged the triumph of the professional sports model.

10

The Death of Amateur Sports

As late as the 1948 Olympics, Bob Mathias won the gold medal in the decathalon—emblematic of the world's best athlete—after only a few months of special training. Never again. Twenty-eight years later, Bruce Jenner set aside four years of his life (and the life of his wife) to devote to the single-minded pursuit of the decathalon. Each day, he worked out from six to seven hours. Driven not by the joy of play nor by patriotic sentiment, Jenner frankly acknowledged that he engaged in such arduous training only in anticipation of future gains. After winning at Montreal, he resolved to never again set foot on a track. Even in the most traditionally relaxed sports, rigorous training and large sums of money were essential to success. For example, preparation for the 1983 America's Cup race—in which a cup was the only tangible reward—cost yachtsmen in excess of $7 million. "I just a little bit deplore that you've got to work for two years—every working day—to prepare for a sailboat race," commented Bob Bavier, president of *Yachting* magazine.

Television and the large sums of money that seemed to invariably accompany the medium led to the demise of amateur sports in America. The amateur model of sports had probably never prevailed in pristine form. Yet before the middle of the twentieth century the preoccupation with winning at all costs had not been the dominant characteristic of track and field, college sports, and preadolescent youth sports. Only on rare occasions did coaches and athletes make these sports the all-absorbing end of their lives. In principle, sports should simply supplement other activities, such as work or school. By and large, amateur sports should be primarily a form of play rather than work. One played for the joy of the game, perhaps for improved health, for the team, or for the alma mater, but not as a means of enhancing one's personal fortunes.

Perhaps such values and behavior could be retained only as long as the possible personal rewards from playing such sports remained modest. At any rate, in the age of television athletes and those coaching athletes found the direct financial rewards in track and field, college sports, golf, tennis, figure skating, and gymnastics suddenly escalating beyond belief. Money and the high visibility furnished by television transformed college football into virtually a professional sport and turned what had been largely a regionally oriented sport into a national spectacle. The Olympic Games became international media spectacles in which athletes, nations, and bureaucracies enlisted sports on behalf of self-aggrandizement, national self-interest, and the enhancement of existing international sports organizations. Golf and tennis, once primarily country club sports, developed lucrative professional circuits. And youth programs increasingly resembled their professional models. Little League baseball, for example, had outfield fences, dugouts, grandstands, and even a "draft" system.

Historically, no athletic movement had resisted the professional model in sports more adamantly than the modern Olympic Games. Baron Pierre de Coubertin, the aristocratic French Anglophile who founded the modern Games, had insisted upon the rigid Anglo-American definition of amateurism. The Olympics should be held for the pleasure that it afforded to the athletes and to encourage pacific international relations through athletic competition. "The most important thing is not to win but to take part," wrote the Baron, "just as the most important thing in life is not the triumph but the struggle." Presumably athletic competition would insulate the Games from politics and avarice. "Sport," said Avery Brundage, the Chicago construction magnate who served as president of the International Olympic Committee (IOC) from 1952 to 1972, "like music and other fine arts, transcends politics. We are concerned with sports, not politics or business."

Yet the Games never fully escaped the exigencies of politics or business. Even at the first revived Games, held in Athens in 1896, the Greek royal family seized the opportunity to enhance their power. The first Games also inaugurated the practice of having the athletes represent nations rather than simply themselves and the custom of raising the national flags of the winning athletes at a victory ceremony. On the eve of the 1908 Games, James E. Sullivan, leader of the American Olympic delegation—with characteristically American bluntness—declared: "We have come here to win the championship in the field sports." For the 1908 Games, the American press devised an unofficial point system so that national achievements could be easily compared. Political animosities arising from World War I drove the IOC to exclude the losers of the war—the Central Powers of Germany, Austria, Hungary, and Turkey—from the Games of 1920 and 1924. Neither did the IOC extend an invitation to the newly established regime in Russia to compete in the postwar Games; Soviet Russia did not participate in the Games until 1952. And in the 1936 Games, held in Berlin, the Nazis in Germany brazenly used the games to solidify support of their rule at home and abroad.

But the professional model achieved a complete triumph in the Olympics only with the advent of television—and of the Cold War between the United States and the Soviet Union. In due time the Cold War, television, and big money pushed each Olympiad a bit farther away from the amateurism which, even in the past, had been present in a pure form only in the imaginations of Olympic spokesmen. Eventually, each nation, including the United States, devised efficient systems for subsidizing their "amateurs." Olympic officials accepted this hypocrisy, partly to perpetuate their own jobs and the Olympic bureaucracy. The lords of the Olympics also continued to preserve the illusion that the Games were immune from politics.

The Cold War first spilled over into the Olympic Games in 1952. When the Soviets announced that they would send a team to the Games in Helsinki, Finland, both American athletic and government officials became alarmed. To raise funds to counteract the "Red Menace," the United States Olympic Committee arranged for an Olympic Telethon, starring Bing Crosby and Bob Hope. Hope set the tone for the American effort when he cracked: "I guess Joe Stalin thinks he is going to show up our soft capitalist Americans. We've got to cut him down to size." At the 1952

Games, each power devised ingenious, self-serving scoring systems. Athletic success, the two nations implied, demonstrated the superiority of their respective social and political systems. The athletes began to conceive of themselves as surrogate warriors in the Soviet-American battle for prestige and influence. "There are many more pressures on the American athletes [in 1952] because of the Russians than in 1948," declared Bob Mathias. "They were in a sense the real enemies. You just loved to beat 'em. You just had to beat 'em. It wasn't like beating some friendly country like Australia."

The degree to which the subsequent rivalry between the two superpowers impinged upon the Games depended on the intensity of the Cold War. The Games of 1956 at Melbourne, Australia, and of 1960 at Rome reflected the easing of the classic phase of the Cold War. At Melbourne, American and Soviet track officials announced a tentative agreement for an exchange of track meets, to begin in Moscow in 1957. At the Rome Games of 1960, East-West goodwill abounded; Soviet and American athletes openly fraternized. The chairman of the Soviet Olympic Committee was even moved to say, "Politics is one thing, sport another. We are sportsmen." In the 1960s and 1970s, regularly scheduled athletic competition between the Soviet Union and the United States constituted part of a wide-ranging program of cultural exchanges between the two nations. Yet latent antagonisms again surfaced after the Soviets invaded Afghanistan in 1979. In retaliation, President Jimmy Carter called for a worldwide boycott of the 1980 Games, to be held in Moscow. Although only a few nations supported the American move, the boycott did deny the Soviets access to the immense American television audience.

In the 1960s, television began to radically alter the shape of the Olympics. Television enormously increased the number of people who could see the Games, intensified national rivalries, became a favorite medium for advertisers who wanted to identify with the Olympics, gave athletes additional opportunities to become celebrities and launch successful commercial careers, and eventually became essential to the financial solvency of the Games. (The payment from American television now amounts to about two-thirds of the host city's revenue from the Games.)

The numbers in the contracts between the Olympics and American television networks grew slowly until the 1970s, when they soared to astronomical heights. ABC's bid of $225 million for the 1984 Summer Games at Los Angeles and $91.5 million for the rights to the Winter Games at Sarajevo astonished many veteran observers of the broadcasting industry, but video rights for the 1988 Winter Games at Calgary were bought by ABC for the spectacular sum of $309 million—after an eleven-hour bidding process that James Spence, senior vice president of ABC Sports, called "degrading." The *Wall Street Journal* noted that "the 1988 Calgary games may be a trophy of questionable value"; ABC, it reports, "may have trouble selling commercial time" at rates commensurate with its winning bid. And audience ratings for the Sarajevo Olympics fell below those for the 1980 Winter Games. Originally the Koreans had hoped to realize at least $750 million for the rights to the 1988 Summer Games, but the withdrawal of the Communist bloc nations from the 1984 Los Angeles Games and the expectation that they would also boycott the Seoul Games dampened the enthusiasm of the networks. Before submitting final bids, they anxiously awaited the ratings for the Los Angeles Games.

Corporations found in the Games a wonderful opportunity to sell their products. They spent large sums of money to get their wares identified with the Olympics. Traditionally, American athletes had not been issued coordinated apparel; but in 1964, clothing firms began providing free, coordinated outfits for the entire American team. Clothing manufacturers believed that Olympic team outfits exerted a particularly strong influence on the purchases of youths, especially in the fall season following the Games. By the time of the 1976 Games, Olympics fans could purchase official Olympic butter, beer, sugar, gasoline, cameras, watches, and a host of other products. At Montreal, Coca-Cola alone paid $1.3 million to supply the athletes with free, Olympic-endorsed soda. With the costs of the Olympics skyrocketing and financial considerations becoming daily more complex, Olympic organizations found that business matters took up far more of their time and attention than did sport itself.

By the 1980s, the IOC, the international bodies that supervised competition at the Games, and the national Olympic committees had become increasingly absorbed in the tasks required to maintain their own existences. (In most cases—at least in the West—the sports bodies were self-perpetuating, responsible to no one but themselves.) The Olympic movement had become a huge, unwieldy network of bureaucracies. The IOC itself reflected the trend toward bureaucratization. Until 1964 the permanent staff of the IOC consisted of only the president and two part-time assistants in Chicago (Brundage's home) and a chancellor and two part-time assistants in Lausanne, Switzerland, the IOC headquarters. Until 1960 the entire expenses of the IOC had been less than $10,000 per year. But in 1980 the administrative head of the IOC alone (Monique Berlioux) received an annual salary of $100,000, and the Lausanne office included more than thirty-five full-time employees. A similar bureaucratization occurred in the United States, where the USOC typically spent over half of its budget on administration.

Until 1972, Americans accepted an uncoordinated Olympics program and a rampantly hypocritical system of "amateur" athletics without noticeable concern. Except for a two-week interlude every four years, the media and most Americans simply ignored the Olympic Games. Television, more than any other phenomenon, transformed American interest in the Games. The drama of the 1972 Munich Games riveted the attention of the American people to their television sets as nothing had done since the assassination of President Kennedy and the moon shot.

The Munich Games offered incomparable television drama— monumental blunders, sparkling heroes, and genuine tragedy. Sprinters Eddie Hart and Ray Robinson failed to show up for the second round of the quarterfinals of the 100-meter race. Howard Cosell doggedly pursued (and after locating him, hounded) their coach, Stan Wright, for an explanation. (Wright had relied upon an antiquated schedule printed eighteen months earlier.) Before a worldwide television audience, runners Vince Matthews and Wayne Collett fidgeted irreverently on the victory stand during the playing of the National Anthem. (Olympic officials fumed and eventually barred them from further competition.) The United States lost to the Soviet Union in a basketball game in which the Americans had apparently been cheated out of victory twice by inept or prejudiced officials.

The Games had their heroes: Mark Spitz, handsome American swimmer, and Olga Korbut, an endearing Soviet gymnast. And their horrors. Located just nine miles and thirty years from Dachau, the Olympic village was visited with a reminder of earlier outrages. Arab terrorists invaded the Israeli compound, leading eventually to the deaths of nine Israeli hostages and all but three of the terrorists.

Both at the 1972 Games and at the 1976 Montreal Olympics, television magnified the victories of the Communist-bloc countries and made millions of Americans acutely aware of the deficiencies of their nation's Olympic effort. President Gerald Ford, himself a former college football player and an ardent fan, appointed a special presidential commission to study the American system of amateur athletics and make recommendations for a total overhaul. "In international sport," the presidential commission concluded in its final report, "American performances are deteriorating. Against athletes from nations for whom Olympic medals are as precious as moon rocks, U.S. competitors seem to have steadily diminishing chances of success."

Often presidents seem to appoint special commissions in order to give the appearance of taking action on a problem without doing anything substantively, but both Presidents Ford and Carter and a large congressional majority endorsed the recommendations of the Olympic Sports Commission. The resultant Amateur Sports Act of 1978 represented a sharp departure from the traditions of American amateur sports. To eliminate long-standing disputes between amateur sports governing bodies for hegemony over the American Olympic effort, the act empowered the United States Olympic Committee (USOC) to act as a coordinating authority. This provision especially trimmed the power of the once-powerful Amateur Athletic Union. To develop minor sports and sports medicine, Congress appropriated $16 million. Subsequently, the USOC set up permanent quarters in Colorado Springs, Colorado, for research and athletic training. For several months of each year, promising Olympic hopefuls in several sports could now train—all expenses paid—at Colorado Springs.

The nation also moved closer to the professional model in its subsidization of the athletes competing in Olympic sports. Until the mid-1970s, amateur athletes technically could not benefit monetarily in any way from their sports activities. However, nearly all of the world-class athletes received some sort of subsidy. Those attending colleges usually enjoyed athletic scholarships, and an athlete in the military might be granted additional time off for training. Since at least the 1920s, promoters of track and field meets in both the United States and Europe had paid well-known athletes generous "travel" expenses to participate in their meets. And in the 1960s, endorsements of sporting equipment by "amateur" athletes became something of a worldwide scandal. Manufacturers offered Olympic participants free equipment plus cash payments to prominently display skis, vaulting poles, clothing, and the like before the omnipresent television cameras. "Most of us are aware," declared Jack Kelly, president of the Amateur Athletic Union, "that as many as two-thirds of the athletes signing the Olympic oath are committing perjury."

Gradually practice and principle came closer together. In 1974 the IOC modified its strict rules: It permitted "amateur" athletes to receive their regular salaries when in training for international competition even though the athletes might not actually be working at a job. In the United States, the Amateur Sports Act of 1978 and additional changes in IOC rules allowed Olympic hopefuls to accept guaranteed appearance money, earn "Grand Prix" points on the international track circuit which could be translated into dollars, serve as highly paid consultants to corporations, and even do television commercials without losing their amateur status. Suddenly, several of the world-class athletes in the Olympic sports began to make as much money as the typical professional athlete in team sports. The richest of the "nonprofessionals" in the 1980s was probably marathoner Alberto Salazar, who could command as much as $20,000 for appearing in a race and reportedly earned $200,000 annually.

Amateur athletes, however, could not take the money directly. Funds first went to the national sports organization to which the athlete belonged. For example, the Athletic Congress (TAC), the governing body of track and field, placed athletes' earnings in a trust fund that could technically be tapped only for essential living and training expenses. But TAC, like the other regulatory organizations, was generous in its definition of "expenses," allowing the athletes in effect to earn as much as they could. Such an artifice made it possible to retain a tissue-thin illusion of amateurism while in fact providing for a system of professional sports. Whether the professionalization of the American Olympic effort would produce more athletic victories over the Communist countries remained to be seen.

Before World War II, winning conference championships and defeating traditional rivals had usually satisfied all but the most rabid fans of a college's football team. But no longer. Television prompted fans to ask for more. Especially in states without professional teams, fans sought in their college teams sources of national recognition and pride. And a team succeeded nationally only when it ranked highly in the wire-service polls and appeared regularly on network television. To join the vaunted ranks of the Top Ten required the generation of vast sums of money, the hiring of a winning coach, fancy athletic facilities, a national recruiting system, a burgeoning bureaucracy, and the perpetuation of the myth of the student-athlete—in short, the full-scale professionalization of a college's athletic program.

Success in joining the ranks of the Top Ten began with a highly specialized, well-managed bureaucracy. While the number of players in varsity sports rose by 11.8 percent between 1966 and 1972, the number of full-time personnel involved in administration climbed 35.9 percent. The 1966 ratio of players to coaches in college football stood at thirty to one; seven years later, it was eight to one. Similar ratio changes occurred in other sports. Athletic directors who once performed multiple roles as business managers, sports information directors, fund-raisers, and coaches all but disappeared from the college scene. Almost no coaches or players applied their skills to more than one sport. In season the athletes often spent up to forty hours a week in practice, chalk talks, film sessions, and travel. Out of season, they typically engaged in a program of supervised daily weight lifting. Such a regimen made a mockery of the idea that college players were students who happened to be athletes.

The pressure to join the Top Ten intensified the effort to recruit "blue-chip" athletes. "Recruiting, not coaching, is the name of the game," explained Oklahoma's Barry Switzer, the nation's most successful college football coach in the 1970s. Oklahoma has "built its tradition with Texas high school players—and I'm proud of it. We've got to get where the players are. Texas has 1,400 high schools playing football. There are just 200 in the entire state of Oklahoma." Schools located in sparsely populated areas had to recruit nationwide, but in the 1970s, even the University of Southern California, which was located amidst a rich pool of football talent, extended its recruiting effort to the entire nation. Furthermore, since basketball could offer a relatively simple and inexpensive means for a college to attract national attention, and since only one quality player might reverse the fortunes of an otherwise mediocre team, competition for the top high school basketball players was even more pronounced than for football players.

Effective recruitment required a systematic, well-coordinated effort. Coaches spent countless hours poring over the films of high school games and some 100 days of each year jetting about the country visiting callow high school youths. Recruiters relied heavily upon personal contacts. Local alumni, especially celebrities—including state governors, astronauts, singers, actors, and professional athletes—often lent their assistance to their alma maters. Colleges increasingly tried to appeal to rising ethnic, racial, and regional consciousness. Big-time football powers usually hired at least one black, one Irish-American or representative of another Catholic ethnic group, and coaches who had a strong identification with regions outside of the state in which the university was located. Once the prospective athlete arrived on campus, he might be greeted by members of the "Gibson Girls," "Husker Honies," or "Gater Getters," organizations of comely coeds especially recruited by the athletic departments to act as official hostesses.

Recruiters might promise prospects legal or illegal benefits. Without violating NCAA rules, a recruiter could emphasize to the potential recruit the likelihood of a good job after graduation, the quality of the school's coaching staff, the number of past bowl invitations or past television appearances, or improbably, the quality of education offered by his university. Above all, the prospect of appearing on television attracted recruits. "We haven't been on TV even regionally for years," groused a losing Big Ten football coach in 1978, "but some of the schools we recruit against, like Notre Dame, Nebraska and Ohio State, are on national TV twice or three times a year. National TV is where the youngsters want to be," he added, "and they know our school isn't likely to get them there."

Playing on television also enhanced the prospects of the athlete eventually joining the professional ranks. When eighteen-year-old Marcus Dupree, generally considered to be his year's outstanding college football prospect in America, was asked at a 1982 press conference why he had selected the University of Oklahoma, he responded: "They have a winnin' tradition. They'll be on TV a lot. They'll be a national contender. I can win the Heisman . . . [and] I believe I can fit in there."

Any college with a goal of joining the Top Ten had to provide its athletes with lush facilities. These might include special athletic dormitories (complete with a television set in each room, recreation rooms, a special dining hall, and a swimming pool), carpeted locker and shower rooms, the latest weight-training equipment, and a battery of private tutors to assist the players in their academic programs. At the University of Oklahoma athletic dormitory—known locally as the "Sooner Hilton"—two athletes shared a suite consisting of a bedroom, living room, and private bath. As on most campuses, the dormitory was strictly off limits to everyone but Oklahoma athletes; the players spent four years closeted only with fellow athletes. "I believe in first-class facilities for my players," said coach Barry Switzer. "I think they should be able to live together, play together, win together, and lose together." College accommodations were so luxurious that when players first joined the pro ranks, they were sometimes astonished to find the pro facilities inferior to those they had enjoyed in college. Unlike the colleges, the pro leagues (having a draft system) did not have to worry about appealing to recruits.

Illegal inducements took several forms. Alumni and booster groups, often with the tacit approval or at least the knowledge of the coaching staff, might grant cash, cars, clothes, rent-free apartments, unlimited use of charge accounts, or high-paying jobs. One of the most common abuses was the sale by college athletes of tickets given to them by the athletic department. Ostensibly, the athlete gave such tickets to members of his family or to friends. But athletes often sold the tickets, sometimes generating more than a thousand dollars in income. To obtain the admission of an athlete with a poor academic record, coaches might also tamper with transcripts. To make up deficiencies in college credits or grades, coaches might arrange for snap courses offered through correspondence or by college extension divisions.

Given the intense competition among colleges for top-flight athletes, the NCAA faced an insuperable enforcement problem. A thin line sometimes separated legal from illegal practices. Coaches often complained that minor infractions were impossible to avoid. Some of the rules seemed petty; for example, a coach could not technically purchase his players ice cream cones from the local Dairy Queen. Although the NCAA acted as policeman, prosecutor, and judge, it had no subpoena powers. To have been effective in supervising the athletic operations of the some 600 colleges under its jurisdiction, the NCAA would have needed powers equivalent to those of the Soviet KGB or the FBI. (Even within these limits, as of 1982, 73 of the 139 schools playing Division 1A football had at one time or another been placed on probation.) Apparently most coaches had a tacit understanding to ignore all but the most blatant forms of cheating. Consequently, those close to the college athletic scene, including coaches and athletes, estimated that only a small fraction of the total number of violations resulted in punishment.

Many colleges sought quick entry into the Top Ten by hiring a coach with a proven record as a winner. To seize such opportunities, coaches broke their existing contracts with impunity. Rather than have their school face legal hassles, booster clubs sometimes paid off the former employees of the new coach. Salaries of such coaches soared. In 1982, Texas A & M stunned the college football world by luring Jackie Sherrill away from the University of Pittsburgh for $1.7 million over six years. Sherill's base pay of $95,000 ($5,000 more than the university's president made) came from the coffers of the athletic department. A television show and A & M boosters furnished the rest of Sherrill's income. Wealthy boosters "can make it so attractive that even a high-principled guy could be tempted to do anything to be in the top 10 every year," asserted Donald B. Canham, director of athletics at the University of Michigan. "I'm fearful that more and more. . .wealthy people are trying to use their money to control a college football team or a basketball team as if it were a professional franchise."

Paying the bills for the splendor of a big-time athletic program taxed the wits of the shrewdest athletic administrators. Of course, consistently winning teams generated large sums from gate receipts; several colleges raised the ticket prices of choice seats to astronomical heights. But the gate alone could not finance the athletic programs of even the most successful schools. State universities often received some direct or indirect assistance from the taxpayers. And television revenues were critical to the financial solvency of big-time schools. As noted earlier, how the television pie was to be shared sharply divided the college ranks.

Apart from television, donations from boosters grew more quickly than any other source of income. In 1982, at the University of Florida, according to the *Wall Street Journal*, 6,400 members of the Gator Boosters contributed $2.5 million of the school's $9.5 million sports budget. "How important is that money?" rhetorically queried Bill Carr, the school's athletic director. "Only about as important as blood to the human body." Like most big-time schools, Florida tied gifts to season tickets. Seats between the thirty-five yard lines on the west side of the stadium, the one facing away from the afternoon sun, cost the boosters $275 each. The twenty-eight Bull Gators—twenty-seven men and one woman—who stood at the top echelon of the Gator Boosters contributed at least $10,000 each a year to the university's sports program. On football game days, Bull Gators and their guests sat in a glass-enclosed, air-conditioned box at Florida Stadium. (The university's president and his guests sat outdoors.) Boosters received other "perks," such as preferred parking for sports events, free press guides and free newsletters, having their pictures in scorecards, and special meetings with coaches. Many observers feared that boosters had become overly involved in the management of athletic programs; boosters played conspicuous roles in nearly every recruiting scandal.

In the 1980s, college sports entered a crisis perhaps more serious than that of the great scandal of 1950. In 1980 a string of ugly stories leaped to the headlines of the nation's press. In the Southwest, reports indicated that Arizona State football players received credits for unattended, off-campus extension courses. A sordid story of forgery and fakery (revealed only because of an unrelated FBI investigation) wrecked the University of New Mexico basketball team. Then came even more startling revelations. Half of the Pacific Ten Conference schools admitted that they had "laundered" academic transcripts and granted false credits to athletes. The culprits included UCLA, for many years the nation's premier college basketball team, and the University of Southern California, a perennial contender for the national football crown. Given the nature of big-time college sports, there seemed no easy way of avoiding corruption. Doug Barfield, football coach at Auburn University, put the choices confronted by many college coaches succinctly: "Go on as you have been and eventually get fired. Cheat more and survive. Or quit." Shortly after Barfield made these observations, Auburn fired him for failing to win enough games.

Not even the most sympathetic observer could any longer believe that college sports were simply an activity played by student athletes for the joy of the game and the glory of the school. The ethos of college games differed little from that of professional sports. In both instances, the values of entertainment superseded those of sport. College football, as Frank Broyles, the dapper and articulate athletic director of the University of Arkansas explained, "is in competition for the entertainment dollar and [teams have] . . . to put on a good performance if they want their share." The traditional spirit of college sports survived only at the smaller colleges, which made no effort to join the big time and rarely if ever had their games appear on network television.

Every fall, thousands of mothers and fathers gather along the sidelines to encourage their eight- and nine-year-old boys to "play" with more intensity. Many are confident that playing football has detoured their youngsters from lives of crime and drugs. Not only have their children evaded the clutches of the juvenile authorities, the parents reason, but the boys are learning discipline, respect for authority, teamwork, zone defenses, veer offenses, and how to make more effective use of their ninety-pound bodies— heads, forearms, and shoulders. Perhaps they are even learning the skills that will one day carry them to a glamorous career in the National Football League.

Towering over the helmeted, shoulder-padded boys are adult officials in striped shirts. To maintain order, they must frequently blow their whistles. Coaches, and sometimes the officials as well, yell and scream at their little warriors. "I've been asked if I sometimes think I'm Vince Lombardi," said a Pop Warner football coach in Boston. "I say that sometimes I think I'm Lombardi and other times I think I'm Knute Rockne." On the sidelines, eight- and nine-year-old girls noisily cheer on their diminutive heroes.

Such a scene reflects the general triumph of the professional model in youth sports programs. In an earlier era, youth had played pick-up games on empty lots, schoolgrounds, or cow pastures, or in the supervised programs of the "boy workers" in city recreation departments, YMCAs, and schools. But, during the age of television, adult volunteers organized athletic programs in football, baseball, and basketball that reached nearly every preadolescent youth in the nation. Invariably, the volunteers adopted a scaled-down version of the corresponding professional sport. In the individual sports of tennis, golf, gymnastics, swimming, skating, and track and field, pre-teenagers with the financial wherewithal and parents bent upon a professional athletic career for their children sought out personal coaches, athletic boarding schools, and special summer camps.

Likewise, many high school athletic programs moved toward a more professional orientation. Scandals arose in most states over the transfer of star athletes from one school district to another; some high schools permitted students to "redshirt," holding the student back a year in school so he or she would gain an additional year of athletic maturity. The number of professionally trained coaches proliferated. "I only had one [coach] in high school," recalled Red Grange, football hero of the 1920s. "Today, there are two or three in grade school, five in high school, and the last time I visited the University of Illinois, there was a coach for every specialty." Many of the athletes themselves saw high school as merely a way station on their road to the college and pro ranks.

The earliest adult-directed youth sports programs conscientiously avoided copying professional models. Indeed, the reformers in the Y's, the city recreation programs, and the schools were uncompromising adherents of the amateur sports tradition. They sought to build non-spectator-centered programs suited to the physical, mental, and moral maturation of their young charges. In the playing of games (and regardless of their outcome), the youngsters, they hoped, would learn self-control, steadfastness, and teamwork. Thus they abhorred a winning-at-all costs ethos and using sport as a springboard for becoming professional athletes. Although the unbridled competition prevalent in the marketplace inevitably spilled over into youth programs, the reformers enjoyed a remarkable degree of success. Even at the high school level, they often blocked the holding of state championships in football, abolished all varsity sports for girls, and eliminated all varsity sports for children in the elementary and junior high schools.

Since neither the schools nor city governments encouraged highly competitive sports for preadolescent youths, adult volunteers gradually filled the void with their own programs. Volunteers founded the Pop Warner Football League in 1929 and Little League Baseball in 1939. These programs grew slowly until after World War II. Then an amazing burst of growth accompanied the burgeoning of suburbs and the increased privatization of leisure. The home-centered fathers and mothers of the suburbs passed up regular dinner hours and even relaxation in front of the family television set to transport their children to ball fields, to coach them, to serve as umpires, and to shout encouragement, instructions, and sometimes insults at their children.

Uninhibited by an allegiance to the amateur tradition and influenced by what they saw on television, the volunteers tried to simulate as closely as they could the professional sports model. Ironically, while the distance that a high school football team could travel for a game was usually limited to 200 miles or less, eight- and nine-year-olds trekked all over the nation to play in such "midget" bowls as the Junior Liberty (in Memphis), Junior Orange (in Miami), Auto (in Grosse Point, Michigan), Carnation Milk, Santa Claus, Sunshine, Mighty Mite, and even the Honolulu Bowl. No national championships existed in any high school sports, but Little League Baseball held an annual World Series at Williamsport, Pennsylvania.

While television alone was not responsible for the demise of the amateur model in youth sports, it contributed immensely to the growing seriousness which pervaded youth programs nearly everywhere. The cool medium flooded homes with positive images of professional sports and packaged athletes as celebrities who earned mind-boggling financial rewards. The "up-close and personal" style of television interviews transformed stars into living room intimates, personalizing their accomplishments while stoking the illusion that anyone could make it to the top. "It starts from the day a [well-meaning] Little League coach takes a youngster under his wing and tells the boy he can be a great baseball player," explained Bill Walsh, coach of the San Francisco 49ers. " 'But to do it,' he tells the boy, 'you've got to forgo all other sports—no tennis, no swimming. Never mind the piano, practice your baseball!' "

Such dreams sometimes turned preadolescent sports into grotesque enterprises. To make the weight limits in junior wrestling and junior football programs, players submitted themselves to a regimen of diet pills and low-calorie diets. The coaches—many of whom had had little or no previous experience in sports—often inappropriately tried to employ the latest techniques they had observed on television. They might urge midget lineman to use their football helmets to "spear" opponents, or tiny pitchers to throw curve balls. The experience of coaching sometimes turned otherwise humane and reasonable men into raging animals. "They want to win at any cost," reported Chuck Ortmann, a former Michigan All-American who quit as chairman of a midget football league at Glen Ellyn, Illinois. "They tell their players, 'Go out there and break that guy's arm.' They won't even let all their kids play." In many places, children with inferior athletic talents rode the bench or played only briefly.

Parents, while enthusiastically endorsing opportunities for their children to play in organized programs, did worry about an overemphasis upon winning. In the 1983 Miller Lite survey of American attitudes toward sports, 86 percent of all parents agreed that there was too much emphasis placed upon winning and not enough upon the physical and psychological development of their children; 82 percent agreed that the amateur team coaches often took the game too seriously. In response to widespread criticism, several preadolescent programs introduced reforms, such as requiring that all the youngsters be permitted to play at least briefly. Yet these minor reforms failed to transform the main outlines of the organized youth sports programs.

Television may have had an even larger impact on youth in individual sports. Prior to television, pre-teenaged youth had rarely given tennis, track, gymnastics, figure skating, skiing, or swimming much of their attention or time. Perhaps during the summer months, they might take a few lessons at the country club to which their parents belonged or participate in a city recreation program. Otherwise they simply played for fun or in a few meets scheduled over the summer. But all of that changed with television. Television made celebrities out of such athletes as Chris Evert, Jimmy Connors, Mark Spitz, Olga Korbut, and Nadia Comaneci. Within a decade following the 1972 Olympics, the level of competition in individual sports improved almost beyond belief. In tennis, tiny teenaged girls developed powerful, dependable ground strokes. Track and field records seemed to fall almost daily. The record time which won Mark Spitz the gold medal in the 100-meter race in the 1972 Olympics would not have even qualified him for the event in the 1980 Olympics. In diving, gymnastics, and figure skating, execution of new, complex maneuvers—some of which were previously thought to be humanly impossible—were necessary before one could even qualify to compete at the international level. (Incidentally, most of the new movements were also more physically dangerous, leaving in their wake a larger toll of permanent physical injuries.)

Youngsters with a goal of becoming world-class athletes now had to make their sport the end-all of their existence. They had to begin systematic training at the age of five or six or even younger. Tracy Austin received her first tennis racket and first lesson at the age of two; three years later, *World Tennis* magazine featured her on its cover. Such children had to practice three or four hours daily, their training carefully supervised by an individual coach. In order to train during the school year, they might have to begin practice at 6:00 in the morning; evening practices might not conclude until 9:00 at night. On weekends and during the summer months, these children engaged in an endless round of organized competition with others, often embarking upon long trips away from home that sometimes even took them to foreign countries. Not only did the youths have to devote themselves to a single-minded pursuit, but their families had to make enormous sacrifices in time and money as well. No one knew what the long-range effects of such rigorously focused childhoods might be. There were disturbing reports of occasional suicides and aimlessness in later life; yet, surveys of children competing at the national and international levels indicated that most of them performed well above average in their schoolwork and seemed to be better adjusted psychologically than non-sporting youth of a comparable age.

The demise of the amateur sports model had far-reaching implications for American sports. For more and more athletes, sports became a form of work rather than play; athletes "played" for the external rewards rather than the satisfaction of the experience itself. "If all the year were playing holidays, / To sport would be as tedious as to work," said Prince Hal in *Henry IV, Part 1*. Such values as good sportsmanship and teamwork, thought to inhere in the playing experience itself, could also no longer be sustained. All other values tended to be subordinated to winning or being "Number One."

The death of the amateur model and the ubiquity of television also reduced the propensity of children to engage in spontaneous, informal sport. Observers everywhere noted a sharp decline in games organized by youths themselves. The loss of such experiences meant that youngsters had fewer opportunities to learn valuable lessons in improvisation and cooperation, or to experience for themselves the sheer fun to be found in sports.

11

Where Have Our Heroes Gone?

At mid-century there was Bobby Thomson, who won the National League playoff for the New York Giants with a clutch home run; Joe DiMaggio, who played with a painful bonespur in his heel so that his team might have a shot at the pennant; Joe Louis, who at the peak of his professional career volunteered for the Armed Services; Jackie Robinson, who spurned insults while integrating the National Game of baseball; Connie Mack, a skipper who was revered by all; and Phillip Wrigley, the chewing gum magnate and owner of the Chicago Cubs, who placed the interests of the fans before his own ego gratification. Such men were admired as much for their dignity as for their feats in sports; they inspired others to act nobly.

Some three decades later, there were countless coaches repeating Vince Lombardi's dictum: "Winning is not the most important thing; it's everything." There was John McEnroe—loud, vulgar, rude, and vain, "a spoiled child only his mother could love"—all exposed on television. The poor loser: "I'd play my heart out . . . and someone else would blow the game," sulked Wilt Chamberlain. There were players and their agents demanding multi-million-dollar, no-cut, long-term contracts. And there were beleaguered skippers and self-indulgent owners. Such men tarnished the traditional sporting experience. If they inspired people at all, it was to act with exquisite selfishness.

Between mid-century and today, then, the behavior and images of athletes, managers, and coaches—the main actors in the sports drama—have undergone sharp changes. At mid-century, the managers and coaches of professional and college teams held esteemed positions, owners conveyed an aura of being public benefactors, and certain athletes enjoyed the role of being national heroes. In the 1960s such images began to fade. In that divisive decade, sports idols no longer commanded universal reverence; instead, each major social grouping claimed its own athletic champion. Thus, Vince Lombardi inspired "Middle Americans" who held what they considered to be traditional, "conservative" values, while Joe Namath spoke to both the hipsters and the playboys, Muhammad Ali to black Americans, and Billie Jean King to militant feminists. The 1970s eventually witnessed the virtual death of the sports hero of old and the emergence of athletes as mere celebrities. That is, athletes were recognized simply for being "well known." And being well known was increasingly an outgrowth of the kind of media images projected by the athletes rather than of their feats on the playing field.

The presence of a set of national sports heroes from the 1930s through the 1950s reflected a widespread quest for national unity. First the Great Depression, then the Second World War, and finally the Cold War encouraged support for common symbols and heroes, and a common national creed. Blacks began to join the mainstream of American life, and everyone (including minorities themselves) urged ethnics on to faster and greater assimilation. Scholars in history, philosophy, political science, and sociology claimed to have discovered a broad consensus in American beliefs. A hero of World War II, Dwight D. Eisenhower, elected President in 1952, perfectly fitted the temper of the time. So did the national sports heroes. They came of age with the belief that the United States was one nation with a single set of values—that it was a nation in which any boy might succeed, and where one could say "Wow" without embarrassment.

Nearly all Americans idolized Joe DiMaggio, Joe Louis, Stan Musial, Bobby Feller, Mickey Mantle, and Willie Mays. Not only had all of them performed magnificently on the field of play; they had played with dignity and grace. They had won a share of the American dream under adverse circumstances: DiMaggio up from the fishing wharves of San Francisco, Louis from the Detroit ghetto, Musial from the coal mines of Pennsylvania, Feller from the corn fields of Iowa, Mantle from the red-dirt country of Oklahoma, and Mays from the cotton patches of Alabama. Few thought of DiMaggio first as an Italian and then as an American; he was an American who happened to be of Italian descent. In sports, if nowhere else, Americans believed that the great melting pot worked. Assimilation was, of course, not so complete for black men like Joe Louis and Willie Mays; yet, they too became heroes for black and white alike.

The national hero of mid-century combined the best of both amateur and professional traditions in American sports; he somehow—almost magically—contained such wildly opposing impulses as play versus work, excess versus control, and the community versus the individual. Perhaps the most perfect hybrid hero was Joe DiMaggio. He won his poetic nickname, "The Yankee Clipper," first because of the understated elegance manifested in his style of play and secondly because he exuded an image of solid, consistent support of his team. DiMaggio's Yankees were winners. When DiMaggio realized that his skills (and thus his contributions to the team) were slipping, he promptly retired. He refused the last contract offered him by the Yankees: "I didn't think I could give them a hundred-thousand-dollar year," he said. The perfect antithesis in personality appeared to be Ted Williams, a perfectionist at bat but one who disdained the fans; he appeared to be an irresponsible boy who cared nothing for the fate of his mates. (Later, after Williams was recalled to active duty in the Korean War, he finally received his due as a hero.)

Mickey Mantle, an Oklahoman and thus a geographical and spiritual neighbor of President Dwight D. Eisenhower of Abilene, Kansas, replaced DiMaggio both as the Yankee centerfielder and as perhaps the nation's leading sports hero. He came from plain folk: simple, humble, unlettered, down-to-earth people. Arriving at the Yankee training camp in 1951 carrying a cardboard suitcase, he proceeded to hit a baseball harder than Babe Ruth and to run faster than anyone else in the game. But his awesome power and speed were marred. Osteomyelitis curtailed his performance while it enhanced his heroism. Everyone knew that he played with bandages and pain, and everyone wondered about what might have been.

Although Jackie Robinson had integrated the National

Game, Willie Mays was the first black baseball player to gain full acceptance by whites. Mays, the centerfielder of the New York/San Francisco Giants, rivaled Mantle as a hero. In fact, many preferred the more expressive style of Mays. He brought an enthusiasm and flair to the game reminiscent of the players of old. "No one who ever saw Willie on the field in his best days could have been misled into thinking that Willie looked on baseball as work," Robert Smith has written. "He greeted each base hit for his side with whoops of pleasure. . . . He galloped along from base to base like a small boy celebrating the end of school."

Nurtured on Frank Merriwell stories and traditional values, nearly all of the athletes of the 1940s and 1950s conceived of themselves as role models for the nation's youth. They rather self-consciously cultivated an image of conventionality. In a 1958 piece for the *New York Times Magazine*, Gay Talese summed up a common suspicion that modern baseball players were, in fact, rather dull men who were less colorful than their predecessors. As described by Talese, nearly all of the players eschewed late hours, poker games, pinball machines, and chewing tobacco. They obeyed the Boy Scout Law, baby-sat, subscribed to the *Wall Street Journal*, and "would not think of tripping their mothers, even if Mom were rounding third on her way home with the winning run."

In the 1960s the quest for national unity and personal security gave way to struggles by individuals for greater personal expression and fulfillment, to specific social groups seeking a larger share of the promise of American life, and to some groups trying desperately to hold on to what they already had. Traditionally, the world of sports had rarely become entangled in larger social issues; indeed, part of the appeal of sports has stemmed from its capacity to resist intrusions from the outside world. And athletes were among the last public figures to become identified as supporters or opponents of the civil rights movement, the feminist movement, and the Vietnam War. Yet in due time, each cause found athletes who helped unite and inspire its followers.

Arnold Palmer, a golf hero, probably represented the broadest constituency of any athlete in the 1960s. Both the Associated Press and *Sports Illustrated* chose Palmer as their "Athlete of the Decade." Palmer brought to golf high drama and a charismatic personality. Before a nationwide television audience on a searingly hot afternoon at the U.S. Open in Denver in 1960, Palmer established his reputation for the "Palmer charge," which was described by Joseph Durso in *The All-American Dollar* as "a heart-attack approach to golf that demanded the situation look hopeless before one really begins to play." Entering the last round of the tourney trailing by seven strokes and fourteen players, Palmer exploded, scoring one birdie after another to finish with an epic 65, a score low enough to take the title. Golf fans never forgot the 1960 Open, but Palmer added to his own legend by fashioning an incredible string of come-from-behind victories. Few experiences in sports provided the sheer drama of the Palmer charge.

Palmer, more than any other athlete of the 1960s, effectively embodied the opposing tensions evident in earlier sports idols. On the one hand, he was the son of a local golf pro, hailed from a small town, dressed conservatively, and enjoyed the friendship of corporate executives and of President Richard M. Nixon. On the other hand, he played with an exuberant recklessness. He acted and looked like a "regular guy" who needed the help of fans. Palmer's face, unlike that of the typical stony-faced pro, registered his emotions. He celebrated his good shots with a wide, disarming grin and by raising his club high in the air as if to say, "We did it!"; bad shots produced painful grimaces. Long after Palmer stopped winning many championships, "Arnie's Army," as the immense throngs who accompanied him were dubbed, continued to follow him around the course as he played. He exuded trust; he was an ad man's dream.

By far the best-known instance of a sports figure becoming the hero of a cause was Muhammad Ali. While Jackie Robinson had breached the color ban in the National Game (1947) well before the momentous Supreme Court decision of 1954 (which with one stroke undercut the entire edifice of Jim Crow segregation), black athletes had been conspicuously absent from the sit-ins of the early 1960s, the Freedom Riders, and the March on Washington in 1963. To protest racism in sport or elsewhere might have jeopardized their newly won status. Ali's early career fit the mold established by other black athletes. As Cassius Clay, he had won the light heavyweight gold medal at the 1960 Olympic Games in Rome by defeating a more experienced Russian boxer. Asked by a Soviet reporter about racial prejudice in the United States, he responded with a statement that could have been authorized by the press secretary of the State Department. "Tell your readers we got qualified people working on that, and I'm not worried about the outcome. To me, the U.S.A. is still the best country in the world, counting yours."

After the triumph in Rome, Ali began a rapid climb to the heavyweight championship. His good looks, enthusiasm, and loquacity attracted more than the usual attention given to an aspiring heavyweight boxer. Ali himself exhibited a penchant for self-promotion. Soon known as the "Louisville Lip," he asserted in 1961 that "boxing is dying because everybody's so quiet." In 1964, in a revealing self-description, he told a reporter: "Cassius Clay is a boxer who can throw the jive better than anybody you will probably meet anywhere." Prior to his fight with Sonny Liston for the heavyweight title in 1964, he proclaimed, "I am the greatest!" Unlike the more reticent black athletes who preceded him, Ali brought to the attention of the nation an expressive, candid, self-indulgent black cultural style. Soon other blacks, and even a few "white" athletes, followed Ali's lead.

After his defeat of Liston in 1964, in the presence of a nation-wide television audience, Ali shocked boxing fans by renouncing his "slave name" of Clay in favor of Ali and proclaiming his conversion to the Black Muslim faith. The world of boxing had always tried to cloak its athletes in the mantle of orthodox religion, conventional morality, and patriotism, to counter its negative images of fixers, thugs, racketeers, and hit men. By rejecting Christianity and joining a militant black religious sect opposed to racial integration, Ali had defied one of the traditional formulas for heroism. Most white Americans feared the Muslims; in a series of press and television reports, the sect was described as highly disciplined, pious, and violent and as believing in black superiority. Ironically, the fact that Ali, consistent with his new faith, renounced coffee, liquor, drugs, and sexual liaisons with white women failed to allay white fears; indeed, it only intensified them.

Ali's announcement of his conversion coincided with mounting social conflict. In the summer of 1964 riots broke out in Harlem, three white civil rights activists were murdered in Mississippi, and the Senate adopted the Gulf of Tonkin resolution, which opened the way for a large American troop buildup in Vietnam. Ali himself became increasingly iconoclastic; he expressed an utter contempt for past boxing heroes, declaring them to be slow, inept, and above all, ugly. His outrageous doggerel often satirized American ideals. Ali's fight in 1965 with Floyd Patterson, a former heavyweight crown holder, took on the character of a "holy war": Christian versus Muslim, loyal American versus one whose loyalty was suspect. Patterson, a recent convert to Roman Catholicism, determined "to give the title back to America." "The image of a Black Muslim as the world heavyweight champion disgraces the sport and the nation. Cassius Clay must be beaten and the Black Muslim's scourge removed from Boxing." In the ring, Ali dashed all such hopes. He totally outclassed Patterson, mocking and humiliating him before the referee finally called a halt to the mismatch in the twelfth round. To Elridge Cleaver, Floyd Patterson was the "leader of the mythical legions of faithful darkies who inhabited the white imagination," while Ali was a "genuine revolutionary, the black Fidel Castro of boxing," who had inflicted a "psychological chastisement on 'white' white America similar in shock value to Fidel Castro's at the Bay of Pigs."

When shortly thereafter Ali refused to be inducted into the Army, was peremptorily (on that account) stripped of his livelihood by the custodians of boxing, and faced a possible prison term, he became one of the most powerful symbols of the troubled decade. While he was under suspension and while court appeals were being prepared, Ali appeared frequently with Howard Cosell as a boxing commentator on ABC's Wide World of Sports. Engaging in mock battles and extravagant bantering, they assisted one another in becoming national media celebrities. Ali's influence extended far beyond militant black Americans; he now inspired blacks worldwide, along with white opponents of the war in Vietnam, participants in the counterculture, and civil libertarians. On the other hand, supporters of the war and adherents of traditional values found in Ali a highly visible target of their frustration and anger.

Only slightly less important as the hero of a cause was Billie Jean King. Traditionally, tennis had been a bastion of genteel sexism. Women had been permitted by the social elites to play the sport, but only within the confines of "proper" female behavior. In mixed doubles the male player played the most conspicuous and dominant role. Proper decorum, circumspection, and subordination had been imposed on women athletes, though the emphasis

placed upon winning by Suzanne Lenglen in the 1920s and by
Maureen Connolly in the 1940s had threatened to upset the delicate role assigned to women players. In the 1960s and 1970s King,
a California athlete from a lower-middle-income family, led a
two-pronged crusade: against the stiff formality and pomposity of
tennis in general, and against sex discrimination in tennis in particular. King was not only a superb player, but was also articulate,
confident, and, like Ali, expressive. In the words of Robert Lipsyte, she "gave soul" and "personalized" the "bringing of tennis—classiest of sports—to the people."

King led the movement for equal opportunity for women in
professional tennis. Although women's matches sometimes attracted audiences almost as large as those for men, until the 1970s
the prize money available to women was only about 10 percent of
men's purses. With the advent of open tennis in the 1970s, several
promoters, assuming that women could not draw financially re-
warding gates, had dropped women from their tournaments. In
response to this exclusion, King and seven other players collabo-
rated with Gladys Heldman, publisher of *World Tennis* magazine,
in 1971 to form the Virginia Slims tournaments, a separate circuit
for women. At the urging of Heldman, the Philip Morris Tobacco
Company decided to underwrite the circuit and promote it as part
of the growing feminist movement. The Slims acquired a substantial television contract and by 1975 awarded nearly a million dollars in prize money. By threatening to withdraw from Forest Hills
and Wimbledon, the women also obtained far more equitable
purses. As an arena offering opportunities to women in professional sports, tennis was the most lucrative of all. In 1971 King became the first woman athlete to earn $100,000 in a single year;
four years later, Chris Evert won more than $300,000.

King's significance, like that of Muhammad Ali, extended far
beyond the world of sports. She became one of the most important heroes of the revived feminist movement of the 1970s. Har-
rassed by reporters for her frank pursuit of tennis as a profession
and her decision not to have children, she insisted upon her right
to be a full-time professional athlete. "Almost every day for the
last four years," she told a reporter, "someone comes up to me
and says, 'Hey, when are you going to have children?' I say, 'I'm
not ready yet.' They say, 'Why aren't you at home?' I say, 'Why

don't you go ask Rod Laver why he isn't at home?' '' By equating herself with a male professional athlete, King aroused the wrath of all those who maintained traditional notions of feminity.

The 1973 tennis match between King and Bobby Riggs probably focused public attention more sharply on the "battle of the sexes" than any other single event in the decade. Fifty-five-year-old Riggs, a former triple-crown winner at Wimbledon (1939) and a long-time sports hustler, publicly claimed that women players were inferior to men and thus overpaid. He boasted that, despite his age, he could defeat the best of the women players. He first challenged King, but she refused, arguing that, regardless of the outcome, such a match could not benefit the cause of women's tennis. Nonetheless, Margaret Court, another top-flight women's player, accepted Riggs's challenge. On Mother's Day, 1973, a nervous Court, who had recently become a mother—this fact became part of the hype for the match—lost to Riggs, 6–2, 6–1. To the surprise of television producers, but as an omen of how important the contest was in terms of larger cultural divisions, the rating for the match topped that of the men's World Championship Tennis finals, played on the same day.

Riggs then issued King a new challenge. "I'll set women's tennis back 20 years," Riggs boasted. The humiliating defeat of Court, the flamboyant chauvinism of Riggs, and the offer of $100,000 in television rights plus $100,000 more if she won led King to agree to a match with Riggs. In a circuslike atmosphere, she confronted Riggs in Houston's Astrodome before a crowd of 30,472, the largest audience ever to attend a tennis match. Millions more watched on prime time television—which, via satellite, extended coverage of the match to thirty-six nations. In a contest advertised as "The Battle of the Sexes," King routed Riggs, 6–4, 6–3, 6–3. Perhaps no single sports event in history had been so loaded with symbolic and cultural significance.

The match was also important in terms of the traditional sports experience. For it violated a fundamental premise of sports—that the conditions of competition should be the same for all contestants. True, large men played against small men. But from the time of the ancient Greeks, the principle of equality in the conditions of competition barred contests between men and boys and between men and women. Without such a standard, sports were no longer true contests; they were mere spectacles. By featuring a contest between the sexes, the Riggs–King match abandoned this tradition.

The difference in King's and Riggs's ages probably made the match more acceptable to knowledgeable sports fans, but television quickly exploited the public interest stimulated by the Riggs–King match by putting together a synthetic "sports" show, "The Battle of the Sexes." The Battle of the Sexes made a complete mockery of traditional sports. Given a handicap, women "competed" against men in various kinds of games. Neither the male nor the female athletes took the games seriously. Television viewers, perhaps unconsciously aware of the violation done to authentic sports, quickly tired of these contests, and they soon disappeared from television.

Professional football offered perfect heroes for two major segments of the American population in the 1960s. A coach, Vince Lombardi, became the hero of those troubled by the cultural unrest of the 1960s. Not since Knute Rockne's reign at Notre Dame in the 1920s had a coach been as idolized as Lombardi. As with Rockne, tragedy cut short Lombardi's career and added to its mythic dimensions; Lombardi died from cancer in 1969 at the age of fifty-seven. Like Rockne, Lombardi was a winner. The Green Bay Packers, representatives of the smallest city in the NFL and winner of only one game in 1958, appointed Lombardi, a former assistant coach with the Giants, to the position of head coach and general manager in 1959. Over the next nine years he led the team to ninety-nine victories, six conference titles, and five championships.

Lombardi's Packers resembled a paramilitary organization. "He's the general and we're the privates," one of his players aptly said. Another player remarked: "He treated us all equally—like dogs." Lombardi insisted upon strict discipline, perfection in technique, and professional pride. Yet he was a highly emotional man; he often resorted to old-fashioned rhetoric and saw his team as members of "one big family." He implicitly condemned the counterculture. "Everywhere you look," he said, "there is a call for freedom, independence, or whatever you wish to call it . . . [but] we must learn again to respect authority, because to disavow it is contrary to our individual natures." To many Americans,

Lombardi demonstrated that, even amidst the turmoil of the 1960s, adherence to traditional virtues still paid dividends. Yet Lombardi popularized a value antithetical to the traditional spirit of American sports: to wit, that the sole purpose of play was victory. For those inspired by Lombardi—and they were many—anything less than being number one was utterly unacceptable. Anything less than being number one suggested personal failure.

"Broadway Joe" Namath, a celebrity lionized both on and off the field, seemed to embody the perfect contrast to Lombardi. If Lombardi represented a father figure, then Namath symbolized the rebellious youth of the 1960s. Johnny Sample, a teammate of Namath's, said: "Our heroes were a new breed of players. Men like Joe Namath who wore their hair long and bragged about how good they were had replaced men like Johnny Unitas, the clean-cut All-American-Kid type." Namath projected multiple, sometimes contradictory, images. He was personable and handsome, an ideal subject for television. He was an ethnic (Italian) in a decade of rising ethnic consciousness. He had a mythic wound—a damaged knee. He was iconoclastic. On the one hand he seemed to be the "hippie" of the sports world: He wore a Fu Manchu mustache and could not abide schedules, discipline, authority, or Commissioner Rozelle. Yet he shaved off his mustache for a price—a commercial on television—drank Johnnie Walker Red, and wore with pride a Persian lamb coat. He was also Hugh Hefner's ultimate playboy, the quintessential bachelor. He openly celebrated his indulgence in tall blonde "broads," booze, clothes, and parties; he supposedly laid to rest forever the ancient myth that sex the night before a big game impaired one's performance on the field of play. For rather different reasons, he, like Palmer, was an ad man's Messiah. At the same time, he was a precursor of the self-indulgent athlete of the 1970s and 1980s.

While in the 1960s each group had its own hero, in the seventies and eighties heroes—both in sports and elsewhere—seemed to disappear. For the entire 1960s, the *Reader's Guide to Periodical Literature* listed only one article—and that in 1969—suggesting the demise of heroes; in the 1970s and early 1980s the *Guide* listed more than a half-dozen essays entitled either "Where Have Our Heroes Gone?" or "Where Have All Our Heroes Gone?" The titles of other articles struck equally ominous notes: "What's Hap-

pened to Our Heroes?'' ''The Need for Heroes,'' ''Heroes: Do
We Need Them?'' ''Do Teens Hunger for Heroes?'' ''Let's Bring
Back Heroes,'' ''What Price Heroes?'' ''Death of Heroes,'' and
''Youth Heroes Have No Haloes.'' Nearly every author particularly mourned the passing of sports heroes. ''Where Have You
Gone, Joe DiMaggio?'' lamented Simon and Garfunkel in their
hit song ''Mrs. Robinson.'' (DiMaggio was in California, selling
automatic coffee makers.) Perhaps even more serious was the disappearance of heroes among the young. In a 1977 survey of 1,200
junior-high-school children, the most popular response to the
question: ''Who is your hero?'' was ''None.'' Answers farther
down the line in this and other polls revealed the devaluation of
the hero. When students did name heroes, they most often cited
rock musicians, television's Bionic Man or Woman, Evel Knievel,
and other celebrities.

The departure of sports heroes was part of a larger cultural
disillusionment. In the 1970s, public opinion polls indicated a
growing distrust by Americans of authority generally, and of such
major institutions as government, universities, business, and the
professions. This distrust apparently had many sources: the Vietnam War, the Watergate scandal, and the inability of the Federal
government to solve such problems as inflation, unemployment,
energy shortages, and pollution. Moreover, post-Watergate journalism seemed to revel in the most intimate and sordid details in
the lives of would-be heroes; the age took a special delight in
smashing false idols. Some suggested that decisions by committees
of experts, bureaucracies, and computers simply made the individual hero obsolete. The astronauts may have been the logical heirs
of Charles A. Lindbergh, but their heroism had been submerged
in complex team efforts. Finally, the bullets of assassins had
brought down potential heroes John F. Kennedy, Martin Luther
King, Malcolm X, and Robert Kennedy. Perhaps Americans were
afraid of what would happen if they admired somebody too much.
At any rate, many turned inward, to themselves, rather than to
public figures to find inspiration and fulfillment.

The invasion of sports by the realities of the outside world
contributed more directly and perhaps more tellingly to the dimi-
nution of the aura surrounding athletes, coaches, and team owners. In the past, the actors in the sports drama had often been able
to convey the impression that they possessed a certain nobility of

character, that they hitched their own purposes to something larger than themselves, to something that demanded endurance, sacrifice, or courage. But in the 1960s athletes had become increasingly politicized; and in the same decade, talk and images of money began to pervade sports as never before. In due time, reports of strikes, free agents, and soaring salaries overwhelmed the stories of the games themselves. Furthermore, in seeking the elusive goal of self-fulfillment, the players abandoned earlier roles and images. Following the leads of Muhammad Ali and Joe Namath, they became more expressive, often conveying an impression of mere self-indulgence. Likewise, their private lives, down to the most minute details, became the stuff of public knowledge.

Although professional athletes had certainly worried about their salaries in the past, they could do little to change them. The draft, by which a franchise received the exclusive rights to negotiate with a new player, and the reserve system, by which a team held an option on a player's services for his entire playing career, prevented athletes from selling their services to the highest bidder. The player had only two weapons at his disposal: He could "hold out" or quit. Holding out usually failed to work, for owners simply refused to negotiate. Take the case of Joe DiMaggio in 1937. On the opening day of the 1937 baseball season, hold-out DiMaggio told a reporter that he had not been contacted by the Yankees for five weeks. Colonel Jacob Ruppert, owner of the Yankees, said of DiMaggio: "I don't want to hear from him until he's ready to sign on our terms. I won't pay him a penny more than $25,000. I stake my word of honor on it." DiMaggio came to terms for the $25,000 offered by Ruppert. Owners and managers also exercised unbridled authority over both the private and public lives of their charges. Behavior thought to be inappropriate or in violation of club rules could be punished with heavy fines, suspensions without pay, a trade, or being blackballed from the sport entirely.

In the 1960s and 1970s, the props fell out, in rapid succession, from under the player control system of professional sports, and player salaries escalated to undreamed-of heights. For a time, competition between leagues for player talent nullified player reservation systems and drove up player salaries in football and basketball. However, the merger of the AFL and the NFL in 1966 quickly reversed the upward trend in salaries. Limited competition from the Canadian Football League in the 1970s and 1980s and from the United States Football League (beginning in 1983) kept NFL salaries higher than they otherwise would have been. (Salaries climbed from an annual average of about $42,000 in 1975 to over $125,000 in 1983.)

In 1975, professional basketball players approved a merger between the American Basketball Association and the National Basketball Association only upon condition that the classic forms of the draft and the reserve system be abolished. With clubs bidding against one another for players, salaries rose from an average of slightly over $20,000 in 1967 to an average in excess of $185,000 in 1980.

When a grievance arbitration struck down baseball's venerable reserve clause in 1975, salaries increased phenomenally in that sport. As in the case of basketball, the players union negotiated a modified reserve system. Their new contract (or Basic Agreement) also included a complex salary arbitration procedure, first negotiated in 1973. When a case went to arbitration, management and the player each submitted proposed salary figures; the arbitrator then chose one of the two figures as binding. As the owners vigorously bid for the services of free agents and players took their salary disputes to arbitration, salaries shot up from an average of $45,000 in 1975 to almost $145,000 five years later, to twice *that* figure in 1983.

Similarly, in 1983, each player on the Baltimore Orioles received $65,487.70 as his share of the World Series winnings, and each losing Phillies player earned $44,473.32; these figures were almost three and a half times the winning and losing shares for 1975. Only the bonanza television contracts made such spectacular increases possible, for salaries jumped much faster than gate receipts but simply paralleled the increases in television receipts.

The collapse of the player reservation systems in professional sports introduced an entirely new image of the athlete. Although teams had earlier sold and traded players to other franchises, it had been much easier to maintain the illusion that a player had a loyalty to his team roughly equivalent to that of a citizen to his country. Free agency shattered that illusion. Now players in baseball and basketball (football is a unique case) could and did seek out the highest bidder for their services. Many players resembled nomads. Slugger Reggie Jackson, for example, moved from Oakland to Baltimore, then to the New York Yankees, and finally to the California Angels. The players hired personal agents, both to negotiate their complex contracts and to handle endorsements and other business.

An incident in 1964 reveals how much the status of players and their agents had changed. A man arrived at Vince Lombardi's office and identified himself as an agent representing center Jim Ringo. He told Lombardi, the head man of the Green Bay Packers, that he wanted to negotiate a new contract for his client. "Agent?" snarled Lombardi, who immediately retired to his office, made a phone call, and reemerged. "You're in the wrong place," Lombardi told the man. "Mr. Ringo has just been traded to Philadelphia." By the late 1970s, such a cavalier treatment of players and their agents would have been unthinkable. By then, agents, most of whom were lawyers specializing in sports contract negotiations, had become a conspicuous part of the sports scene. For weeks at a time, fans might find on the sports pages endless discussions of the progress of negotiations between agents and owners.

Player unions and player strikes also altered the image of players. In the past, both football and baseball had promoted the myth that the commissioners of their respective sports represented the owners and the players alike—this, despite the obvious fact that only the owners hired and fired the commissioner. Likewise, the owners claimed to place the interest of the sport ahead of their personal welfare. Nonetheless, players in the past had formed associations to represent their interests; in fact, in 1890, baseball players had even formed a separate major league. Yet such player militancy had been rare, and in the long run, unionization efforts in professional sports had failed.

Until the mid-1960s, the player associations in football and baseball were moribund organizations; they had limited their activities mostly to efforts to obtain better pensions for veteran players. Probably the reaction to unions by Bob Friend, a player representative in the National League in 1963, was typical. "If the structure of our players association was changed to a union, I believe it would result in ill will for the players. It would tend to destroy the image of the baseball star for the youngsters because of the haggling between players and owners. Stan Musial picketing a ball park would look great, wouldn't it?"

Yet in the mid-1960s, rising player expectations, stemming partly from the cascading dollars pouring into sports from television contracts, the civil rights movement and other examples of social activism, and the almost simultaneous appointment of new labor leadership in baseball, basketball, and hockey, induced a growing player militancy. Fans were most shocked by the unionization of baseball. In 1966 the Players Association hired a full-time executive director, Marvin J. Miller, who had worked for many years with the United Steelworkers Union. Miller brought to the association discipline, factual knowledge, and a keen, painstaking mind. "To a disinterested observer," reported Robert H. Boyle in 1974, "Miller comes on like a David with an ICBM in his sling while the owners stumble around like so many befuddled Gladiators." Ironically, the adamant opposition of the owners to Miller helped unite the players behind the union. Under Miller's firm guidance, the union won a series of victories, including a huge increase in pension funds, mandatory salary arbitration, and the preservation of a free agency system. In 1972 and 1982, the union conducted costly but effective strikes.

Players had the most difficulty in organizing an effective union in the sport that prospered the most—pro football. Several obstacles confronted those seeking to organize the football players. First, an individual player was not as crucial to the success of a football team as he might be to a basketball or baseball team. Thus, football owners were reluctant to sign expensive free agents. Second, unlike the baseball and basketball owners, the football moguls were a close-knit group, headed by a shrewd and powerful commissioner, Pete Rozelle. Although the players won a minor victory in a strike/lockout in 1968, a 1974 strike failed miserably. Unable to force the owners to bid for free agents, the union abandoned free agency in its 1982 contract negotiations. Instead, the union demanded that 55 percent of the teams' gross revenues go to player salaries. After a long strike in 1982, the players won a limited victory.

The salary explosion (which was far greater than the rate of inflation in the 1970s and 1980s), long-term contracts, free agency, unions, and strikes had significant implications for the status of players as heroes. Before free agency, management had imposed an iron curtain of silence on salary figures, but after free agency both the players and the owners often turned to the press to assist them in their negotiations. And the press fully chronicled salary controversies. Salaries, rather than home runs, touchdowns, or field goal percentages, often became the bottom line for defining a player's identity and status. Little wonder, then, that the players became more concerned with salaries. Upon hearing that a teammate, or a player elsewhere of similar caliber, enjoyed a more lucrative contract, grievances of the imagination mounted. Resentful players frequently demanded that their salaries be renegotiated. Salary disputes also eroded a sense of community among the players and sometimes led to the spectacle of wide-open team feuds, such as the highly publicized one in the late 1970s involving George Steinbrenner, Billy Martin, Reggie Jackson, and Thurman Munson of the New York Yankees. The fans sensed, meanwhile, that the preoccupation with money reduced the players' enthusiasm for the game and loyalty to their team.

Fans also suspected that the players did not put out the same energy they once had and that high salaries may have changed the way the games were played. "Regardless of what the athlete says, if he has total security and is put in a tough spot, he may go through the motions and say, 'The hell with it. I've got mine,'" said Thomas Tutko, noted sports psychologist. "Kids have the wrong idea about basketball," declared Rick Barry, NBA star. "They are now all hungry to score points. They read that the high scorers are making the money and it's true. . . . I'll tell you what money has done. It's changed the philosophy of the game. Pro basketball is not played as well today as it was ten years ago. Players don't know the fundamentals." Under such circumstances, fans found it more difficult to identify with their highly paid, financially secure stars. According to a 1983 poll, three out of four Americans believed that professional athletes were overpaid, while about half believed that the athletes were more dedicated to their own gain than to the sport or their team.

There has always been a tension between the playing of sports and the external rewards—money, trophies, public acclaim—but television and escalating revenues made such rewards much more obtrusive. Sports "are modeling greed, egotism, self-centeredness," said Thomas Tutko. "We're modeling things that potentially threaten the fiber of this country. There's no such thing as loyalty to *anybody*." Many shared Tutko's grim conclusion. When running back Herschel Walker decided to pass up his senior year at the University of Georgia in 1983 and join the professional ranks, *Newsweek* implored: "Say it ain't so, Herschel." For

Walker had, for money, betrayed the image of the amateur athlete as innocent. "He was so straight—the quintessential All-Everything," continued *Newsweek*. "And everybody not only admired Herschel Walker, they believed. In the sublime order of things, he would finish out his record-shattering college career, gathering still more honors, the very perfect gentle scholar-athlete, and move with dignity into the professional game." In a major cover story, *Time* magazine conveyed a similar sense of betrayal.

For decades fans had been able to find in the sports page a retreat from the world of money and the anxiety that it always seems to create. There the fan could be comforted with accounts of Bobby Feller's "flaming fastball," Dolph Camilli's "fancy footwork" at first base, or the "basket catches" of Willie Mays in center field. But free agency brought a creeping invasion of financial news onto the sports page. The losing struggle of nineteen-year-old Fernando Valenzuela, Dodger pitcher, to become a juvenile millionaire in 1982 drew fifty times more space than his victory over the Yankees in the 1981 World Series. "Money stories tend to drive poetry, vibrant description—in short the best pieces—out of the sports pages," Roger Kahn has written. "An excess of financial stories is to the sporting spirit what an excess of gypsy moth caterpillars is to a white birch. Death or at least defoliation."

The press also gave much more attention to the private lives of athletes. Driven by competition from television and perhaps inspired by a post-Watergate, post-Abscam era of journalistic skepticism, reporters began to reveal everything. "If Bill Tilden were playing today," Osborne Elliot, dean of the Graduate School of Journalism at Columbia noted in 1982, "he'd be more known for his homosexual leanings than as a tennis player." "When I came up [in 1965]," recalled California Angels pitcher Tommy John, "people who covered baseball were fans. They probably knew so-and-so was hung over when he pitched, but they didn't expose it to the whole world. They had the Ring Lardner, 'boys will be boys' attitude. Now reporters aren't holding back to protect the image of ballplayers." Indeed. Modern athletes may not be behaving any worse than their predecessors, but the media, by detailing their salary grabbing, alcoholism, cocaine sniffing, fights, and sexual assaults, dashed all prospects of their being elevated to the status of national heroes.

In the 1980s, the apparently widespread use of drugs in professional sports particularly damaged the image of athletes. Some used drugs to improve performance; virtually every world-class weight lifter, shot-putter, and discus thrower turned to steroids. Many other athletes, perhaps reflecting their "celebrity"-level salaries and status, experimented with the "glamour drug," cocaine. In 1983, five members of "America's Team"—the Dallas Cowboys—were implicated in a federal drug investigation. SOUTH AMERICA'S TEAM and DRUGSTORE COWBOYS read cynical headlines in 1983. Dallas veterans, like those on other pro football teams, hazed rookies by requiring them to sing for the rest of the team in the preseason training camp dining hall; the Cowboys' number-one draft pick, Jim Jeffcoat, chose to sing "Santa Claus is Comin' to Town"—but he changed the words to "The FBI Is Comin' to Town." Unlike the crooning efforts of the other rookies, Jeffcoat's was met by his teammates with a stony silence. In 1984 the commissioner of baseball suspended several players for using cocaine.

In professional sports (though not at the college level), big money reduced the prestige of the once powerful and revered skipper. Overnight superstars began to receive five or six times as much money as their coaches. And since many of the players enjoyed no-cut, long-term contracts, how they performed often did not directly affect them financially. Thus, neither the coaches nor management had much leverage on the star athletes. If a team began to lose, it was the coach rather than the superstar who was sent packing. Noting the widespread loss of status by coaches, Kansas City Chiefs Coach John Mackovic only half-humorously cited the following changes in the way that coaches have addressed their players over the years:

"Go over and stand in the corner."
"Please stand in the corner."
"How about if you went over and stood in the corner?"
"How about us talking about you standing in the corner?"
"Why don't I go over and stand in the corner for you?"

Television made myth making, which is essential to hero making, far more difficult than in the past. For one thing, it obliterated much of the distance between the potential hero and the hero worshipper. Physical distance disguises imperfections; it permits fantasy. But television filled the screen with close-up shots of athletes. Sometimes the fan felt like a Lilliputian examining the craters in Gulliver's face. Television revealed would-be heroes to be all too human.

Many of the athletes, not knowing how to behave, adopted a media "persona." Some donned nonexpressive "media faces"; some engaged in strenuous gesturing to attract the attention of the cameras; and still others retreated into frozen self-consciousness. In 1970, Tony Kubek, announcer for NBC's Saturday Game of the Week, carefully briefed Yogi Berra on three questions. The cameras started rolling. Kubek asked the first question. A total absence of response. The producer became frantic, and Kubek fidgeted. Finally, Berra blurted out, "Let's go to the second question." Broadcaster Ralph Kiner once asked the Mets' "Choo Choo" Coleman how he got his nickname. "I don't know," came the chilling reply. Post-game interviews disclosed the existence of many college seniors whose pronunciation bordered on incomprehensibility and whose vocabularies appeared to be at about a third-grade level. Overacting, however, was probably more damaging to potential heroism. Close-up shots encouraged the players to act foolishly and brag about their achievements, even while the game was in progress.

Television also produced a diffusion of images that was detrimental to the nurture of sports heroes. Instead of the clear profile of a solitary athletic hero generated in the imagination, television served up a bleary succession of endless candidates for heroism. Certainly in earlier times professional athletes had hawked products; but shilling chewing tobacco and breakfast cereals in print was an entirely different matter from doing so on television. For television had an enormous power to magnify, distort, and confuse images. The image of O. J. Simpson, star running back of the Buffalo Bills, barreling down the sidelines competed with images of Simpson futilely trying to hit a backhand shot on "Celebrity Tennis" and gracefully leaping through airports for Hertz Rent-A-Car advertisements. As athletes assumed multiple media roles, the line between the sports hero and the celebrity tended to vanish.

Reducing the performances of athletes to a tiny screen somehow made their feats less noteworthy. On television, completing a long pass, returning a wide-angle groundstroke on the tennis court, and scooping up a hard-hit ground ball all seemed deceptively easy. A wide-ranging survey—underwritten by Miller Lite beer and released in 1983—on the attitudes of Americans toward sports found that 45 percent of the respondents sometimes felt that, given the right training, they could do as well as the athletes on television. The figure shot up to a startling 74 percent among those aged fourteen to seventeen and was as high as 25 percent even among those sixty-five and over. Given such beliefs, it was little wonder that many spectators refused to elevate athletes into heroes anymore.

12

In the Twilight of Our Games

Television could broaden and deepen the experience of sports. With multiple cameras, replays, slow motion shots, and announcers, television directors produced dramatic creations unavailable to the fan in the stands. By quickly shifting images—from close-ups to long distance shots, from players to spectators, from spectators to cheerleaders, from live action to replays—directors tried to lace the events with a continual series of visual surprises. Close-up and replay shots could add to the fan's appreciation of beautifully executed plays. Perhaps for these reasons, a majority of Americans, according to a nationwide poll conducted by *TV Guide* in 1978, preferred to watch sports (except baseball) on television instead of being in the stands.

Yet, paradoxically, while television furnished the viewer with an experience in some ways superior to that available to the live fan, the medium ultimately trivialized and diluted the traditional sporting experience. Dilution and trivialization took the form of too much hype, too many "big plays," too many extraneous sensations, and too many games. Once the miracle of seeing major sporting events (and "big plays") became commonplace, viewers began to lose some of their enthusiasm for the games. No longer did the sensations arising from the immediacy of the sports event exert the same poignancy, the same urgency, or the same power to inspire. Commas and semicolons, rather than periods and exclamation marks, punctuated the drama of sports.

Indirectly, television contributed to the nationalization of

American sports and the rise of a new set of values in sports. The traditional values of sportsmanship, civility, the suppression of the individual ego for a higher cause, play for the joy of the game—all tended to give way to winning at all costs, "number oneism," incivility, self-indulgence, and the blatant enlistment of the games on behalf of monetary interests. Such values weakened the capacity of sports to foster bonds of comradery and community among its followers.

Since the nineteenth century, sports teams have helped define the identity of cities and towns. Joint rooting for a team tied citizens together. Even in the age of television, a tight baseball pennant race continued to evoke passionate fan support. Perhaps the most striking instance was the "amazin' " New York Mets, an expansion team which lost 100 or more games for five of their first six seasons in the National League. In 1968, they finished ninth in a ten-team league. Then in 1969, the Mets surprised everyone by winning the pennant and then the World Series (from the powerful Baltimore Orioles). Blasé New Yorkers gave the team a celebration unequaled in the Big Apple since the armistice ending World War II. Similar outbursts of civic pride erupted in St. Louis (in 1967) and Detroit (in 1968), two cities that may have escaped massive race riots because of the pennant drives of their respective ball teams. In 1979, the Pirates and the entire city of Pittsburgh rallied behind their aging star, Willie Stargell, to chant repeatedly the team's (and the city's) credo, taken from a hit song: "We Are Family."

But baseball's power to evoke rootedness declined sharply in the age of television. Several teams did not even represent clearly definable communities. The California Angels, Texas Rangers, and Minnesota Twins, for example, built stadiums in suburbs adjacent to one or more metropolitan areas. Both the New York Giants and the New York Jets football teams moved (in 1976 and 1984, respectively) to the Meadowlands sports complex in East Rutherford, New Jersey. (In 1983 the New York State Senate considered a resolution forcing the teams to drop "New York" from their titles. The use of "New York" by the two teams, the resolution stated, added "a note of affrontery and, indeed, insult to the fans of the great city and state which [the owners] . . . have so callously abandoned.")

In the stands of many sports events, casual spectators re-placed fierce partisans. The California Angels, Heywood Hale Broun concluded, "played to a revolving collection of fans largely made up of those who were going to Disneyland tomorrow or had been yesterday and wanted to see a ball game before returning to the Middle West and real life." Revolving spectators and week-end excursionists with only a passing interest in a team's fate made up a large segment of the audience for all baseball teams. If a fam-ily from Lincoln, Nebraska, or Topeka, Kansas, visited Kansas City during the baseball season, they were expected to watch the Royals play, take their children to Worlds of Fun—the Kansas City equivalent of Disneyland—shop at the Crown Center, and perhaps visit the Nelson Art Gallery.

Telecasts of games by the major networks, superstations, and cable systems also tended to erode local loyalties. As early as the 1950s, network telecasts favored teams from New York and other large cities over those from smaller cities. Consequently, some spectators began to identify with these teams, perhaps even at the expense of the team located in their own community. Supersta-tions represented a different kind of threat to local allegiances. "I live in Del Mar, California, and I can see the Chicago Cubs now [in 1982] more often than as a kid in Chicago," explained profes-sor of communications Michael Real of San Diego State Univer-sity, "because WGN carries them, and WGN is picked up on ca-ble. So I can remain a Cub fan, even living on the West Coast."

Bouncing signals off of a satellite, Ted Turner, owner of the Atlanta Braves and of superstation WTBS, aggressively sold WTBS's television rights to the Braves games to the some 4,000 cable systems found in all fifty states. By 1984, over 28 million Americans could see the Braves play. In Valdez, Alaska, an oil town on the North Slope, about fifty men gathered at the Totem Inn four afternoons a week to watch the Braves play. Thanks to WTBS, the citizens of Storm Lake, Iowa, once loyal to the St. Louis Cardinals and the Minnesota Twins, switched their alle-giance to the Braves. And so it was in hundreds of other hamlets.

The Braves became a national team—"America's Team," Ted Turner liked to say. The other big-league owners "thought I was a dumb rich sucker, who stepped up with $10 million to buy a losing franchise with only one-tenth of the people to draw on as the big cities," said the tobacco-chewing Turner. "But I'm giving

Atlanta to the nation—to the world. . . . When they [the Braves] start to win, and get into some playoffs, they're going to take America by storm.'' The intrusion of Braves games into regions traditionally loyal to other teams alarmed the other owners. ''The fact that we cannot yet produce a corpse . . . is beside the point,'' Commissioner Kuhn told a congressional committee in 1982. ''Do they [WTBS] want an autopsy and a few bankrupt clubs,'' he asked, before they ceased their nationwide telecasts?

Professional football had never engendered quite the same sense of community as baseball, and television further undermined its capacity to encourage rootedness. Before television the sport had appealed to a limited ethnic, working-class audience; the season was short and a team played less than a dozen games. Television quickly transformed football games into national spectacles. In fact, after 1961 the league did not permit local franchises to sell television rights. In the 1960s, such winning teams as the Green Bay Packers and Baltimore Colts developed large national constituencies of Sunday afternoon television viewers.

In the 1970s and 1980s, the television history of the Dallas Cowboys reflected even more sharply the nationalization of pro football. Although the Cowboys represented a population base far smaller than that of several other pro franchises, by the 1970s their average television ratings exceeded those of any other pro football team. The Cowboys were the darlings of CBS Sports. The network's slogan: ''When in doubt, give 'em Dallas.'' Spectators could not escape the Cowboys even when they turned the television set off. Even in New York City, half a continent from Dallas, The Dallas Cowboy, a restaurant, did—for a time—a hefty business. Cowboy jewelry, posters, and other baubles marketed by NFL Properties far outsold those of any other team. Though costing $15.95 annually in 1982, the *Dallas Cowboys Official Weekly* had a paid circulation of over 100,000. ''We're the largest newspaperlike sports weekly in the country except for the *Sporting News*,'' proudly declared Tex Schramm, president and general manager of the Cowboys. The Cowboys' radio network of 200 stations also far exceeded that of any other franchise.

A winning record accounted for part of the national appeal of the Cowboys. Since joining the NFL in 1960 as an expansion team, Dallas had the best regular season record in pro football. Whereas other teams experienced streaks of greatness, Dallas was consistently excellent, having missed the playoffs only once in 18 years since 1965 and played in five Super Bowls.

The Cowboys generated a national audience of either lovers or haters; few spectators could remain neutral. Cowboy philia or phobia arose from the sharp images projected by the franchise and its team. Cowboy phobia often sprang from the team's Texas base. "Who wants to root for an oil well?" queried Paul Zimmerman in *Sports Illustrated*. Yet the Cowboys projected images of patriotism. They wore silver and blue uniforms; their long-time quarterback, Roger Staubach, had attended the Naval Academy and served in the Navy, wore his hair short when it was unfashionable, and publicly proclaimed his religiosity. The team even had the audacity to describe itself (well before the Braves) as "America's Team." Subjected to ridicule for such pretension, the team nonetheless entitled their 1981 highlight film *The Star Spangled Cowboys*. Using the media to enhance the image of the Cowboys was "not just an ego trip," explained Cowboy president Tex Schramm; it gave Dallas "a competitive edge." It assisted the team in the signing of free agents and made playing for Dallas special ("like the Yankees," said Schramm), so that players put out more.

The team also projected an image of modernity. The success of the Cowboys was due, it appeared, to something appropriately referred to as The Dallas Organization. For many, the mere mention of the Cowboys conjured up images of such giants as the Ewings, IBM, and the Pentagon. The approach of the Dallas Organization to football appeared to be coldly rational; it was a pioneer in the use of computers to identify and select recruits, scout opponents, and prepare game plans. Beano Cook, a CBS publicist, allegedly once told Tex Schramm, "You're one of the two most efficient organizations in the 20th century." "What's the other?" asked Schramm. "The Third Reich," responded Cook.

Television and the nationalization of sports aroused expectations among fans of seeing only the best. "A diet of the best only increases the appetite for nothing but the best," Sol Yurick has written in *Esquire*. "There is no sense of patience for what went into the effort that was finished in a few seconds." Consequently, televised sports diminished the significance of, or completely destroyed, sports at the grass roots level. Hence the death of minor league baseball, of semi-pro baseball, and of local fight clubs. Except for a few remote areas such as west Texas, attendance and interest in high school sports sank to all-time lows.

Television encouraged the introduction of sensations external to the core of the traditional sporting experience. Interviews with players and coaches while the games were in progress represented a particularly odious example. The instant that the first half of play at NCAA football games came to a close, the viewer witnessed the spectacle of a desperate television announcer tugging at the sleeve of one of the coaches for a quick interview. Such interruptions damaged the integrity of the game. For the coach now devoted some of his time and energy to entertaining the fans rather than preparing for the next half of play.

Breaks in the action for commercials—the numbers crept ever upward—broke up the continuity of all sports experiences. The fan at a game could bridge lapses in the action on the field by looking at other fans, players, or cheerleaders, or by speculating on the course of the game to date and on what was likely to come next. But television did not permit the luxury of such reflection. It interfered with the pace of the game itself by requiring time-outs for commercials, and then bombarded the viewer with alluring ads for an endless array of automobiles, tires, gasolines, airline flights, razor blades, shaving creams, and brands of beer. The ads did not give the viewer a single moment of breathing and seeing space; they became an integral part of the total experience of witnessing games. Images of the games merged with the slick images of the commercials.

The television commercials were sometimes more exciting than the games themselves. The battle of the breweries represented a classic instance. Given the reputation of sports fans as beer drinkers, breweries had long been major sponsors of sports on both radio and television. But no brewery had fully realized the potential of the television-sports coupling until 1975, when the Miller Brewing Company decided to launch a huge campaign to sell its new low-calorie beer, Miller Lite. In the past, said Bob Lenz of the Backer & Spielvogel ad agency, which handled the Miller account, "all the low-cal beers . . . were diet-related. You got the weight-watcher crowd, women, white-collar types. Low-cal was considered a sissy product." While riding home on a bus in Manhattan, Lenz noticed a picture of a smiling Matt Snell, a New

York Jet running back. Then it came to him: Have athletes sell
Miller Lite. Not star athletes, but athletes with a sense of humor
and with whom beer drinkers could easily imagine themselves
joshing at a corner tavern.

The Miller Lite commercials soon became the most popular
ads on television. The intention of the commercials, according to
director Robert Giraldi, was to entertain first and advertise secondly. The big hook was the clever employment of self-mocking
humor, as when big Dick Butkus, former Chicago Bears linebacker, and even bigger Bubba Smith, former Baltimore Colts
lineman, tiptoe through a bar in their tiny, tight shorts and Smith
rips open a can of balls, saying, "Tennis anyone?" With each ad,
Butkus and Smith became more culturally pretentious and consequently more ludicrous. In the next ad, the viewer found them fin-
ishing a round of golf, after which they described themselves as
"us linksters" and Smith unconsciously revealed that he did not
know what a "birdie" was. In a still later spot, Butkus and Smith
arrived at a bar decked out in tuxedos. Butkus explained to the bar
patrons and the television audience that "us impresarios have just
been to the opera" and that next week they planned to attend the
ballet. "This time I sure hope they do it in English," said Smith.
"Yeah, me too," responded Butkus. The barflies laughed. Puzzled
by the laughter, Butkus eventually smiled in an endearingly sheep-
ish way. The commercials boosted Miller Lite sales far ahead of
those for all other low-calorie beers; after only six years of the campaign, Miller Lite rose to number three in total sales for all beers.
Many viewers echoed the sentiments of a Greensboro, North Carolina, man who said, "I can't leave these commercials even to go to
the refrigerator to get a beer."

With television's immense capacity for creating instant celebrities, everyone from the spectators at the games to the owners of
the franchises scrambled for the attention of the cameras. The media spawned outrageous behavior. Apart from wide smiles, waves,
and endless repetitions of "Hi, Mom!" by the players, coaches,
especially basketball coaches, sometimes behaved like raging ma-
niacs. Such behavior on the streets would have quickly called forth
the police, not to mention an ambulance crew from the local mental hospital.

Even the owners of many sports franchises elbowed their way
into the spotlight. Men of new wealth, such as George Steinbren-

ner (shipbuilding), Ray Kroc (McDonald's hamburgers), Charlie Finley (insurance), Ewing Kauffman (ground-up oyster shells), and Ted Turner (advertising and broadcasting), replaced many of the "sportsmen owners," such as Tom Yawkey of the Boston Red Sox and Philip K. Wrigley of the Chicago Cubs. Many of the men of new wealth apparently purchased big-league sports franchises as an "ego trip"—i.e., so that they could become celebrities. When the television cameras recorded victory celebrations, there invariably stood the owner, "brushing aside his sweaty hirelings to pose as the humble man of vision who made it all happen," reported a *Sports Illustrated* writer. "In defeat he rages—right there in the headlines for all to see—about the gutless sluggards who are ruining his fun."

In order to hold center stage, the new owners often abandoned the direct management of all their other enterprises so they could devote full time to their sports franchise(s). Located as he was—or at least his New York Yankees were—in the media capital of the world, perhaps no owner exceeded the ability of George Steinbrenner to command the attention of the media. When his highly paid minions failed to win an adequate number of games, he publicly bullied and harangued them. When this strategy also failed, he turned to quick-fix trades, the free agent market, and the shuffling and reshuffling of management personnel. He hired and fired a record three managers in one season (1981), and over a six-year period he hired Billy Martin three times and fired him three times. He haunted the Yankee dugout, directed changes in the lineup, and personally ordered special player workouts.

Perhaps the least tolerable form of excess was to be found among the sports commentators themselves. Nearly all of the viewers agreed that sportcasters over explained, overresearched, and oversold sports events. To fill presumed gaps in the excitement, announcers tended to resort to idle chitchat or too much analysis. In football, volumes of analysis and several replay shots seemed to accompany every play, no matter how routine. Listening to such analysis during a Wimbledon tennis telecast, one viewer complained that he "felt the annoyance that one would feel at the theater when those behind one talked throughout the performance and spoiled good entertainment with their rudeness."

In his first years as an announcer, Howard Cosell, though sometimes blunt and excessive, had brought a refreshing candor to sportscasts. But as David Halberstam noted in a 1982 issue of *Playboy*, Cosell became increasingly less restrained. "He had become his own historian, and he footnoted himself faithfully," wrote Halberstam; "every broadcast was now filled with Howard reminding us endlessly of his insights and of his predictions that had been fulfilled." With Cosell behind the microphone, "there was a theme, and it was this: *Howard was always right.*"

As with Cosell, the premium placed on excessive behavior and drama frequently took the form of an assault upon civility. The assault may have begun with the boxing hype of Muhammad Ali. But one sensed that when Ali asserted that he was the greatest, he was mocking white culture, making a social/political statement, as it were; no one detected a higher mockery in the churlish pouting and exhibitionism of most of the other athletes. In the 1970s and 1980s, conspicuous displays of bad manners became almost commonplace. In tennis, Jimmy Connors expressed his disgust with vulgar gestures; in college football, veteran coach Woody Hayes of Ohio State University slugged a Clemson University player during a bowl game; and on two different occasions in 1982, Big Eight head football coaches, believing the University of Nebraska team was "running up the score" for higher poll ratings, refused to extend the traditional post-game handshake to Cornhusker head coach Tom Osborne. Evel Knievel, angry about the remarks of a writer, proceeded to break the arm of the offender with a baseball bat.

John Leonard, writing as "Cyclops," the media reviewer for the *New York Times*, suggested in 1975 that television had created a group of "media brats," who, lacking a belief in themselves as either heroes or celebrities, compensated with strenuous gesturing and posturing. They seemed to be thinking to themselves, "Golly, I'm famous, and I love being famous, but it happened so quickly—what if it goes away?" The media brats were not sure whether they were celebrities because of their achievements on the playing field or merely media creations ("personalities"). In either case, throwing punches, using vulgarity, loudly proclaiming oneself "number one," spiking balls in the end zone, dancing over sacked quarterbacks, and constant whining made for more exciting telecasts than exercising the restraint called for by "good sportsmanship."

In 1978, Jennings Bryant, chairman of the communications

department at the University of Evansville in Indiana, conducted a study in which he asked a group of about 100 college students to listen to dubbed commentary of a routine tennis match between Torben Ulrich and Sven Davidson. Then they were asked to report how much they enjoyed the match and how intense they thought the match was. One-third of the group listened to a commentary in which the players were said to be good friends; one-third heard a commentary in which the players were said to be bitter enemies; and a third group heard a commentary in which the relationship between the players was not specified. The viewers who were told that the players were hostile to one another found the match far more interesting, exciting, and enjoyable.

Television sports producers may have been ignorant of Bryant's findings, but they knew that sports events drew better ratings when they were presented as a running soap opera of feuds. The feuds could be between opposing players, coaches, or owners— even between cities. For purposes of promotion, feuds that could be reduced to individuals rather than teams were most effective. Thus televised sports focused on individual duels, even in the team sports and even when the individuals might never be on the playing field at the same time. Such distortions invariably damaged the integrity of the games themselves.

Consciously or unconsciously, athletes recognized that television rewarded uncivil behavior in the sports arena. Television advertisers even capitalized on the negative images of athletes and managers. Abrasive Yankee manager Billy Martin appeared in a variety of ads designed to appeal to "the blue-collar crowd," as his ad agency put it. A 1982 ad agency poll found tennis player John McEnroe the "least liked" of a list of twenty-five athletes, and he was "found believable" by only 16 percent of the public. Yet, in 1982 the BIC corporation began a series of television advertisements starring John McEnroe, well known for his temper tantrums off and on the court. "BIC corporation has tapped the terror of tennis to tout its disposable shaver," said a BIC press release. "Taking full off-court advantage of McEnroe's feisty image, the 30-second commercial opens with a seemingly familiar on-court confrontation between McEnroe and an umpire." David Furman, BIC's advertising manager, said, "We are trying to use him as an authority figure. . . . A demanding sort of person. It's a device, just as his temper is a device. He has a certain credibility."

The requirements of the media for visual drama and spectacle destroyed the traditional balance in sports—always a delicate one—between play and work, expression and control, community and the individual. The values of obtaining attention and being number one came before respect for authority, a sense of duty, and self-restraint. Losing, even if it did presumably teach a desirable set of values, was no longer acceptable; rather, it became the nation's greatest single sin. Writer Willie Morris wrote of a "tough-eyed" coach from the University of Nebraska "who considered winning in college football a moral equivalent of the survival of the earth, in an American state where many nuclear-headed missiles were aimed toward . . . Soviet Russia."

Jim Lynch, a former Notre Dame and Kansas City Chiefs linebacker, told of being introduced to the father of a Chiefs rookie. Lynch told the father that he had heard good things about his son. The father snorted back: "He's not starting, is he? He's not Number 1. That's what it's all about, isn't it?" Paradoxically, the obsession with winning often robbed winning of its joys.

Despite television's dilution of the traditional sporting experience with extrinsic sensations, Americans could still find in televised sports a unique form of entertainment. For the suspense of games, while not as poignant as it once was, continued to be real, not fictive. The courage of the gimpy-kneed quarterback was genuine, not that of a Clint Eastwood firing blanks at a wall of falling movie extras. On television, viewers could still see athletes perform their artistry at the highest levels of excellence.

But taken in their totality, televised sports overwhelmed and flattened the fan's sensibilities. Before television, a trip to the ball park—or to the movies or the opera, for that matter—was, for most, a special occasion. Even for those who lived within easy reach of a big-league ball park and had ample financial means, going to a big-league game was usually much more than a casual excursion; for those living many miles away, it might amount to an experience remembered throughout a lifetime. The anticipation of attending a game added immeasurably to the excitement. Once at the stadium, fellow members of the audience became part of the fun; the sharing of emotions heightened the intensity of the experience.

With television, seeing a big-league sporting event became an everyday experience. Viewers could see sports on the major networks every weekend from morning till night and on cable channels twenty-four hours a day, seven days a week. On separate channels, one could see basketball, hockey, golf, baseball, and tennis—all on a single Sunday afternoon. By increasing the sheer quantity of games available, the moguls of professional sports unintentionally debased the significance of each single sport, and each single game. Between 1960 and 1980 major league baseball added 868 games, basketball 614, hockey 510, and football 124 games to each season. With so many games, one game seemed to merge into another; the games became virtually indistinguishable.

Debasement also took the form of flooding viewers with more and more "big games" and endless "championships." The quantity of championships proliferated beyond the imagination of the boldest dreamers of the pre-television era. In the 1950s boxing had had only eight world championships, each representing distinct weight divisions. The sport could be "managed" mentally; one could know the names of the champions and the major challengers, and something of the past achievements of both. By the mid-1980s—principally so that television could promote more fights as title bouts—boxing offered twenty-eight international championships. Now fans could see a championship fight nearly every weekend. Mental management of the sport became impossible for all but the most persistent.

In the major team sports, the burgeoning number of playoff games sharply reduced the importance of regular season games. Baseball, more than any of the traditional sports, retained the integrity of the regular season. Before television, baseball's only "playoff"—unless teams in the same league had identical records at the end of regular season play—had been the World Series between the winners of the National and the American leagues. In 1969 baseball divided each league into eastern and western divisions. At the end of the season, division winners engaged in a playoff; the winners of the playoffs then played in the World Series.

Although college football did not have a playoff system, the number of post-season bowl games increased. The number of teams in the NCAA college basketball playoffs also mushroomed. Until the 1970s, only eight teams qualified for the playoffs; in the

1980s, one out of every five major college teams in the country received a berth in the playoffs. In the National Football League, fourteen of the twenty-eight teams competed in the playoffs.

Regular season play in professional hockey and basketball was even more meaningless. In the NBA, twenty-three teams labored through an eighty-two game schedule for the sole purpose of eliminating seven of them for the playoffs; in the National Hockey League, twenty-one clubs played an eighty-game schedule to eliminate only five teams. Since the playoff games were more lucrative in gate and television receipts than regular season games, Jerry Kirshenbaum of *Sports Illustrated* suggested that the pro leagues simply dispense with regular season play and launch immediately into playoffs, with all the clubs qualifying.

The combination of jazzed-up offenses and the hyperbole of television announcers resulted in a plethora of "big plays" in each game. Sometimes announcers tried to retain the attention of the marginal enthusiast by breathlessly describing the performance of a routine play. The cheapening of the big play was especially the case in both professional and college football. With the new rule changes in the late 1970s—which permitted what had once been offensive holding—jumbo-sized weight lifters took over the offensive lines. The defenses did not catch up. Quarterbacks filled the air with passes, breaking all records at both the college and pro levels. "Remember when there were only two or three big plays a [pro] game?" asked Paul Zimmerman in *Sports Illustrated* in 1983. "Now there are a dozen, two dozen—so many that they all blur, become indistinguishable."

To the championships in bona fide sports, television added a host of championships in synthetic sports. Now fans could witness on television such unmemorable spectacles as world bubble gum–blowing and world refrigerator-carrying championships. Satirizing the prevalence of such created-for-television championships, along with the skimpily dressed cheerleaders at sporting events, "Saturday Night Live"—the late-night television comedy show—once featured a mock "World Championship of the T's and the A's."

To exploit the additional opportunities for profit presented by television, traditional sports seasons vanished. Prior to the advent of television, each major sport had established its own season: baseball presided in the spring and summer, football in the fall, and basketball in the winter. Baseball, being the National Game, even had its own kind of non-playing winter season, the "Hot Stove League," which consisted of long debates and speculation by fans about the past and forthcoming seasons. Boxing championships—especially fights for the heavyweight title—came rarely enough to excite nearly universal interest. By the 1970s, however, the lengthened football, basketball, and hockey schedules invaded baseball's expanded schedule, leaving only June and July free of competition for baseball from the other major team sports. With the establishment of the United States Football League in 1983, baseball lost even this privileged position. For many, season overlapping had destroyed an important cultural clock.

Once viewers could see big-league games, championship games, and "big plays" every day and in every season, each event lost a measure of its intrinsic excitement. Few could experience the games with the same sense of wonderment that those in the pre-television age of sport had been able to do. The mysterious, the spectacular, and the unexpected became the routine. For many, "watching" a game on television became so casual that they simultaneously glanced through magazines, did housework, played cards, conversed, or simply daydreamed. For many viewers, television flattened the experience of sports; "seeing" a big-league game was now no more exciting than watching the vast wasteland of other trivial entertainment found on television.

Consciously or unconsciously, Americans began to revolt against television's attenuation of the traditional sporting experience. Many refused to watch televised sports or restricted themselves only to the major events. Television sports ratings in the 1980s began to slide downward. In 1983, CBS's audience for its NFL telecasts declined by 400,000 households, while NBC's fell by almost a million and ABC (for its prime time Monday night games) lost over three million. The shrinkage may have been only temporary, but advertisers were already seeking compensation from the networks for lost viewers. The networks, in turn, sought a reduction in their payments to the NFL for television rights.

Some fans watched principally only the so-called "amateur" sports, as played by the colleges or at the Olympic Games. "A lot of fans are turning to college athletics and amateur sports for heroes—like our Olympic hockey team which brought back national pride and patriotism. They were 21 kids who got together and did the impossible," said Don Ohlmeyer in 1980 as director of NBC Sports. In these sports, the athletes sometimes continued to display open enthusiasm for the game itself, and to convey a sense of playing on behalf of a team or the nation rather than simply for personal rewards.

Countless millions began to experience the joy of sports directly: They flocked to the playing fields. In the 1950s and 1960s American presidents had urged the nation's citizens to engage in sports as a way of promoting physical fitness, but it was not until the 1970s that participation jumped markedly. In the 1970s tennis bubbles and racket clubs sprouted up nearly everywhere, and newspapers introduced special sections for those who played sports rather than watched them on television. Manufacturers of sports equipment cited impressive data indicating the growth of squash, racquetball, handball, platform tennis, gymnastics, cycling, and even roller skating.

But all these physical activities paled beside the growth in running. The *New York Times* estimated that twenty million Americans took up running in the 1970s. In 1970, 126 men entered the first New York Marathon; in 1980, over 12,000 men and women ran in the event. In 1978 even the President of the United States, Jimmy Carter, began to jog between forty and fifty miles a week. Most joggers ran noncompetitively; many claimed that long-distance running not only reduced the likelihood of cardiovascular disease but also generated a sense of euphoria. For some, daily jogging apparently replaced weekly visits to a psychoanalyst.

While the value of this participatory revolution in sports cannot be denied, much has been lost. Television, more than any other single force, has transformed spectator sports into trivial affairs. Sports will never again be an arena populated by pristine heroes. No longer are sports as effective in enacting the rituals embodying traditional American values, and no longer do they evoke the same intensity, the same loyalty, or the same commitment. For sports are no longer so transcendent in American life.

A Note on Sources

A complete list of sources relevant to television and sports would require a book in itself. Fortunately, Robert J. Higgs, *Sports: A Reference Guide* (Westport, CT: Greenwood Press, 1982) already provides nearly all of the major sources. Yet specifically for television and sports see William O. Johnson, Jr., *Super Spectator and the Electric Lilliputians* (Boston: Little Brown, 1971), Donald Parente, "A History of Sports and Television" (Ph.D. diss., University of Illinois, 1974), and Harvey Frommer, "A Description of How Professional Football Employed the Medium of Television to Increase the Sport's Economic Growth and Cultural Impact, 1960-1970" (Ph.D. diss., New York University, 1974). Ron Powers, *Supertube: The Rise of Television Sports* (New York: Coward-McCann, 1984) focuses upon the internal history of the networks' involvement in sports. Other secondary works that are useful include Ira Horowitz, "Sports Broadcasting," in Roger C. Noll, ed., *Government and the Sports Business* (Washington, D.C.: Brookings Institution, 1974), and Bert Randolph Sugar, *"The Thrill of Victory": The Inside Story of ABC Sports* (New York: Hawthorne, 1978).

Several books and essays have recently appeared which address the fundamental nature of sports. Books that I have cited or used to form my ideas include: Paul Gallico, *Farewell to Sports* (New York: Alfred A. Knopf, 1941) and *The Golden People* (New York: Doubleday, 1965); Allen Guttmann, *From Ritual to Record: The Nature of Modern Sports* (New York: Columbia University Press, 1978); Christopher Lasch, "The Degradation of Sport," in *The Culture of Narcissism* (New York: W. W. Norton, 1978); Robert Lipsyte, *SportsWorld: An American Dreamland* (New York: Quadrangle/New York Times, 1975); Richard Lipsky, *How*

We Play the Game: Why Sports Dominate American Life (Boston: Beacon Press, 1981); and Michael Novak, *The Joy of Sports* (New York: Basic Books, 1976). In October, 1974, *Esquire* devoted almost an entire issue to "Super Sports" and in October, 1975, to "The Joy of Sports." These issues contain several marvelous essays. Moreover, Roger Angell's essays in *The New Yorker* consistently offer sensitive insights.

Occasional valuable essays on televised sports appear in a large variety of magazines. I perused the following: *Advertising Age, Broadcasting, Chronicle of Higher Education, Esquire, Inside Sports, Journal of Communication, The New Yorker, Newsweek, Sports Illustrated, The Sporting News, Television Age, Television/Radio Digest, Time, TV Guide, Variety,* and *WomenSports*. Nearly all daily newspaper regularly carry Associated Press stories on television sports. Since the *New York Times* and the *Washington Post* not only often perceptively reported on sports and television but also have easy-to-use indexes, I found them especially useful. Excellent reports on the business side of sports appear in the *Wall Street Journal*.

Primary sources include Congressional testimony of network television personnel and moguls of sport which can be found in Hearings before the Subcommittee on Communications of the Committee on Interstate and Foreign Commerce, House of Representatives, *Network Sports Practices*, 95th Cong., 1st sess., 1978; Hearings before the Antitrust Subcommittee of the Committee on the Judiciary, *Telecasting of Professional Sports Contests*, 87th Cong., 1st sess., 1961; Hearings before the Subcommittee on Antitrust and Monopoly of the Senate Committee on the Judiciary, *Organized Professional Team Sports*, 85th Cong., 2nd sess., 1958; and Hearings before the House Select Committee on Professional Sports, *Inquiry into Professional Sports*, 94th Cong., 2nd sess., 1976. For public attitudes toward sports and television, see A. C. Nielsen, *Televised Sports* (published annually since 1972) and Research & Forecasts, Inc., *The Miller Lite Report on American Attitudes Toward Sports* (Milwaukee: Miller Brewing Co., 1983).

Specific books and articles that I have quoted from, or especially relied upon (apart from those previously cited in the body of this book or in this bibliography) include:

ARLEDGE, ROONE. "Playboy Interview," *Playboy*, October 1976.

——— WITH GILBERT ROGIN. "It's Sport . . . It's Money . . . It's TV," *Sports Illustrated*, April 25, 1966.

AXTHELM, PETE. *The City Game: Basketball in New York from the World Champion Knicks to the World of the Playgrounds.* New York: Harper & Row, 1970.

BAKER, WILLIAM J. *Sports in the Western World.* Totowa, NJ: Rowman and Littlefield, 1982.

BARBER, RED. *The Broadcasters*. New York: Dial Press, 1970.

BARNOUW, ERIC. *The Tube of Plenty: The Evolution of American Television*. New York: Oxford University Press, 1975.

BOORSTIN, DANIEL. *The Americans: The Democratic Experience*. New York: Vintage, 1974.

BROWNE, RAY B. ET AL., EDS. *Heroes of Popular Culture*. Bowling Green: Bowling Green University Popular Press, 1972.

BRYANT, JENNINGS. "Sports and Spectators," *Journal of Communication*, Winter, 1982.

CAPPA, FRANK, ED. *Screen and Society*. Chicago: Nelson-Hall, 1980.

CHANDLER, JOAN M. "TV & Sports: Wedded with a Golden Hoop," *Psychology Today*, April 1977.

COSELL, HOWARD. *Cosell*. New York: Pocket Books, 1974.

DEFORD, FRANK. *Five Strides on the Banked Track*. Boston: Little, Brown & Co., 1971.

———. "Long Live the King," *Sports Illustrated*, January 21, 1980.

DURSO, JOSEPH. *The All-American Dollar: The Big Business of Sports*. Boston: Houghton Mifflin Co., 1971.

———. *The Sports Factory: An Investigation into College Sports*. New York: Quadrangle/New York Times, 1975.

ESPY, RICHARD. *Politics of the Olympic Games*. Berkeley: University of California Press, 1979.

The Final Report of the President's Commission on Olympic Sports. 2 vols. Washington, DC, 1977.

FOWLES, JIB. *Television Viewers Vs. Media Snobs*. New York: Stein & Day, 1982.

GOLDSMITH, ALFRED N. AND AUSTIN C. LESCARBOURA. *This Thing Called Broadcasting*. New York: Henry Holt, 1930.

GREENSPAN, EMILY. *Little Winners: Inside the World of the Child Sports Star*. Boston: Little, Brown and Co., 1983.

HALBERSTAM, DAVID. *The Breaks of the Game*. New York: Alfred A. Knopf, 1981.

———. "The Mouth That Roared [Cosell]," *Playboy*, December 1982.

HOLTZMAN, JEROME, ED. *No Cheering in the Press Box*. New York: Holt, Rinehart & Winston, 1974.

HUIZINGA, JOHN. *Homo Ludens: A Study of the Play Element in Culture*. Boston: Beacon Press, 1938.

HUSING, TED. *My Eyes Are in My Heart*. New York: Bernard Geis Associates, 1959.

JENKINS, DAN. *Saturday's America*. Boston: Little, Brown & Co., 1970.

JORDAN, JERRY N. *The Long Range Effect of Television and Other Factors on Sports Attendance*. Washington: Radio-Television Manufacturers Association, nd.

KENNEDY, RAY AND NANCY WILLIAMSON. "Money in Sports," *Sports Il-*

lustrated, July 17–July 31, 1978.

KIRSHENBAUM, JERRY. "And Here to Bring You the Play by Play . . . ," *Sports Illustrated*, September 13, 1971.

KOPPETT, LEONARD. *All About Baseball*. New York: Quadrangle/New York Times, 1974.

KOSTELANETZ, RICHARD. "Fanfare for TV Football," *Intellectual Digest*, August 1973.

MAYER, MARTIN. *About Television*. New York, Harper & Row, 1972.

METZ, ROBERT. *CBS: Reflections in a Bloodshot Eye*. New York: Playboy Press, 1975.

NAGLER, BARNEY. *James Norris and the Decline of Boxing*. Indianapolis: Bobbs Merrill, 1964.

NEWCOMB, HORACE. *TV: The Most Popular Art*. Garden City, NY: Anchor Press/Doubleday, 1974.

POE, RANDALL. "The Angry Fan," *Harper's*, November 1975.

QUINLAN, STERLING. *Inside ABC*. New York: Hastings House, 1979.

RADER, BENJAMIN G. *American Sports: From the Age of Folk Games to the Age of Spectators*. Englewood Cliffs, NJ: Prentice-Hall, Inc., 1983.

RALBOVSKY, MARTIN. *Lords of the Locker Room: The American Way of Coaching and Its Effect on Youth*. New York: Peter H. Weyden, 1974.

RICE, GRANTLAND. *The Tumult and the Shouting: My Life in Sport*. New York: A. S. Barnes, 1954.

RIESMAN, DAVID. "The Suburban Dislocation," *Annals of the American Academy of Political and Social Science*, 1957.

ROSS, MURRAY. "Football and Baseball in America," in John T. Talamini and Charles H. Page, eds. *Sports and Society*. Boston: Little, Brown & Co., 1973.

SHEATSLEY, PAUL B. AND PAUL N. BORSKY. *The Effects of Television on College Football Attendance*. Chicago: National Opinion Research Center, University of Chicago, 1950-1954.

SMITH, CURT. *America's Dizzy Dean*. St. Louis: Bethany, 1978.

"Sports in America," *National Forum*, Winter 1982.

STERN, BILL. *The Taste of Ashes*. New York: Henry Holt, 1959.

"This Is Howard Cosell," *Newsweek*, October 2, 1972.

UNDERWOOD, JOHN. *The Death of the American Game: The Crisis in Football*. Boston: Little, Brown & Co., 1979.

VOIGT, DAVID QUENTIN. *American Baseball: From Postwar Expansion to the Electronic Age*. University Park and London: Pennsylvania State University Press, 1983.

WEST, ROBERT. *The Rape of Radio*. New York: Rodin Pub. Co., 1941.

YABLONSKY, LEWIS AND JONATHAN BROWER. *The Little League Game*. New York: Times Books, 1979.

YIANNAKIS, ANDREW ET AL. *Sport Sociology: Contemporary Themes.* Dubuque, IA: Kendall/Hunt Pub. Co., 1976.

ZIEGEL, VIC. "It Ain't Heavy, It's My Refrigerator," *Inside Sports,* May 1982.

About the Author

Benjamin G. Rader teaches history at the University of Nebraska–Lincoln. Author of *The Academic Mind and Reform* and *American Sports: From the Age of Folk Games to the Age of Spectators*, he serves on the Board of Editors of the *Journal of Sport History*.

Born and raised on a farm in southern Missouri, Rader lives in Lincoln, Nebraska with his wife and two children. He is an avid tennis player.

Index